Islam and the Tyranny of Authenticity

Islam and the Tyranny of Authenticity

An Inquiry into Disciplinary Apologetics and Self-Deception

Aaron W. Hughes

Sheffield, UK   Bristol, CT

Published by Equinox Publishing Ltd.

UK: Office 415, The Workstation, 15 Paternoster Row, Sheffield,
South Yorkshire S1 2BX
USA: ISD, 70 Enterprise Drive, Bristol, CT 06010
www.equinoxpub.com

First published 2015

© Aaron W. Hughes 2015

All rights reserved. No part of this publication may be reproduced or transmitted in any form or by any means, electronic or mechanical, including photocopying, recording or any information storage or retrieval system, without prior permission in writing from the publishers.

British Library Cataloguing-in-Publication Data

A catalogue record for this book is available from the British Library.

ISBN-13 978 1 78179 216 2 (hardback)
         978 1 78179 217 9 (paperback)

Library of Congress Cataloging-in-Publication Data

Hughes, Aaron W., 1968–
Islam and the tyranny of authenticity: an inquiry into disciplinary apologetics and self-deception / Aaron W. Hughes.
   pages cm
Includes bibliographical references and index.
ISBN 978-1-78179-216-2 (hb) -- ISBN 978-1-78179-217-9 (pb) 1. Islam—Apologetic works. 2. Islam—Study and teaching. I. Title.
BP170.H835 2015
297.2—dc23
      2015010606

Typeset by JS Typesetting Ltd, Porthcawl, Mid Glamorgan
Printed and bound in Great Britain by Lightning Source UK Ltd., Milton Keynes and in the USA by Lightning Source Inc., La Vergne, TN

*For Jacob Neusner
who showed so many of us the path forward,
and who refused to back down.*

Contents

	Acknowledgments	ix
	Preface: Noble Lies	xi
	Introduction: Setting the Problem	1
1.	Islamic Religious Studies and the Politics of Identity	15
2.	Prisoners of Said	37
3.	Insiders, Outsiders, and the Path Between	57
4.	Business as Usual	75
5.	Jacob Neusner Meets Islamic Studies	95
6.	Turf Wars	115
	References	129
	Author Index	139
	Subject Index	141

Acknowledgments

As usual, I am grateful to a group of scholars who share a similar perspective when it comes to the academic study of religion, a group that I am happy to say I find ever expanding. Those who either listened to or read parts of this study and offered important feedback include, in alphabetical order, William E. Arnal, Shahzad Bashir, Herbert Berg, Willi Braun, Jamal J. Elias, William Scott Green, Susannah Heschel, Luther Martin, Matt Sheedy, Randall Styers, Mark Wagner, Donald Wiebe, and Elliot R. Wolfson. At Equinox, I would like to thank Janet Joyce, as always, for supporting my work, in addition to Hamish Ironside and Nick Ascroft for tidying up my prose and the ideas expressed therein.

Parts of this manuscript were delivered orally at Florida State University, Hobart and William Smith Colleges, Stanford University, the University of Miami, the University of Pennsylvania, and the University of Toronto. I am grateful for my hosts and audiences at all of these institutions.

I would like to single out two people in particular for both their generosity and vision. Both are rebels and fighters in the best sense of each word. The first is Jacob Neusner, to whom I dedicate this book, someone I have gotten to know personally over the past couple of years. Neusner, to me, represents a true scholar of religion—someone who refused to accept things the way they were handed down to him and had the chutzpah and indefatigable drive to change them. When his chosen subfield resisted, he pushed back even further. The other is Russell McCutcheon who, since his critical and pathbreaking *Manufacturing Religion* in 1997, has provided many of us with a set of terms and categories to think about "religion" in new ways. Like Neusner, McCutcheon has refused to be intimidated by the pushback from the more irenic and ecumenical types that haunt and still largely define religious studies. If I can be thought of in terms that are similar to the ways that Neusner and McCutcheon are in their chosen subfields, I will consider that I have done my job properly.

I would also like to thank my beautiful wife for all her help and support over the years. Whenever I am with her, I am home. She makes everything possible.

An earlier version of Chapter 5 appeared as "The Formative Period of Islam and the Documentary Approach: A Prolegomenon," in *A Legacy of Learning: Essays*

© Equinox Publishing Ltd. 2015

in Honor of Jacob Neusner, edited by Alan Avery-Peck, Bruce Chilton, William Scott Green, and Gary G. Porton (Leiden: Brill, 2014), pp. 372–85. Finally, parts of the Preface originally appeared as "ISIS: What's a Poor Religionist to Do?" published in *The Marginalia Review of Books* at http://marginalia.lareviewofbooks.org/mrblog-isis-whats-poor-religionist/.

— Preface —

Noble Lies

"Now," said [Socrates], "can we devise one of those lies—the kind that crop up as the occasion demands which we were talking about not long ago—so that with a single noble lie we can indoctrinate the rulers themselves, preferably, but at least the rest of the community?"

"What sort of lie?" said [Glaucon].

"Nothing too outlandish," said [Socrates], "just a tall story about something that happened all over the place in times past (at least that's what the poets claim and have persuaded us to believe), but which hasn't happened in our lifetimes and I'm not sure it could, and people would need a great deal of convincing about it."

(Plato 1993: 414b–c)

In April 2014 the Congregation of the People of Tradition for Proselytism and Jihad, now made famous by their Hausa name Boko Haram, kidnapped 276 Christian schoolgirls from Borno state, a northeastern province of Nigeria. It is believed some of the girls were sold into slavery and that others were forcefully converted to Islam so that they could be married off to Boko Haram soldiers. It is certainly a disturbing story, and it eventually caught the attention of the media and provoked outrage throughout the world. Although many hostile and politically conservative commentators in the West wanted to make Boko Haram into the latest poster boys for Islam, it would certainly be a mistake to transform these Nigerian Muslim militants into a metonym for Muslims worldwide. It would also be a mistake, however, to argue that they are somehow *not* Muslims, especially given the fact that the members of Boko Haram not only see themselves as such, but also because one of the clearer features of their largely inchoate mandate is to stop the so-called Westernization of Nigeria and implement a Muslim state governed by religious law (*sharia*).

Boko Haram did not last long in the news or in our collective imagination, however. They were quickly eclipsed by the even more outrageous acts of ISIS (also known as ISIL or Da'ish), the self-proclaimed "Islamic State." This group's brutal murder of those who do not share their vision (e.g., Shi`is, Christians, Druze) and its wanton disregard of the material cultural remains of the Ancient Near East quickly cast this group into the spotlight.

© Equinox Publishing Ltd. 2015

Despite Boko Haram's and ISIS's self-proclaimed commitment to a particular version of Islam, many so-called secular scholars of Islamic studies in the West were nevertheless quick to argue that these militant organizations were indeed beyond the pale of real Islam. Such scholars were content to put them at the current top of an ever-growing list that includes the likes of al-Qaeda, al-Shabaab, the Taliban, Jamaat-e-Islami, and Hamas. The Islam of Boko Haram and ISIS, not to mention the Islams of these other groups, conflicted with what these Western scholars believed to be the authentic version of the religion—one that was, for example, liberal, inclusive, pluralistic, feminist, gay-friendly, and so on—that they had largely created in their own pluralistic image. They used terms such as "vile," "repulsive," and "evil" to describe Boko Haram and ISIS, and many went so far as to proclaim that the members of these organizations were simply terrorists, not Muslims.

There is, however, a real problem with this scenario. The job of religious studies scholars—as opposed to, say, theologians—is to contextualize religion as a social phenomenon, not to judge who is or is not a good practitioner of religion. Religious studies, as I and many others conceptualize the field, is not about articulating the "sacred" or finding eternal meanings of human existence in the world's religion. It is, on the contrary, a critical enterprise, one wherein historically and socially embedded actors accomplish various political, social, and economic activities. One would think, indeed hope, that scholars who spend their time studying Islam within the secular discipline of religious studies would not be so quick to make pronouncements about what is or is not authentic Islam. Rather than judge the Islamic bona fides of groups such as Boko Haram and ISIS, why not attempt to explain and understand such groups within the larger context of globalization, religious fundamentalism, the crisis of Islamic masculinities, and the intersection of politics and religion? Such an understanding and contextualization would be much more helpful to students, to the media, and, I would hope, to the general population in the United States and other countries.

If we did this, we might say that groups like Boko Haram and ISIS are engaged in acts of legitimation based on the manipulation of a set of finite symbols that the tradition of Islam considers normative (e.g., Qur'an, Sunna). In this, they are not any different than any other social group, including those that say such versions of Islam are inauthentic, that sits under the canopy that we often label, monothetically and monovocally, as "Islam." Groups like Boko Haram and ISIS, thus, create and perform their identities in the public domain based on what they perceive to be the actualization of timeless and eternal truths. These acts of identification, though their actors may perceive them to exist outside the realm of history, are preeminently historical and necessarily social.

The question arises, then, why are so many scholars of Islam in the business of adjudicating between "authentic" and "inauthentic" versions of the religion? As a scholar of religion, I was always under the impression that we do not take sides in our analysis of data. On the contrary our goal is to analyze and explain through redescription—that is, taking native or indigenous reports and "redescribing" them in our own scholarly and analytic categories—as opposed to providing simple description or color commentary. The present book seeks to answer this question and, in the process, ask another one: what went wrong in the academic study of Islam? It uses the academic writings of scholars of Islam working within the larger discipline of religious studies—something I refer to pejoratively by the name "Islamic religious studies"—as its data to analyze the spiritual motivations, the rhetorical moves, and the political implications associated with the apologetical discourses that currently define the field. Many of these scholars are Muslims or converts to Islam and, for a variety of reasons to be examined in the pages that follow, they have created an Islam that is egalitarian, progressive and pluralistic, which they not surprisingly label as "authentic." In itself, there is certainly nothing wrong with this. Indeed, Muslims have been creating a variety of Islams, many at cross-purposes with one another, since the death of Muhammad in the sixth century CE until the present. However, when scholars—many of whom are employed by secular universities—do this in the name of the secular study of religion or the secular study of Islam, it is important to examine and critique their actions. It is a politically charged arena, to be sure. In the shadows the specter of Edward Said looms and at stake is who possesses the authority to represent Islam within the North American Academy.

The larger theoretical question that informs this study is what happens when a field or subdiscipline within the academic study of religion thinks that its largely untheorized questions and normative pronouncements are ipso facto important or beyond intellectual justification. We should, at least according to many within Islamic religious studies, simply take their narratives of what "real" Islam consists of and, thereby, take their word for it when they show how it differs from its many "unreal" despisers. The articulators of this authentic Islam claim that rival presentations of Islam are bastardizations that are either based on Orientalism or Islamophobia (if one is a non-Muslim) or misogyny or homophobia (if one is a Muslim that disagrees with them).

At issue is relevance. What are the consequences—intellectually, institutionally, socially, even religiously—of not theorizing data in ways that are of relevance to other scholars in religious studies or even the humanities more generally? If we simply manufacture stories that equate an originary and pristine Islam with notions of democracy, liberalism, gender justice and equality for all regardless of sexual preference, we are not engaging in scholarship, but mythopoesis.

* * *

In Book III of *The Republic*, as quoted above, Plato calls untrue stories made up for popular consumption "noble lies." These refer to stories told by elites for the sake of maintaining social harmony or advancing a particular agenda. I want to suggest in this volume that the Islam that scholars of Islamic religious studies manufacture amounts to little more than a set of noble lies. They are certainly noble in the sense that they seek to provide Islam with a series of benevolent attributes in order to counter what amounts to real hostility against this religion in the West. This benevolence I neither doubt nor is it my problem in the present volume. However, they are also lies in the sense that they do not conform to reality. In a short essay entitled "The Necessary Lie: Duplicity in the Disciplines," Jonathan Z. Smith differentiates between the "white lie" and "disciplinary lying." The former, he remarks, "is done in the name of our students, in the name of simplifying, of generalizing, of speaking to a wide and a diverse audience" (Smith 2007: 77).[1] Disciplinary lying, by contrast "becomes built into the structure of things, in which it becomes that which constitutes a discipline as a discipline over and against other disciplines" (Smith 2007: 77). While Smith acknowledges that a certain amount of disciplinary lying is necessary to carve out room for scientific analysis, he is most opposed to the little white lie:

> Though I think there is something to disciplinary lying, I think there is very little to justify introductory lying. In the case of the introductory courses, we produce incredibly mysterious objects because the students have not seen the legerdemain by which the object has appeared. The students sense that they are not in on the joke, that there is something that they don't get, so they reduce the experience to "Well, it's his or her opinion." (Smith 2007: 80)

It is these white lies (what I am here calling noble lies) that characterize the study of Islam not just at the introductory level, but also at the disciplinary level. Many scholars of Islam who work at major publicly funded universities and who publish in leading academic presses,[2] systematically engage in the misrepresentation of the complexity of Islam in the service of correcting negative stereotypes and of self-aggrandizement. They expect their students and their readers simply to take their word for it.

Certainly there are Muslims who are peaceful, just as there are Muslims who are bellicose; there are Muslims who are gay, just as there are Muslims who are homophobic; there are Muslims who are for granting equality to women, and there are Muslims who are not. One could, of course, apply these attributions to any religion. When the former terms of the aforementioned dyads are held up as authentic, and the latter as inauthentic, as a scholar of religion, I begin to worry for the health of my chosen field. My interest accordingly is with the desires governing such attributions and with the problems to which they inevitably give rise.

It is one thing to say that religious actors do good or bad things in the name of their religion, and that certain teachings within the religion help them to justify or legitimate their actions. In this regard Yigal Amir's use of select rabbinic teachings to justify his assassination of the Israeli Prime Minister Yitzhak Rabin or of James Kopp's use of the religious teachings of the Army of God to legitimate his murder of Dr. Barnett Slepian in my previous hometown of Amherst, NY are certainly grounded in Judaism and Christianity respectively. To claim that Amir or Kopp were crazy or lone "nuts" ignores the larger religious and political rhetoric that both creates and enables such actions. It is quite another thing, however, to say that only certain beliefs and actions—that is, the good ones or, at least, the ones with which we happen to agree—are legitimately religious, and that the bad ones are somehow not.

Yet, this is precisely what many scholars of Islamic religious studies do. They imagine an Islam that is egalitarian, progressive, pluralistic, democratic, and so on, and then maintain that it is the real or authentic version. But every Muslim believes that the Islam that he or she practices is the real or authentic one. This is, after all, the reason why they practice it. Osama bin Laden, no less than the leaders of Boko Haram and ISIS, was convinced that his understanding of Islam was the correct one and, because of this, the most authentic. As scholars of religion, it is our job to discuss the rhetoric of authenticity, not what or whose Islam is more authentic. Teaching in public universities, subsidized by tax dollars in a country that makes a sharp distinction between Church and State, it is not up to us to create "good" religion and differentiate it from so-called "bad" religion, even though many students and others want us to. We need to contextualize and explain, not to adjudicate and deprive. The moment we, as scholars of religion, say what gets to count as an authentically Islamic act, practice, or belief, all those who do not ascribe to them cease to be objects of study. In so doing, we actually end up depriving Muslim actors, whether existing synchronically or diachronically, of their agency.

The problem with these noble lies is that, as it turns out, they were not just meant for popular consumption after the events of 9/11, the point at which they were used with increased frequency as a way to correct woeful ignorance and hostility among Americans. "Why," many Americans naively asked, "do Muslims hate us so much that they would fly airplanes into our buildings?" The generic answer was simple: They were not Muslims, but, like Boko Haram and ISIS, hijackers of the beautiful tradition of Islam. This was again in the news with debates over how Islam should be portrayed at the newly opened 9/11 museum in New York City. In one of the installations, visitors can watch a seven-minute video called "The Rise of Al Qaeda." An interfaith group of New York clergy members argued the film failed to differentiate sufficiently between terrorism and Islam, and asked that changes be made to the presentation. The museum, however, refused. At stake in this little controversy, as we shall see throughout this study, is whose representation and what point of view is deemed authoritative and by whom? Creating Islam as a religion, if not *the* religion of peace, has now become the foundation of the subfield of Islam as taught within departments of religious studies in the United States. Because I find this sort of work to fall considerably short of what scholars should be doing, this volume both examines and critiques the desire to create this strategically partial Islam as it emerged and as it continues to power the engine of academic discourse.

After an introduction where I set out the interpretive ground and articulate the problems to be discussed in the remainder of this study, Chapter 1 defines in detail the characteristics of "Islamic religious studies." Here, we see the manifestation of the worst traits of identity politics wherein critical and historical scholarship can be simply dismissed as the stuff of "Orientalism," an increasingly amorphous and meaningless term. This means that certain topics are avoided (e.g., the redaction of the Qur'an, the early Islamic polity, source criticism of the *sira* literature), whereas others are embraced (e.g., finding a feminist stratum in the Qur'an, showing how Muhammad is an exemplar of modern virtues, making Sufism or Islamic mysticism normative). Certain theorists are mentioned in Islamic religious studies over and above Said, most notably Talal Asad, but his complex notions are reduced to make a Saidian point—"he argued forcefully that Muslim societies must be understood on their own terms and not a superimposed Western model" (Ernst and R. Martin 2010: 9). The invocation, even if problematic, of such theorists is necessary because it seeks to give intellectual legitimation to a project that is little more than apologetics. Such misreadings, moreover, are necessary because if the work of Asad were truly engaged it would ultimately be at cross-purposes with the aims of the constructive project of Islamic religious studies.

Chapter 2 begins with a debate between two scholars of Buddhism, Donald Lopez and Robert Thurman, on the proper representation of Tibet and Tibetan Buddhism. Whereas Lopez accuses Thurman of romanticizing Tibet, the latter suggests that no scholarship on the traditions of that country can ignore Chinese aggression and Tibetan suffering. This becomes my point of departure for thinking more generally about how many in Islamic religious studies believe ardently that the role of scholarship should be to defend a particular version of Islam that is of their own making rather than engage in anything that resembles critical scholarship as conceived in cognate disciplines. Much of the blame for this conceptual and categorical failure can, I argue, be laid squarely at the feet of the late Edward Said. For him, traditional attempts to understand Islam on historical grounds—so-called "Orientalism," something that is now pejoratively referred to as the *"bête noir"* of Islamic studies—amounts to little more than a politically motivated attempt to undermine Islam.

In the place of critical work, we instead witness the creation and dissemination of a liberal form of Islam to counter the version of the tradition linked with terrorism. The personal narratives of liberal Muslim scholars—based on narratives of dispossession, on the complexity of identities—now litter the field, and those critical of this project are often written off as hostile to Islam, as Orientalists, or, even worse, as "Islamophobes." Not surprisingly, those within the field who are uncomfortable with the now regnant discourses know that they are not to challenge them publicly. The problem, though, is that as historians and as critical scholars of religion we are expected to hold our technical skills in abeyance as others develop interpretations of Islam that they consider to be somehow immune from the complications of politics and history. We must, I argue, begin the process of historicizing these apologetic discourses, as opposed simply to assenting to them, within the "rhetoric of authenticity."

Chapter 3 charts a path to begin speaking about converts in the academic study of religion. Although it is a sensitive subject, we cannot overlook the fact that, through conversion, scholars are able to move from "outsiders" to "insiders" fairly rapidly. Rather than regard these two categories as hermetically sealed, conversion shows them to be porous and, ultimately, as artificial as any other category in the field. It is also problematic, it seems to me, when converts to Islam decide to equate Islam with "love" in their scholarly writings, for such an equation cannot be neatly separated from their own religious journeys. My interest is not in the inner states of these converts, such as what Islam offers them on a spiritual level that their previous traditions did not, or how and why this is the case. Rather, I try to respect their religious beliefs but at the same time examine critically their published writings. Here we would do well to remember that personal beliefs in religious studies are an inevitably thorny topic, and my goal here is to try to examine and provide some theoretical modeling to the threads, so tightly knotted, between the personal and the professional.

Chapters 4 and 5 provide two competing models for Islamic studies. Chapter 4 takes as its point of departure a short essay in which Omid Safi, a scholar of religion and a leading player in the progressive Islam movement, offers his opinion on the current state of Islamic religious studies. Therein he is critical of non-Muslims in the field, and instead invokes a number of scholars—Sherman Jackson, Amina Wadud, Jonathan Brown, Kecia Ali, Ingrid Mattson, and others—whom he believes should function as models "to be emulated by the current and future generation of Islamic studies." In this chapter I examine the writings of these scholars with an eye toward asking whether or not they should indeed function as "models." Picking up a theme from Chapter 2, it is worth noting that, as far as I know, all of the scholars that he mentions are converts to Islam and, for the most part, all engage in apologetical readings of the tradition.

If the goal of Chapter 2 was to show how the issues in Islamic religious are not unique, but indicative of larger debates within the academic study of religion, Chapter 5 offers another exemplum, this time from the field of Jewish studies, and focuses on the work, motivations, and relevance of the work of Jacob Neusner. Neusner, a scholar of Jewish studies, did more than anyone to bring the *academic* study of Jewish data into sync with the conversations happening within the larger context of the humanities. He did this not by apologizing for Judaism, but by submitting its traditions to historical, textual, and critical scrutiny. He could do so even though he was also trained as a rabbi (making him an "insider," as it were) and, moreover, he could do so during the 1950s and 1960s, a period of rampant anti-Semitism and at a time when pretty much the only place one could study Judaism was theologically in a seminary. One of the reasons Neusner could do this, and this is why I use him or at least his approach as another possible model, is because he had such respect for his data that he realized he had to make Judaism into a legitimate academic topic using the critical language and categories of other disciplines.

The sixth and final chapter provides an attempt to deal with many of the aforementioned issues, albeit from the perspective of greater theoretic distance. For ultimately many of the problems that I have broached and discussed in the previous chapters are but a set of examples, derived from my own chosen field, that are representative of what I consider to be some of the larger issues endemic to the academic study of religion. The questions that I have asked in the previous chapters, if I have done my job properly, ought to be relevant to those dealing with similar issues, but working in other religious traditions. Since religious studies lacks a consistent and consensual theoretical framework, it should come as no surprise that there are passionate debates about how to negotiate "religious" data. The debate in Islamic religious studies, then, reflects a larger trend in the academic study of religion that revolves around the appropriate place for theory and method. In a discipline governed by status quo, what should the role of new method and theory be? What, framed somewhat differently, is the ultimate price of transgression?

* * *

The chapters that follow seek to criticize the increasingly popular discussion of manufacturing good Islam. My position, as should be clear already, is that the widespread scholarly assumption, operative in so much of North American scholarship on Islam as carried out within departments of religious studies, is best conceptualized as constructively theological as opposed to scholarly. The self-evidence of data—as personal, as driven by identity politics, as immune from various social and political concerns—needs to be held up to critical scrutiny. As things currently stand, much of the scholarship associated with Islamic religious studies exists beyond criticism, is highly personal, and is not subject to independent verification, with the result that the standards of evidence that define scholarship in the contemporary university have little or no bearing on the academic study of Islam.

Notes

1. The essay appears online at http://teaching.uchicago.edu/?/ctl-archive/course-design-tutorials/assessing-and-improving/smith. It also appears in McCutcheon (2007). For the sake of convenience, I quote from the latter.
2. It is for this reason that I frequently mention where these scholars teach and the presses in which they publish. My goal is to alert the non-specialist in Islam, who might not be familiar with the names, to show that I am not talking about a fringe group in marginal institutions. Indeed, these individuals are training the faculty of tomorrow and this is what I find so worrisome.

And still others, convinced of the validity of their own religion beyond any doubt, hold the opinion that they should defend it before others, show it to be fair and free it of suspicion, and ward off their adversaries from it, by using any chance thing. They would not even disdain to use falsehoods, sophistry, confounding, and contentiousness ...

Abu Nasr Alfarabi (870–950; in Alfarabi 1963: 30)

Can we imagine a corner of the modern world in which this state of interpretation—of total confusion, of harmonies, homologies, homogenies, is not found confusing but reassuring? Can we mentally conjure up a social setting for learning in which differentiation is avoided and credulity rewarded? In which analysis is heresy, dismissed as worthless or attacked as "full of mistakes"? Can we conceive of a world in which repetition, in one's own words, of what the sources say is labeled scholarship, and anthologizing is labeled as learning?

Jacob Neusner (1995: 11)

— Introduction —

Setting the Problem

The present volume provides my third installment of a sustained analysis and criticism of the regnant discourses concerning Islam as carried out within departments of religious studies in North America and beyond. I refer to this rather peculiar amalgam of apologetics, political correctness, religious studies, and Islamic studies as "Islamic religious studies," whose first principles and assumptions Chapter 1 will explain in considerable detail. In *Situating Islam* (Hughes 2006), I sought to examine—historically, intellectually, institutionally, and politically—how and why the study of Islam entered the larger disciplinary field of religious studies. My goal in doing this was to show how things in Islamic religious studies had arrived at the state that they currently are in. My conclusion, which will form my point of departure here, is that Islamic religious studies represents an unhealthy commixture of apologetics for Islam with the dominant discourse of religious studies that privileges experience over praxis and the "religious" as if it somehow existed independently from more social or political (i.e., mundane) concerns. Then in *Theorizing Islam* (Hughes 2012d), I simultaneously tried to dismantle these regnant discourses and to reconstruct them in what I considered to be a more theoretically responsible manner. Governing both of these previous works was the notion that the field has become far too apologetical and, in the process, little more than a venue for progressive Muslim theologizing.

This confusion of critical scholarship with constructive theology has created numerous problems for the field. It means, for one thing, that historical and critical questions are largely ignored and are instead replaced with the quest to create a normative Islam that corresponds to that which is perceived to be universally recognized, as opposed to modern Western, values. "Authentic" Islam is defined, as we saw in the preface, as egalitarian and pluralistic; those types of Islam that do not correspond to this model (that of the Taliban, for example, or that found in Saudi Arabia where women are, among other things, forbidden from driving) are regarded as somehow "inauthentic." While I certainly have no problem with young Muslim scholars trying to reform their tradition from within—it has been done, after all, in both Christianity and Judaism—I do worry that this is going on in secular departments of religious studies and being done under the guise of so-called "critical" scholarship.[1]

© Equinox Publishing Ltd. 2015

My interest in the present revolves around the following set of questions: What happens when we use such judgmental and reverential language in the classroom? What happens to an academic field when historical questions retreat into the background and instead become replaced with presentist concerns? What role is there for the non-Muslim scholar of Islam in the contemporary period? These are massive questions that need to be addressed in the field, but currently are not. The present volume is an attempt to generate this larger and necessary conversation.

If Islamic religious studies is to survive as a viable academic field, one that successfully integrates into the larger disciplinary framework of the humanities and social sciences, it must resist the temptation to protect its data from critical intellectual scrutiny. As it stands now, such inquiry can neatly be sidestepped using the language of the late Edward Said, to wit, that since scholarship is politically motivated, the language used to study Islam has been traditionally used in the service of a host of colonial and repressive ends. While I certainly do not doubt for a minute the coupling of scholarship and ideology, I do not think that this should immediately curtail certain modes of analysis or avenues of inquiry simply by its invocation. Perhaps another way of saying all this is that while ideology is certainly a part of scholarship, it is not the only part.

The events of September 11, 2001, have pretty much defined the way we deal with Islam and have, whether we like it or not, created an obsession with all things Muslim in the academy, in the media, and on the "street." Take the veil, for example. Many non-Muslims see it as a sign of the oppression of women in Islam; many scholars of Islamic religious studies, however, seek to counter this stereotype and argue that, *if understood properly*, the veil actually becomes a sign of the freedom of Muslim women, something that enables them to perform their identities in their own privileged sphere (e.g., Ahmed 1993; Ali 2006; Wadud 2006; Kassam 2010; Ahmed 2011; Aslan, Hermansen, and Medeni 2013; Chaudhry 2014; Hidayatullah 2014). Muslim women, for such scholars, are not nearly as oppressed as many would claim. In itself, this is certainly not a problematic claim. Where the argument gets strained, however, is in the assumption that when Islam is *properly understood*, it is a tradition that is clearly egalitarian. Moreover, there is also the assumption that these scholars are the ones who have the wherewithal to engage in this proper understanding. Men oppress women, in their conceptualization, but true Islam does not. This is a variation on the age-old trope that religion spiritualizes and culture or politics pollutes. Problems only occur when people *misunderstand* religion, thereby corrupting it. When Jews, Muslims, or Christians do bad things in the name of their religions, it is a bastardization of a pure or pristine faith, a "political" corruption of a "spiritual" teaching.[2] Yet, the problem with this claim is that it assumes that religions exists somewhere in the ether, that is, independently of social actors and that it cannot be reduced to something else.

The following study is both informed by and hopes to contribute to the ongoing theoretical question carried out by some in the discipline of religious studies—their names will quickly become apparent in the pages that follow—who want to do away with the concept of religion as an academic descriptor. They maintain that the field would be better served by unraveling the various acts, institutions, objects, and claims that we normally collapse into the term "religion" as opposed to reifying a Western term for which most languages (and thus cultures of the globe) have no equivalence.[3] Rather than subsequently distinguish between "authentic" or "inauthentic," terms that are little more than products of the imagination, we need to historicize them, as indeed we must historicize all of our discourses, lest we assume they exist naturally in the world and all that we have to do is discover or bring them to light.

At the center of the contemporary study of Islam, to reiterate, are the events of 9/11. It is important, however, that we not let these events, including the concomitant desire to either denigrate or apologize for Islam cloud our understanding, as I fear it has. These events have thrust Islam into the spotlight and, as a result, everyone—political pundit, politician, scholar, journalist, taxi driver—necessarily has an opinion about it. Islam is this, that, or the other thing. In this myriad of claims, however, we have largely lost sight of the fact that Islam is, like every religious tradition, a canopy under which sit a plethora of *humanly* constructed voices, acts, beliefs, and institutions, many of which are in disagreement with one another. Within this context, I differ from many of those that I critique in this study. Islam, for me, is nothing more (or less) than a fascinating social movement and the human imaginative practices that it has given rise to are certainly worthy of scholarly attention. But when some of these practices are held up as better, more normative, than others, or when some of them are believed to be more in sync with what is perceived to be a pristine quranic message, categorical mistakes will inevitably ensue.

The present volume seeks to focus on the intimate intersection between Islamic religious studies and identity politics. This intersection is a rather recent phenomenon that, like so much in the field, can be traced to the post-9/11 era. We have seen in the past 15 years a growing desire to articulate, as we have already witnessed, an Islam that is believed to be in accord with a set of liberal values that are perceived to exist naturally in the world. Those parts of the tradition that fit well with such a construction are deemed "authentic" and those that do not can be labeled as "inauthentic" and neatly excised. The result is the manufacture of a liberal and progressive Islam that revolves around a set of positive notions such as pluralism, justice, and egalitarianism.[4] The only problem with this is that it is based on the rhetoric of authenticity that confuses narratives of origins with actual origins, and is produced via an elaborate system of privilege and denial in which data are ignored or employed solely on account of their utility to fit with predetermined conclusions.[5]

It is one thing to create a set of noble lies to correct prejudices; however, it is something entirely different to distort the manifold and diverse local traditions that have both synchronically and diachronically gone by the generic term "Islam." Yet, this is precisely what has happened. In their desire to create a progressive Islam, scholars in secular university settings have done what they accuse their critics of: producing a one-sided version of the religion to score a political point. The *ideal* goal of religious studies, however, should not be the manufacture of good religion; rather it ought to analyze how religious narratives are invoked in the formation of identity, a *social* and *political* category that is also related to a host of social, economic, and gendered variables. This has been and continues to be my problem with Islamic religious studies. In their desire to create a pristine Islam, many scholars actually succeed in denying real Muslims, both in the past and in the present, their agency as social and historical actors. Islamic religious studies is about reading the values that contemporary scholars deem valid and finding them, selectively, within the tradition. As active producers of Islam, I chose to examine the writings of these scholars not as secondary sources, but as primary ones.

Yet, if Islamic religious studies is little more than the locus of progressive Muslim constructive theology, where does this leave non-Muslims? It leaves them, I submit, with essentially two options. Either they can convert to the tradition or they can act as voyeurs and cheerleaders. Both options have indeed become the norm. As for the former, many converts to Islam today exist within the field, and a great many of them are deeply involved in the progressive Muslim movement.[6] Rather than pass over this in silence, I think it is high time to theorize "the convert" in religious studies in general and Islamic religious studies in particular. The other or latter option, that of the voyeur or cheerleader, essentially recycles the discourses put forth by the former group without actively engaging in the constructive Muslim theology side of things. In his "Theses on Method," Bruce Lincoln states that

> When one permits those whom one studies to define the terms in which they will be understood, suspends one's interest in the temporal and contingent, or fails to distinguish between "truths," "truth claims," and "regimes of truth," one has ceased to function as historian or scholar. In that moment, a variety of roles are available: some perfectly respectable (amanuensis, collector, friend, and advocate), and some less appealing (cheerleader, voyeur, retailer of import goods). None, however, should be confused with scholarship. (Lincoln 1996: 227)

What powers Islamic religious studies, as I hope to show in the pages that follow, is a selective use of critical theory, an obsession with Orientalism, and the invocation of identity politics. The first, the selective use of critical theory, usually means invoking Said's groundbreaking, though by now increasingly dated, *Orientalism* (1978), in addition to the selective use of more recent scholars, such as Talal Asad and Judith Butler. The second feature, the obsession with Orientalism, is intimately related to the first. It means that anyone or any theory even remotely critical of Islam or the enterprise of creating a good Islam can be summarily ignored and written off as hostile, Eurocentric, or Islamophobic. The third feature, identity politics, allows Muslim scholars—whether by birth or conversion—to imagine a shared experience of injustice that permits them simultaneously to assert or reclaim ways of understanding their distinctiveness and to challenge what they perceive to be dominant oppressive characterizations.

Tearing Down Boundaries Between "Insiders" and "Outsiders"

This book argues that the academic study of Islam as carried out and practiced within departments of religious studies must become more critical and less apologetic. One should be able to be a critical scholar of Islam and, simultaneously be a Muslim or sympathetic to the tradition. They need not be mutually exclusive enterprises. Framed using a set of categories from the larger academic study of religion, one can write about the tradition as an "outsider" while at the same time being an "insider." Whether Muslim or not, one does not have to take up the mantel of religious caretaker. It ought to be possible to engage in historical, philological, and critical scholarship without serving a larger project of reforming Islam within or protecting that which has been reformed from disinterested scrutiny. This is currently the crossroads at which this subfield finds itself, and the present volume seeks to offer an alternative to the type of scholarship that is, at the moment, unfortunately *de riguer* by subjecting it to a sustained critique. Rather than reify Islam, whether "progressive" or otherwise, and use it as the standard by which to judge rival Islams, the subfield of Islamic studies, at least as understood in the broader disciplinary unit of religious studies, must begin to engage with the *critical* discourses of this larger field of study. This is certainly not to say that everything that passes for scholarship in the field of religious studies is critical, however. By "critical discourses" I refer specifically to the likes of Daniel Dubuisson (2003), Bruce Lincoln (1994, 1999, 2003), Tomoko Masuzawa (1993, 2005), Russell McCutcheon (1997), J. Z. Smith (1982, 2003), and Winnifred Sullivan (2005); in addition to the work of scholars from cognate disciplines, such as sociology (e.g., Bourdieu 1984, 1993), anthropology (e.g., Asad 1993, Bayart 2005, Bloch 2013), and philosophy (e.g., Butler [1990]1999; Schatzki 2008).[7]

Many in Islamic religious studies, I submit, undertheorize their data because, in many ways, they serve as their own data. Progressive Muslims create a progressive Islam for consumption for other progressive Muslims, many of whom are professors of Islamic religious studies. The complexity of identity is mentioned—for example that of a gay convert to Islam or an Arab-American scholar—but never queried let alone undermined. If we take the theoreticians mentioned at the end of the last paragraph seriously, it becomes difficult, if not impossible, to write from the perspective of being an "insider" to a tradition because we are all, as the chapters that follow want to suggest, ultimately "outsiders." There is, in other words, no privileged position, no Archimedean point, which permits one immediate or unmediated access to something problematically referred to as Islam. Indeed one of the mandates of this volume is to destabilize and problematize "insider" and "outsider," two hallmark categories in the academic study of religion.

Too often the insider/outsider problem is invoked as a way to establish or signal authority. If one styles oneself as an insider, an outsider will necessarily lack some sort of metaphysical or intangible connection to the tradition in question. But how can circumstance of birth dictate destiny? Framed across the hermeneutical divide, a self-styled outsider sees the insider as someone who is hopelessly incompetent when it comes to understanding his or her own religion objectively.

If the former revolves around identity politics, the latter is based on implicit racism or sexism. Neither, however, need be the case. Returning to the events of 9/11, however, we really see the need on the part of scholars of Islamic religious studies to identify or sympathize with the insider position. Yet the problem with this, as I alluded to above, is that there really can be no "inside" because we all are, whether we admit it or not or whether we like it or not, writing from outside. An Arab-American scholar, for example, may write from his or her own position as an Arab-American, but certainly he or she will no more be "inside" to early or medieval Islam, let alone contemporary Gulf or Levantine Islam.

What happens when identity politics is elevated to the place of a regnant methodology in the field? My goal in the pages that follow is to call to task those who want to pick and choose various ideas from various theoreticians in order to pretend to be more critical than they actually are. It is to ask questions of a subfield that has become mired in apologetic verbiage. It is, in other words, an attempt to offer an anti-essentialist critique aimed at increasingly essentialized and essentializing discourses that now define the field. I blame Edward Said for much of the problems currently besetting Islamic religious studies. Virtually every book in Islamic religious studies opens up with an invocation of his name— "The central point of Said's *Orientalism* is to challenge the authority and political neutrality of self-referential knowledge about the (Muslim) Other" (Grewal 2014: 5); or Said "was able to expose the false assumptions about Middle Eastern (Islamic) societies and the romanticism that was ascribed to them in Orientalist constructions" (Ernst and R. Martin 2010: 3); or

> Said mobilized the theories of Michel Foucault to argue that Western colonial powers engineered the creation of knowledge about Arab and Middle Eastern societies in order to dominate them not just in terms of political power but also cultural productions, artistic imagination, and discursive interaction. Everyone working in the fields of Islamic Studies and Middle Eastern Studies is indebted to Said. (Kugle 2014: 4)

Although I shall discuss the problems associated with Said's approach in Chapter 3 below, it suffices to mention in the present context that Said was no less driven by ideology than those he criticized, and that his selective use of European Orientalism to make a literary point (it is important to remember that he was a Professor of English and Comparative Literature) has largely been translated into a historiographic register by his followers. In these translative acts, Said's corpus is read or is reduced to the claim that, framed in terms of the language of the present study, Europeans function as outsiders and are thus politically motivated in their scholarship on Islam, whereas Muslims or Arabs, as insiders, somehow are not and that they should be granted the authority (by whom it is unclear) to represent themselves.

Despite my criticism of the Saidian project or at least its reception history among scholars of Islamic religious studies, I nonetheless follow his methodology of discourse analysis. Just as he analyzed select passages from the writings of, among others, Orientalists past and present, I do the same. Only the texts that I analyze are all from contemporary scholars of Islamic religious studies. My goal in doing this is to examine some of the assumptions, both tacit and otherwise, in their presentation of Islam.

The "Crisis in the Humanities" and the Study of Islam

Islamic religious studies might well be a sign of what has become vogue to call in recent years the "crisis in the humanities," by which I refer to the decreased enrollments and general lack of interest in the humanities because the disciplines that comprise them are largely thought to be irrelevant or unpractical. Whether there is a crisis or not is the matter of some debate and it is certainly not my desire to wade into it here.[8] What I will comment on, though, is the sheer irrelevance of much of what passes for the academic study of Islam. This is a true paradox because, at a time when Islam is so much in the public spotlight, one would think that the academic study of this religion might actually show others just how relevant the humanities can be. Students want to know about the political, religious, intellectual, and theological *history* of Islam, not listen to faculty actively construct what they consider to be "proper" Islam in front of them. Islamic religious studies is presentist, ideological, and driven by the desire to find, articulate, and disseminate what its practitioners consider to be an authentic expression of their faith. If students at public universities funded by taxpayers want to learn about what might motivate some Muslims to commit violence and murder in the name of Islam, they are quickly told they were not "real" Muslims and are, instead, given faith-based sermons on what this "real" Islam consists of.

Certainly much research in the humanities is based on self-searching and self-discovery. This, indeed, is one of the features that makes it so appealing to those of us lucky enough to gain entrance into the guild. However, we need to be aware that there are certain conventions that govern appropriate intellectual conduct in the university. Since the United States, for example, is governed by a distinction between Church and State, we must be cautious of crossing what is an admittedly very fine line. This is certainly not to claim that religion should not be taught *about*—to use Justice Tom Clark's concurring opinion in *School District of Abington Township, Pennsylvania v. Schempp*—in the university, but it does mean that we should not be in the business of distinguishing between what we as scholars personally believe to be "correct'" and "incorrect" versions of religion (see Orsi 2005: 187–90).[9] The moment we do this, we cease to be scholars of religion and instead become theologians who seek to articulate and disseminate a particular religious perspective. We must speak of regimes of truth, to invoke Bruce Lincoln (1996: 226), as opposed to articulating truth claims.

Students with no oar in this stream do not need to be privy to the theological musings of liberal Muslim professors, especially at state universities. Although we can teach students about the complexity of identity invention and maintenance and introduce them to the nuances of social theory, many enroll in our Introduction to Islam courses to learn the basics of Islam *from a value-neutral perspective*. If we fail to do this, and admittedly a value-neutral position may well prove chimerical, then we fail in our vocation.

Whose "Inside" and Where Exactly Is "Outside"

Before I proceed to my analysis, it might be worthwhile to situate myself personally in this conversation. I am usually not in the habit of beginning monographs in this manner, but I do maintain—indeed, it is one of the premises of this book—that ideology forms an intimate part of scholarship. Scholarship, in other words, is interested and perspectival, and those ideological aspects of it must be uncovered and, where necessary, critically cross-examined. This is not to say that scholarship is simply ideology in drag, but it is to acknowledge that it is situated and, therefore, always incomplete. As a result, the reader needs to know that the author has been self-reflexive and upfront about his or her own situatedness. My colleague Andrew Rippin once accused me, I think correctly, of not letting others know whence I am coming. He argued that anyone engaged in the criticism of an entire subdiscipline, as I presumably am, ought to make clear to readers what motivates his or her criticisms. He contends that

> it is primarily a matter of all of us being willing to situate ourselves within the academy of higher learning as the individuals we are, with our experiences in scholarship and in the classroom, with our networks of colleagues, and in our own relationship to the subject of Islam. (Rippin 2012: 409)

So, without further ado, let me try to begin this process of situation.

I am a Jew, but one with a complicated relationship to the tradition. My maternal grandfather was an Arab and a Shi`i Muslim from South Lebanon.[10] When others ask me what I am, I invoke Derrida and call myself an "Arab-Jew" (Bennington and Derrida 1993: 292–7). I have no idea if this makes me an "insider" or an "outsider," nor, I have to admit, do I particularly care. My point of this disclosure, however, is precisely this complexity—both in myself and in those I study (see, e.g., Hughes 2010, 2013a). Identity, for me is neither an eternal nor assumed essence that is simply and amorphously passed on from one generation to another.[11] Identity (religious or otherwise) is, on the contrary, something imagined, manufactured, contested, and patrolled on account of its porosity. This is why I will never speak of authenticity, the "real," or the like, preferring to take a more positivistic and/or reductionist approach to religious and other identities.

Although a Jew, I consider myself to be an Arab. But does being a Jew disqualify someone from engaging in scholarship in Islam, especially if one does not feel comfort with the regnant discourses of the field? Writing these words in the midst of Israel's most recent bombardment of Gaza (August 2014), comments on social media (including those made by many scholars) would seem to make this difficult, no matter what one's opinion on Israel or Zionism. Regardless, it is not ingenuous when I say that I feel a tremendous affiliation with and respect for Islam and Arab culture. Indeed, I grew up with the latter. I underscore that this was not Sephardic Jewish culture of North Africa as it was, for example, for Derrida, but Arabo-Islamic culture associated with South Lebanon. This permits me, on a fundamental level, to feel like an "insider" to Arab culture, much of which is defined by Islam. However, my own background has *not* led me to try to recuperate some fictive Arab, Lebanese, or Jewish identity, but to appreciate the precariousness both of self and of identity. When others ignore this precariousness and instead try to invent an identity for themselves that is based on selective readings that they subsequently hold up as normative, I believe that I have no option but to engage in critique.

Identity, for me, is extremely complicated and, therefore, highly contested. Although much work in Islamic religious studies claims to study identity, it unfortunately and rarely if ever interrogates it as a social category, preferring instead to compare and contrast identity to some normatively constructed "Islam." Sexual or racial identity is, thus, never examined in all its complexity, say, as regimes of discourse and power that inscribe themselves or are inscribed by others on the body, but as positive traits that can be folded into a pluralistic Islam that is signified as authentic. This pluralistic or progressive Islam is, as we shall see in the following chapters, derived from selectively reading certain texts. In itself, there is nothing wrong with this: Muslims have been doing this since the advent of Islam in the seventh century CE. However, what is problematic for me and for others who share my concerns is that this liberal, pluralistic Islam is being articulated in secular departments of religious studies and subsequently disseminated in the classroom, in scholarly works, and in the public domain as if it were true and authentic.

After I graduated with my PhD, I took a position as a scholar of Islam at the University of Calgary in Canada. My task was to teach classical Arabic, the Qur'an, and early Islamic history. My first week on the job coincided with September 11, 2001. I was, like so many in the field, neither equipped nor sure what to do. I watched as my colleagues in the United States reacted quickly, and one could argue correctly, by claiming that those who engaged in such attacks did not represent all Muslims. Although I do admit that I was uncomfortable with the related proposition that quickly followed this, namely, that the people who perpetrated such crimes were not "real" or "authentic" Muslims. It was quite clear, by contrast, that such individuals not only considered themselves to be Muslims, but the most authentic ones at that. Again, the rhetoric of authenticity was being waged. I recognized this from having recently read Russell McCutcheon's *Manufacturing Religion* (1997), which spoke at length about the trope of authenticity in the academic study of religion.

The situation in Canada, however, was somewhat different than in America in the days after 9/11. Since many Canadian Muslims did not feel they had to genuflect to some amorphous sense of American patriotism, the air was somewhat less clear. In the week after 9/11, for example, at a memorial held in my then university a young, male Muslim student from North Africa, who had been invited to speak by the campus organizers, boldly and cryptically informed a stunned crowd that Islam would always enable the downtrodden to fight back against oppressors. My goal on campus was not so much to defend Muslim students against attacks, but to temper what many perceived to be the potentially hostile rhetoric uttered by some Muslims! I hated doing it. Unlike, I think, most of my colleagues in the field, I disliked being either the on- or off-campus spokesperson for a religious tradition that was not my own. I quickly rebelled and stop engaging in such activity. As coincidence would have it, that semester also coincided with tremendous resistance to my teaching on the part of some conservative Muslim students. They did not want to learn about the redaction of the Qur'an or the problems associated with reconstructing the early Muslim polity. All was clear to them: Islam was eternal and I should not problematize it for them or for non-Muslims. I should simply "tell it as it is" (i.e., in the same manner that they had learned it from religious leaders in places like the Gulf States or Bosnia).

As the months and years passed, it became clear that the study of Islam had changed radically. Some of this had to do with sheer logistics: the number of positions had increased exponentially; the number of groups devoted to the study of Islam at the American Academy of Religion (AAR) had also grown at a rapid rate. To many of these scholars, many of them Muslims or converts to Islam, the AAR now became the place where they could comfort one another and tell their personal journeys with and in Islam to anyone who would listen. Scholarship was slowly giving way to identity politics. I, like many others, felt completely out of place at these self-help sessions. I began to spend more time at panels and with colleagues that were interested in the *critical* as opposed to theological study of religion. Rather than envisage the academic study of religion as a venue of self-discovery within a religious tradition, my new colleagues and I queried the very premise of what constitutes "religion," and the role of authenticity and the creation of identity in such processes.

Much time and energy in those years after 9/11 went into creating a normative Islam, one that—as we have seen—was compatible with notions of liberalism, democracy, and equality. Those who commit violence in the name of Islam, so the master narrative went, were not and could not be true Muslims. Rather than engage in such questions of normativity, I was more interested in asking how so-called discourses of "normativity" bought into the rhetoric of authenticity. This meant that I began to study the study of Islam.

Gradually I began to define myself more as a religionist than an Islamicist. This made me aware that the battle lines drawn in Islamic studies are not sui generis, and that all of us who work in religious studies are embedded in a much larger field as opposed to autonomous regions (i.e., the religion we happen to work on) that only bump against one another at places such as the Annual Meeting of the American Academy of Religion or within a departmental hiring committee. This is why I find the debates between scholars who work in other religions—such as Lopez and Thurman in Buddhist studies, and Neusner and virtually the entire field in Jewish studies—to be so interesting and illuminating. The relationship between insider and outsider, in other words, is endemic to religious studies more broadly and cannot simply be confined to the study of Islam. I, thus, use Islam as but one exemplum to shed light on a larger disciplinary issue.

Since most of my scholarly work, other than my critiques of the field of Islamic studies, involved, as they had since graduate school, the Jews of medieval Islam (many of whom wrote and thought in Arabic), I gradually and increasingly began to turn my attention to Jewish studies.[12] Much to the chagrin of my colleagues at the University of Calgary, I now wanted little to do with teaching Islam. Since changes in curriculum had to be voted on by the department, the majority of my colleagues there voted against my attempts to teach courses dealing with Judaism and the comparative study of Judaisms and Islams, this even after the fact that I had been the victim of anti-Semitic abuse from a non-Muslim student who was infatuated with Arabic and Islam. So, despite the fact that I am a Western Canadian, I left to take up an endowed Chair in Jewish studies, first at the University at Buffalo and now at the University of Rochester.[13]

Personal narratives, I would hope, are only important if they illumine a larger theoretical point. My goal in relating mine is to show, first and foremost, that *all* identity is complex, not just those of African-American Muslims or first-generation Iranians who are also scholars of Islam. Second, that the insider/outside debate is also more complex than we might realize. One can be an Arab (as I consider myself) or a Muslim and still be critical of the field's regnant discourses thereby becoming a so-called "outsider," just as one can be neither a Muslim nor Arab and be, write, and act as an "insider." There are, as I shall examine in the final chapter, a host of political and career reasons for engaging in the latter since they are the regnant discourses after all. Adding further to this complexity is the role of the convert in Islamic religious studies. It, thus, becomes extremely difficult to know who is an "insider" and who is an "outsider." Third, criticism of these regnant discourse are not simply the provenance of neoconservative Islamophobes. Too often critics of Islamic religious studies, such as myself, can be neatly silenced with the claim that we are hostile to Islam. Moreover, our work can unfortunately even be picked up by neocons and used in ways that we never intended. However, this use and abuse of scholarship should not be reason not to mount the critique in the first place. Indeed, it is my respect for the complexity and diversity within the monolithic rubric "Islam" that drives my critique. I refuse to flatten the breadth and diversity of Islamic traditions into a monolith known as "progressive Islam."

There is, I wish to suggest, something at stake in the imagery and language we use to convey impressions and thoughts on the way we, as scholars, imagine Islam. If we fail to acknowledge that we have manufactured this Islam (or, religion more generally) we will obscure the various theoretical and methodological modes of its production. This comes, as I suggest in the pages that follow, with a real intellectual cost.

Notes

1. This, of course, is not unlike what went on within the formation of Jewish studies in Germany in the nineteenth century. Then and there, young German-Jews, many fed up with the traditional religion of their parents and grandparents, began to engage

in critical scholarship of Jewish texts. Although they claimed to be "critical," in the background were a host of political desires, not the least of which was the political emancipation of German-Jews and, indeed, the reformation of their own religion. The only difference between these scholars and contemporary scholars of Islamic religious studies is that the former were not allowed to teach in German universities and, instead, had to make do with teaching in seminaries associated with the new denominational movements (e.g., Reform, Conservative). See, for example, the studies in Schorsch (1994), Wiese (2005), Brenner (2010), and Hughes (2013b).

2. Thus, Karen Armstrong (2000: ix): "The spiritual quest is an interior journey; it is a psychic rather than a political drama. It is preoccupied with liturgy, doctrine, contemplative discipline and an elaboration of the heart, not with the clash of current events ... power struggles are not what religion is really about, but an unworthy distraction from the life of the spirit, which is conducted far from the maddening crowd, unseen, silent, and unobtrusive."

3. According to Daniel Dubuisson (2003: 191), "The history of religions should not have exported this singular notion [i.e., 'religion'], found nowhere else, and issuing from a history that took its own unique course, without having subjected it beforehand to a rigorous critical examination. But it did not do so. Instead, it exported it, along with the West's doxa, without the least doubt or scruple, as if it were inconceivable that other cultures should not possess, if only in primitive, incomplete or aberrant, monstrous form, what seemed to every Western mind the very sign of humanity and civilization."

4. A representative sampling of such treatments includes Soroush (2002), Safi (2003), Abou El Fadl (2005), Jackson (2005), Moosa (2005), Hussain (2006), Wadud (2006), Ramadan (2007), Haj (2008), Esack (2009), Jackson (2009), Safi (2009), Ernst and R. Martin (2010), Kassam (2010), Kugle (2010), Ramadan (2010), Hammer (2012), Shaikh (2012), Aslan, Hermansen, and Medeni (2013), Mattson (2013), Chaudhry (2014), Grewal (2014), Hidayatullah (2014), and Kugle (2014).

5. Of course, we must not lose sight of the many hostile and politically motivated books (e.g., Emerson 2002; Pipes 2002; Manji 2003; Spencer 2007; in addition to websites such as campus-watch.org) that seek to define Islam as a religion of violence and as a tradition that is incompatible with the modern world. The great paradox, of course, is that both apologists and critics of Islam engage in the same selective reading of texts to make their point.

6. See, for examples Chapters 2 and 4 below.

7. This list is certainly not complete; it will expand in the coming pages. I mention these theorists here simply to situate myself and the project that follows within an intellectual genealogy.

8. See, for example the collection of essays in Bérubé and Nelson (1995).

9. I have written about the *School District of Abington Township, Pennsylvania v. Schempp* at greater length in Hughes (2013c).

10. Indeed my grandfather—Muhammad Ali ibn Khalil al-Nijdi (aka Bud Alley)—was one of the founding fathers of the first mosque in Canada, the masjid al-rashid in Edmonton, Alberta, built in 1938.

11. Here I follow the list of theorists mentioned on p. 5 above.

12. With, I should add, the same critical edge (see, for example, Hughes 2010, 2013b, 2014a).

13. My leaving Calgary has recently garnered attention in the Canadian media on account of several Canadian-born Muslims leaving that city to fight with ISIS. Despite the

problematic title, see "University of Calgary Refused to Remove Student Spreading Pro-Jihad Views from Jewish Professor's Class," *National Post*, June 26, 2014. This may be accessed online at http://news.nationalpost.com/news/canada/university-of-calgary-refused-to-remove-student-spreading-pro-jihad-messages-from-jewish-professors-class.

— 1 —

Islamic Religious Studies and the Politics of Identity

The present chapter seeks to define in greater detail the term that I have already alluded to in the previous pages, "Islamic religious studies." I use the term in a negative sense to denote a type of apologetical and theory-light work carried out by scholars of Islam who inhabit departments of religious studies.[1] It is also a term that conveniently permits me to distinguish the largely uncritical work carried out in religious studies with more historical and text-critical work done on Islamic data in cognate departments, such as history, political science, or Near Eastern studies. It is certainly not meant to imply that everyone who works on Islamic data within departments of religious studies is guilty of trafficking the claims of Islamic religious studies, nor is it to assume that those in other disciplines are somehow free of its grasp.

I also do not want to claim that the problem resides solely or simply with the study of Islam. Religious studies, as many have duly noted, is a discipline in considerable intellectual disarray.[2] Indeed some would not even go so far as to call it a discipline since it is largely devoid of any clear and consensual theoretical or methodological focus. Much of these criticisms revolve around the very term or category "religion," arguing that it artificially isolates an entity or phenomenon that is believed to be somehow meaningfully distinct from other types of human cultural production. The unfortunate result of all of this, such critics argue, is that religion is thought to have some sort of independent or autonomous existence that can neither be confused with nor reduced to politics, economics, and so on (see Arnal and McCutcheon 2014: 27).

Despite such attempts at critically rethinking the field and its constituent terms, religious studies, whether we like it or not, is predominantly a theological undertaking—perhaps crypto-theological might be more appropriate—in terms of its overwhelming desire to articulate as opposed to query truth claims on behalf of the various religions of the globe. The result is little more than a form of liberal ecumenicism in which all "religions" are assumed to contribute to the betterment of human civilization.[3] Truth claims are rarely interrogated, let alone undermined, because to do so would be tantamount to "insensitivity." Instead religion, defined by some common and vague notion of "the sacred," is thought by many to exist

© Equinox Publishing Ltd. 2015

timelessly and as somehow immune from historical, cultural, and political forces. A set of phenomenological comparisons based on a faulty comparative framework (all religions have prayer, for example, therefore all religions must by necessity share a common notion of "the sacred") is subsequently employed to bring this shared notion of the sacred to light.[4] Even recently, Robert Orsi could write in a way that overlooks social construction, ideological taint, and largely Western terms of reference,

> The holy still seems to me to name both a reality and an approach to religion that scholars of religion ought to think about. For one thing, people all over the world and in different historical periods have experienced something out of the ordinary in certain persons, places, or things, and they know what they mean, or enough of what they mean, to use the word "holy" (or one like it), even feel compelled to use it, as the only possible word for what they have experienced. This is the empirical warrant for continued interest in the term. (Orsi 2011: 85–6)

If subfields are only as good as the fields in which they find themselves located, it should perhaps come as little surprise to learn that Islamic religious studies is also in considerable intellectual disarray, mistaking as it does truth claims for timeless truths, myths of origins for origins, and so on. Things get considerably worse with the study of Islam, however, when we add to the mixture the role of identity politics. By this latter term I follow the lead of those who argue that it is a phenomenon predicated on theorizing that emerges from what are perceived to be the shared experiences of injustice among members of certain social groups (e.g., Ericson 2011: 1–10). Members of this constituency—in the case of this study, scholars of Islamic religious studies—seek to assert or reclaim ways of understanding their distinctiveness in the face of traditional scholarly categories that they hold to be responsible for, among other things, their malevolent representation.

The problem, however, as I tried to show in the Introduction, is that when the apologetical discourses of Islamic religious studies combine with identity-based criticism of traditional scholarship, some of which is certainly justified, more sober-minded scholarly inquiry can be written off and/or systematically avoided.[5] However, to dismiss an entire field of scholarly study on account of its perceived associations with an ill-defined and reified "Orientalism," a term that is never analyzed but that instead functions as little more than a red herring, is problematic in the extreme. Certainly Said was correct to point out the racialist assumptions of French Orientalists in the nineteenth century—how, for example, it objectifies and feminizes "*the* Orient." However, it is something entirely different to write off if not completely ignore, say, contemporary source and redactional criticism (e.g., Wansbrough 1977; Powers 2009) of the Qur'an as "orientalist" because it is "insensitive" to Muslims (see, for example, the comments in Denny 1994: 148). This last example, of course, could be critiqued along Saidian lines: Which Muslims? Muslims do, after all, believe a lot of things, and the implication here, as it is throughout this study, is that it is fine to generalize some things (i.e., that which suits us) but not others (i.e., that which does not).

The result of the admixture of Islamic religious studies with identity politics has real intellectual repercussions. It means that certain subject matters are eschewed—for example, the formation of the Qur'an or early Islam—because such topics in the past have traditionally been used to show that Islam is simply the sum of its monotheistic parts, namely, Judaism and Christianity.[6] Yet rather than attempt to counter such assumptions with a set of arguments that we should not assume that either Judaism or Christianity were stable, well-defined, and already fully articulated in the sixth century CE, there is a tendency in Islamic religious studies simply to ignore this period. Instead of demonstrating the complexity of religious, cultural, or ethnic identity in the Red Sea basin in late antiquity, such topics are largely avoided because they deal with the thorny issues of origins.[7] Indeed, identity is so messy and complex in this period that it might well potentially complicate an Ur-Islamic message into which modern commentators seek to tap. If the Qur'an is a text that, like all other texts, does not fall from heaven, then much of the energy that is expended in showing what it really has to say about gender, equality, or sexuality might be thought to be for nothing. This is why Islamic religious studies is less interested in the complexity of ethnic, racial, and religious distinctions—all incidentally of modern provenance—at the time of Muhammad than in extrapolating about what an idealized and historically inaccurate Muhammad means personally to the modern interpreter.[8] The results are anything but scholarly.

Defining Islamic Religious Studies

We might say that the academic study of Islam, especially as articulated in departments of religious studies, is currently undergoing a set of growing pains. The events of September 11, 2001, created, albeit for all the wrong reasons, an interest in things Muslim and Islamic. Although Islam has traditionally occupied a place, even if a somewhat minor place, within the religious studies curriculum (see, e.g., Adams 1967, and more recently R. Martin 2010), it has now become the religion in vogue. This popularity is based, as so much in the humanities, not on intrinsic value or worth but upon the larger context of geopolitical events. The areas, languages, and religions of those with whom we are at war necessarily receive greater interest and thus increased federal funding and media attention.[9]

In the years immediately following 9/11 every religious studies department in the country suddenly wanted—and usually received funding for—someone who could talk to students, and presumably faculty, about this religion and those who practiced it.[10] This was presumably with the aim of articulating what exactly motivated Muslims to act the way they did, to answer the nagging if problematic question "why do they hate us?," and, of course, to try to show that those who flew their planes into the Twin Towers and the Pentagon could not have been real Muslims but practitioners of a bastardized or hijacked Islam.[11] It was certainly better and more authentic if the scholar doing the explaining was of the religion so that he or she could show in his or her very comportment that not all Muslims are bad. As the debris, both literal and metaphorical, cleared from those uncertain days, a new generation of Islamicists was born. If the older generation had been primarily white, male, and interested in historical questions, the new generation was young, both male and female, and tended to be Muslim, whether by birth or conversion.[12] This new scholar of Islam was less interested in historical or textual problems and more interested in showing others (students, colleagues, the media) that Islam was not violent and hostile to the West. In the place of this violent and seemingly omnipresent Islam, these scholars saw it as their main goal to articulate a safe and liberal version, something they referred to as "progressive," that is, an Islam that was imagined to be compatible with the best of modern virtues with which they had grown up in, say, the United States or Canada. This is not to deny that a certain amount of apologetical caricature was not needed in the immediate aftermath of 9/11. Many of these scholars can certainly be credited with correcting both misinformed and overtly hostile stereotypes. This, however, is not the issue I wish to focus on. My focus instead is on how many of these scholars began to believe their own rhetoric and really did consider themselves to be leading a "reformation" (see, for example, the essays and language found in Safi 2003, and the work of Abou El Fadl 2005). The result was that almost overnight the study of Islam went from being a scholarly activity to a constructive theological and apologetical one.

Scholars of Islamic religious studies now had to articulate what constituted and defined their particular version of Islam. The Qur'an was good, medieval interpreters were bad; Sufism (= mysticism) was in, Salafism (= fundamentalism) was the problem. According to Kecia Ali (Boston University), we must "expose reductive and misogynist understandings of the Qur'an and hadith, refusing to see medieval interpretations as coextensive with revelation" (Ali 2006: 153). Scott Siraj al-Haqq Kugle (Emory University) likewise writes that "it is possible for homosexual relationships to be based on ethical reciprocity, trust, justice, and love, just as heterosexual relationships ought to be based on these values in the ethical vision of the Qur'an" (2010: 3). Or, again, Gwendolyn Zoharah Simmons (University of Florida) writes,

> I am further strengthened in my belief about the equality of women by the fact that I was graced by God to meet a Sufi mystic, Sheikh Muhammad Raheem Bawa Muhaiyadden, who by his teachings, his example, and his very being introduced me to Islam, an Islam of justice, truth, beauty, and grace. The Islam that my Sheikh taught and exemplified is a gender, racial, and religiously egalitarian Islam. It is an Islam that teaches that all human beings are created from a divine ray of God, are all God's children and are completely equal in God's sight. (Simmons 2003: 238)

Zareena Grewal (Yale University), although less interested in finding the real Islam, nonetheless articulates her problem with Orientalism:

> the discipline of anthropology has been intimately linked to the history of colonialization that haunts my family, that haunts Pakistan, and that continues to aid the imperial interests of the US government. Immediately after the

attacks of 9/11, I watched an earlier generation of discredited anthropological scholarship become reenergized as weapons for use by the US military's wars in Iraq and Afghanistan. (Grewal 2014: 14)

The names of certain theorists, most notably Talal Asad and Judith Butler, are frequently invoked, after Said of course, to help justify or legitimate a particular perspective or point of view, but there is never a systematic or sustained use of their scholarship. There cannot be, as I shall argue in the following chapter, because scholars like Asad and Butler are not interested in the types of essentialized and reified readings of religion that those in Islamic religious studies manufacture for consumption. Although names such as Asad and Butler are mentioned, Islamic religious studies is surprisingly uninterested in the discourses that drive critical scholarship in its parent discipline, religious studies.[13] Scholars such as Jonathan Z. Smith, Bruce Lincoln, Russell McCutcheon, Timothy Fitzgerald, Daniel Dubuisson, to name only a few, are largely ignored. My hunch is that this is the case because they are all white males. In a subfield that is mired in identity politics, premised on self-constructed narratives of exclusion, such theorists are mistakenly believed to have little or nothing to offer to narratives of dispossession. Moreover, many of these scholars query the very term "religion," and all that follows in its wake, as little more than an untheorized folk taxon, something that conveniently but problematically permits what we study, to wit, religion, to occupy a socially and politically autonomous zone. Rather than construct good religion, such scholars have encouraged us to demystify the traditional categories associated with religious studies by translating them into social and cultural terms that others in the humanities and social sciences should be able to understand. We must, they tell us, be explicitly and self-consciously aware of the theoretical moves we make with our data. Indeed, data only appear as such by our theoretical moves, which privilege, deny, and so on. We must, among other things, ask ourselves, why we study what we do, and for what purposes? What baggage, epistemological and personal, do we carry with us that, in turn, informs what we even regard as valid data in the first place?

These questions, however, are unfortunately not the types that scholars of Islamic religious studies are interested in asking themselves. Perhaps the field is too young in its development to ask such questions. Or, I think more accurately, perhaps such questions might uncomfortably expose the assumptions behind their work. These questions, for example, are potentially problematic to those who simultaneously want to be both theorists and the data they theorize. If religion is a social and political construct, where does this leave the constructive theologian? My fear is that the types of questions asked by critical scholars of religion have been and continue to be ignored or, worse, written off as part of the Orientalist project that follows in the wake of what is perceived to be traditional Eurocentric scholarship. That is, such imagined Eurocentric scholarship provides a set of questions that make scholars of Islamic religious studies uncomfortable because they might well provoke them to ask more difficult questions of themselves and their data.

Instead of such questions, scholars within Islamic religious studies confess their allegiance to a tradition that they have largely manufactured in their own images. The result is further mythologizing. It is the scholarship of self-aggrandizement, one wherein the scholar seeks to show how his or her personal narrative and even pain of being a Muslim post-9/11 trumps that of his or her non-Muslim colleagues. Supporting this new Islamic religious studies are amorphous and meaningless terms that are thrown about with considerable regularity: "love," "progressive," "equality," and "gender justice." Islamic religious studies is presentist to a fault. The past, if it is even examined, is interpreted in terms of modern values and concepts. To quote Tariq Ramadan of the University of Oxford:

> Because Muhammad's life expressed the manifested and experienced essence of Islam's message, getting to know the Prophet is a privileged means of acceding to the spiritual universe of Islam. From his birth to his death, the Messenger's experience—devoid of any human tragic dimension—allies the call of faith, trial among people, humility, and the quest for peace with the One. (Ramadan 2007: 7)

Since it is so invested in personal narratives, one is encouraged not to historicize the tradition. However, it is worth noting that Islamic religious studies does reserve its criticism, at times vehement, for Islamic fundamentalism (often referred to as Wahhabism or Salafism) that is perceived to corrupt, "hijack" is often a term that is used, Islam's eternal and pristine message. To counter this "hijacking," the perennial topic in many media outlets, scholars of Islamic religious studies are heavily invested in creating, propagating, and disseminating their authentic "Islam" in the classroom, in public, and in their scholarly personae. The only problem, though, is that their elaborate system of privilege and denial, in addition to their selective reading of the past, means that they engage in the exact same hermeneutical enterprise as those Muslim fundamentalists of which they are so critical.

Within Islamic religious studies, hard questions that concern premodern Muslims and their texts largely go unstudied because such questions prove irrelevant or politically inexpedient to their own personal narratives. If they are studied, premoderns become symbols for modern reform.[14] All of this might be okay if such scholars also engaged in more critical scholarship. Perhaps this does not go on in Islamic religious studies yet because of its infancy. Perhaps in 50 years we might look back on this period, the generation of Islamic religious studies scholars writing in the immediate aftermath of 9/11, as a blip or as a natural progression in the formation of a field of study. Perhaps. My goal here, as indeed it is in many of my publications, is to offer an alternative in the present. This alternative is not, to reiterate, neoconservativism; rather, it tries to point towards a path—the cross-pollination of Islamic data and the critical study of religion—that is surely a desideratum at the current moment and, indeed, will be for some time in the future.

Historically grounded scholarship ought to be interested, at least in part, in the formative processes that went into the origins of the message that Muhammad and his followers created in seventh-century Arabia.[15] Instead, Islamic religious studies has a tendency to dismiss such scholarship as the stuff of Orientalism, as part of "a rejectionist camp, which has based its contrarian position on its own rather tendentious reading of the sources and unsubstantial speculations" (Afsaruddin 2008: xx).[16] Rather than engage critically with the real and thorny problems associated with early Islam, there is instead a tendency to speculate about what Muhammad means to them personally (e.g., Afsaruddin 2008; Ramadan 2007; Safi 2009). The study of Christian origins, by way of comparison, is not about what Jesus as the Christ means to either the scholar or Christians, but about social formation and the way "religious traditions" come to be. Sober scholarship based on the critical examination of documents, on understanding the manuscript tradition, and on making sense of later sources that masquerade as earlier ones all give way in Islamic religious studies to what I like to call a set of variations on the "Muhammad and me" genre.[17] Within this genre supposed scholars of Islam relate to their readers what Muhammad means to them personally by expatiating, for example, on how they live their lives in relationship to him. Again, there is much talk of love and the desire to make the world a better place, but no critical scholarship on the historical sources that conjure Muhammad into existence in the first place.

I certainly do not wish to imply that all work in the critical study of Islam ought to be devoted to reconstructing the earliest sources. Far from it. However, research on premodern Islam has repercussions on what we do in the present. It tells us, for example, about the complexity of identity formation, how communities form as social movements, and so on. In fact, if scholars of Islamic religious studies are as serious about interrogating identity as they claim to be, one would think that such questions and such texts would be important to them. The result of all this is that Islam is no longer analyzed and analyzable as a set of social facts that are interpretable or made interesting to other fields in the humanities and social sciences. On the contrary, Islam, understood as something existing naturally and unproblematically in the world, provides a set of narratives to which scholars make sense of their own gender, sexuality, ethnicity, color, and politics. Although this passes for some as scholarship, it is anything but disinterested. Indeed, disinterested scholarship, it is assumed, is what Orientalists thought they did and do. Rather, what we see is constructive theology that makes claims to an interest in identity, but refuses to ask the types of sober questions that query and dismantle identity. Framed simply, if starkly, as a set of questions that I hope those who want to enter the field begin to ask themselves: How should the academic, as opposed to theological, study of Islam relate to other, well-established scholarly disciplines? What should the *academic* study of Islam look like? Is it the goal of scholarship to engage in a sympathetic treatment of Islam, or is it to call attention to the ways that Muslims—in different times and places, among practitioners and scholar-practitioners—make sense of themselves and create manifold identities using inherited social narratives?

Identity Politics

Identity politics signifies a wide range of political activity and theorizing grounded in the shared experiences of injustice among members that perceive themselves to comprise certain social groups (e.g., women, blacks, Jews). These members seek to assert or reclaim ways of understanding their uniqueness with the aim of challenging oppression, and seeking greater self-determination (Laden 2001: 1–8; Heyes 2007: 15–22). Such processes can take place not only in political organizations and movements, but also in politically charged academic fields, such as Women's studies, African American studies, and Jewish studies.[18] In these academic fields, various entrenched disciplines—history, sociology, philosophy—are invoked and used to resist and undermine traditional scholarly activity with an aim of asserting and reclaiming those groups that scholarship has historically marginalized as unimportant. Scholarship and group identity, then, become intimately intertwined with the one seeking to justify and legitimate the other and vice versa. Differences between the members of these groups and their traditional oppressors is not infrequently defined by appeals to ontological uniqueness, and the language of authenticity is appealed to with the aim of describing conditions or ways of living that are believed to be true to imagined historical and marginalized identities. In the words of Sonia Kruks,

> What makes identity politics a significant departure from earlier, pre-identarian forms of the politics of recognition is its demand for recognition on the basis of the very grounds on which recognition has previously been denied: it is *qua* women, *qua* blacks, *qua* lesbians that groups demand recognition. The demand is not for inclusion within the fold of "universal humankind" on the basis of shared human attributes; nor is it for respect "in spite of" one's differences. Rather, what is demanded is respect for oneself *as* different. (Kruks 2001: 85)

This can translate into the notion that not only are certain groups now imagined as unique, but, from a scholarly perspective, traditional modes of scholarship that have been invested in their marginalization must be avoided. Yet, as others have argued, there can be no real identity that is separable from its conditions of possibility, and political or scholarly appeal to identity formations must engage with the paradox of acting from the very subjectivity it must also oppose (Connolly 2002: 64–6). Judith Butler, for example, has argued that identity politics rests on a mistaken view of the subject that assumes a metaphysics of substance. To what extent, for example, is "identity" a normative ideal rather than an accurate descriptor of experience? Can the regulatory practices that govern, say, gender also govern culturally intelligible notions of identity (see Brubaker and Cooper 2000)? Must the so-called coherence and continuity of what constitutes "the person" be a logical feature of personhood or are they socially instituted and maintained norms of intelligibility?

If critical theory has largely marginalized identity politics, Islamic religious studies is nevertheless content to hold on to outmoded notions of identity and its performance. In Islamic religious studies, identity politics continues to work on the proposition that Islam, perceived as the traditional archenemy of the West, has been historically misrepresented (see, e.g., Said 1978, 1993). This misrepresentation legitimated, justified, and resulted, in the past, in colonialism and imperialism and, in the present (especially post-9/11), with the general mistrust and hatred of Islam and Muslims that now is enveloped into the term "Islamophobia." Much scholarship is accordingly interested in showing how the vocabularies and categories used to study Islam are, whether we are conscious of it or not, invested in hostility towards Islam and misrepresenting it in order to define the so-called "West." The antidote to this negativity, especially today among scholars of Islamic religious studies, is to point out this hostility and to avoid traditional scholarly categories in favor of using so-called "indigenous" taxonomies and vocabularies—which usually function as code for uncritical—to articulate the beauty of Islam, equating it, for example, with peace (since the root of Islam, s-l-m, is the same as peace, Islam = salaam), love, Sufism, or gender equality (also known as, gender jihad).

Those, like myself, who are critical of the politics of identity point to its inherent essentialism, which can be defined as the belief that an object possesses a certain quality that defines it or is perceived to make it what it is. The problem is that essentialism provides an illegitimate generalization about identity. It assumes that one aspect of one's identity is discrete and takes priority in representation. For example, it assumes that being a "Muslim" either takes precedence or is separable from being a woman, from being from a certain culture (Lebanese as opposed to, say, Bangladeshi), or a particular socioeconomic class. When this is translated onto a disciplinary register—for example, Islamic religious studies—identity politics risks dictating the self-understanding that its members should have. Those that do not have it are, by various means, ignored, criticized, or prevented from entry into the guild.

It is also worth noting, within this context, that identity politics risks attributing "authentic" to the self or to the group an identity that in fact is defined by its opposition to an Other (e.g., "maleness," "*the* West," "colonialism"). The reclamation of such an identity as one's own, however, ultimately reinforces dependence on the perceived dominances of the Other, thereby further internalizing and reinforcing an oppressive hierarchy (See Butler [1990]1999: 11–25).

The Danger: Where Are the Footnotes?

I now wish to take this discussion and apply it more directly to the intersection of identity and scholarship in the academic study of religion. This field—I refer not just to the study of Islam, but pretty much every other religion that inhabits its disciplinary canopy—risks becoming overly invested in identity politics. This has to do, it seems to me, with the fact that much scholarship within this larger discipline is now but a variation on the theme of the personal. Indicative of this is the rise in recent years of social media. We blog to appear *au courant*; we are content to offer opinions on topics for which we have very little academic training, and we offer them, moreover, even when they are not asked for. Facebook, Twitter, the blogosphere have now become venues in which scholars increasingly articulate and disseminate ideas that were traditionally done in other places. The problem, though, with many of these new venues of dissemination is that they do not require peer review, by which I refer to the practice of having one's work evaluated by at least one person of similar competence with the aim of maintaining standards and providing credibility. In addition to the lack of peer review, blogs rarely, if ever, rely on footnotes, that institution which historically governs scholarly practice. It is footnotes, to invoke Bruce Lincoln, that keep us honest by showing others how we got from there to here. According to him, footnotes

> mark the fact that a scholarly text is not a discourse of free invention, wherein ideological interests escape all controls. Rather, they serve as a visible reminder that scholarly texts result from a dialectic encounter between an interested inquirer, a body of evidence, and a community of other competent and interested researchers, past, present, and future. All who participated are committed to a sustained engagement with the data and also with one another, their engagements being mediated by shared principles of theory and method ... (Lincoln 1999: 208)

Footnotes, ideally, function as the mechanism that keeps us honest. Remove them from the bottom of the page and we take away a discourse that simultaneously conditions and defines the scholarly project. Historically, scholarship is that activity that enables scholars to make valid and testable claims about the world and subsequently make them known to colleagues. Ideally, scholarship is comprised of disciplinary methods that systemically advance the teaching, research, and practice of an academic field through rigorous inquiry. Without peer review and without footnotes scholarship risks becoming ideology that is so invested in self-promotion that the line is blurred between scholarly activity and informed (or uninformed) opinion. This is certainly not to say that there is or can be an Archimedean point that permits us an objective gaze at some perspectiveless "truth." Nor is it to say that peer review and footnotes aid in the articulation of this so-called truth. It is to make the point, though, that often our claims are invested in a variety of ideologies that not infrequently go by the names of "truth claims." Unless aware of this, unless we show our work, we fail to be honest with ourselves as scholars and we risk engaging in a variety of scholarly activities for what amounts to little more than ideological manipulation.

The scrutiny and criticism of others is what drives scholarship, and makes it possible to do what we do. If academic fields consist of rigorous inquiry, which they must do in order to reject ties to or takeover by politics or ideology, it is necessary to be honest, self-reflexive, and responsive to would-be critics. If we fail to do this, we exist in a jungle wherein everyone plays by their own rules. If scholarly discourse is skin deep, challenges to data, method, or results are taken as personal, and every disagreement becomes an intractable and often nasty battle that is insoluble because it cannot make appeals to externals texts, commentary traditions, or external scholarship. When scholarship becomes intertwined with identity politics, opinion masquerades as analysis and perceived wrongs grounded either in history or memory trump collegial accountability.

Any attempt to bridge the gap between world and interpretation must ultimately face the conundrum that our words, our vocabularies, and our categories are not natural descriptors, but of our own invention. The claim that we must be true to scholarly canons, then, is not an "old-fashioned" or, even worse, a "Eurocentric" claim. It is, to the contrary, to acknowledge that scholarship must have integrity and purpose that transcends skin color, religion or ethnicity. Without analytical rigor and intellectual honesty, we elevate the personal to the universal. This is, perhaps, another of way of saying that if we begin with the conclusions we ultimately want to find in our data set, we will predictably and inevitably find them therein.

Islamic Religious Studies and Identity Politics

Much scholarship in religious studies, but especially in the subfield of Islam, has recently become, what I like to call, "skin deep." That is, Islamic religious studies is largely superficial, based on what one perceives to be one's own unique identity and how it intersects with or is given definition by some amorphous or ethereal concept, namely, Islam. Rather than take critical theory seriously, Islamic religious studies is content to do little more than uphold or reify a set of slogans that, when repeated with sufficient regularity, risk being mistaken for eternal truths. Frequently, for example, we are told that Islam is "inherently liberal," is founded upon "gender justice," is "compatible with democracy," is "pluralistic," and so on. While certain traditions that sit uncomfortably under the canopy "Islam" may well coincide with such claims, to infer that Islam, writ large, does so is extremely problematic, and is ultimately based on an often elaborate system of privilege and denial. It is also extremely presentist, taking a set of modern concerns and then finding them in the historical record and in a set of texts.

Despite—or, perhaps better, because of—such appeals to categories that are of the scholar's own making, much contemporary scholarship in Islamic religious studies ultimately ends up reifying identity (often the identity of those making such appeals) as opposed to querying it. In their desire to show the liberal face of Islam, too many scholars of the tradition do taxonomical violence to the many Islams that have existed in the past and that continue to exist in the present because they write rival Islams out of the tradition that they have created in their own images. Moreover, since their overwhelming desire is to counter hostility to Islam in mainstream society, they refuse to engage in the *critical* discussion of identity that goes on in other disciplines. Perhaps, if Islamic religious studies engaged in community outreach to show the positive side of Islam in the community,[19] and then engaged in critical scholarship in the library it might be better. But the lack of critical awareness in the former, and the way it has now bled into the latter, are a matter of real concern. In the midst of all the glossy rhetoric about what "real" Islam consists of, it seems to me, is the self-conscious maneuvering on the part of these scholars to position themselves as the de facto authorities. The stakes are high, both inside and outside the classroom, where the boundary between the two is always permeable, but perhaps even more so in religious studies.

These and other issues revolve around authority and the rhetoric of authenticity. Who, for instance, is most qualified to speak for Muslims? For Muslim scholars of Islam, the answer is easy: Muslims, at least those of the progressive variety. For those who are not Muslim, like myself, this creates certain tensions. One can be accused, for example, of not understanding the tradition from within or of not having sufficient sympathy for the tradition. At stake in these debates is what counts as valid scholarly method. For those in Islamic religious studies, critical scholarship (e.g., historical and philological study of early Islam) is intellectually bankrupt on account of its outmoded (or old-fashioned or Orientalist) scholarly categories. For those who want to engage in such scholarship, be they Muslim or non-Muslim, the reverential language produced by those in Islamic religious studies is over the top and prevents any sort of critical examination.

Examples: Islam and Gender Justice

In what remains of this chapter, I would like to examine several recent representative works from scholars of Islamic religious studies that, I trust, will reinforce my larger point about the unhealthy intersection between scholarship and apologetics. Informing them all is the assumption that there exists a pristine Islamic message that has been corrupted by various non-religious forces (e.g., sexism, racism, political radicalism). All revolve around the hope that their scholarship can uncover or advance this originary Islamic message by unfettering it from the control of those who seek to harness it for various personally and politically motivated ends.

In her *Domestic Violence and the Islamic Tradition* (note the singular "Islamic tradition" as opposed to "traditions"), published by Oxford University Press, Ayesha Chaudhry (2014) of the University of British Columbia struggles with the quranic verse that grants men authority over women, and permits a Muslim man to hit (*wa-dribūhunna*) a woman if she disobeys him (Q 4:34). The major question driving her research is "how does a believer derive egalitarian ethics from revealed sources, such as the Qur'ān, while still remaining a member of a believing community whose 'tradition' holds a contradictory theology" (Chaudhry 2014: 14)? She argues that the verse can and ought to be read non-violently, and that the interpretation a Muslim chooses, either violent or non-violent, says more about the individual interpreter and his or her community than it does about the Qur'an itself. Following Ebrahim Moosa (2003), she calls this a "performative relationship" with the Qur'an and the Islamic tradition: "The struggle in modern discussions is not so much with the Qur'anic text itself but with the tradition of interpretation that attributed patriarchal meanings to the Qur'ān" (Chaudhry 2014: 195).

The sacred text of Islam, for Chaudhry, seems to be in some privileged non-historical or non-political realm where it exists in an uncontaminated state. Since the Qur'an was revealed in a patriarchal society, she reasons, there was only one way to interpret this verse *at that time*. This does not rule out the notion, though, that the Qur'an (or, presumably its divine author) did not know that things might be different at some point in the future (Chaudhry 2014: 6–7). She writes that

> This transformation is due in large part to a new, egalitarian idealized cosmology that has caused Muslim scholars to adjust their expectations of the divine text and a just God ... This in turn depends on the ability of Muslim scholars to allow the Qur'ān to be a performative text, so that Muslims can struggle with and determine its contemporary meanings. The greatest hurdle to transferring authority from a mythic "Islamic tradition" to the living community of believers is the "Islamic tradition" itself; its unquestioned authority has become stifling for contemporary Muslims. (Chaudhry 2014: 222)

Note that she implies that the Islamic tradition has become "stifling" for all contemporary Muslims, not just those, like herself, who are trying to reform the tradition using a progressive agenda. This agenda assumes, for Chaudhry, that "men and women possess equal human worth before God" (Chaudhry 2014: 12). Originally surprised that she could not find such egalitarian readers of the Qur'an in the precolonial period, Chaudhry reasons that "if scholars rely on the patriarchal tradition in order to maintain authority and legitimacy, then they must compromise their commitment to gender-egalitarianism" (2014: 11). Whereas gender-egalitarianism is a modern virtue, she wants to make it into an eternal truth, binding in all times and places. To get out of this dilemma she proposes that Muslim communities, if they so desire, have the ability to embrace non-violent interpretations, because religious texts mean what religious communities say they mean. According to her, we need to demonstrate that "precolonial legal and exegetical scholars did not attempt to interpret Q. 4:34 in a way that eliminated violence against wives [and that this] can help Muslims to make informed decisions about whether they would like to cling to the pre-colonial Islamic tradition in an uncritical manner" (Chaudhry 2014: 223). If "the Islamic tradition" disagrees with her interpretation, it becomes uncritical. Presumably this means that her own constructive reading represents the critical one.

The problem with this argument, however, is that even though she had begun her argument saying that there is no proper way to interpret the Qur'an, and that there are only communities of interpretation and performative relationships to the text, she ultimately ends up making her interpretation the proper one. "In the end," she writes, "the argument of this book is that readers and their expectations determine the meaning of any given piece of Qur'anic text. In studying the interpretations of Q. 4:34, we learn about the idealized cosmology of its interpreters because interpretations tell us more about the interpreters than the text itself" (Chaudhry 2014: 224). She can either mean by this that there is no text, only interpretations. Yet, if this is the case, then why even bother with the Qur'an? Or, if all there are is interpretations that come out of communities—what she calls "idealized cosmologies"—who gets to adjudicate which interpretation is the correct one? Apparently she does. The same argument that she levels at those whose interpretations she does not like can be applied to hers, as well. The argument is circular, but, like so many arguments we will encounter in the pages that follow, valid argumentation is less important than saving Islam from conservatives or "neo-traditionalists," something that is often lumped under the generic term "*the* Islamic tradition." "Thus, contemporary Muslims may fully belong to a religious tradition that they love," she concludes, "in the face of enduring challenges posed by texts whose precolonial plain-sense meanings they cannot abide" (Chaudhry 2014: 224).

Another, relatively more sophisticated monograph on the same topic is *Feminist Edges of the Qur'an* by Aysha Hidayatullah (2014) of the University of San Francisco and also published by Oxford University Press. Like Chaudhry, her work is informed by the fact that men can and do commit violence against women in the name of Islam (or any other religious tradition) and do so, moreover, using justification derived from sacred texts. I certainly share their concern. My problem is only that Western academics, from the protection offered by the Western academy, believe that they can save real Muslim women by means of their progressive reading of the Qur'an and other texts that are disseminated by Western university presses. Moreover, the fact that none of these scholars have training in traditional Islamic jurisprudence (*fiqh*) and that instead their degrees in religious studies come from secular Western universities means that they will never be taken seriously as authoritative interpreters of the tradition. This means, as I have implied throughout, that they are basically writing for one another. Hidayatullah, however, begins her work by not being as optimistic as Chaudhry, and she is critical of those who want to reclaim the Qur'an by arguing that its misogynist and violent passages are not essential to it. She asks:

> What would it mean if we, as feminist, believing Muslims, eventually found that the text of the Qur'an *does* sanction gender hierarchy and male authority over women? What would happen if we were forced to concede that this is the case—would feminist exegesis of the Qur'an come to an end? What would that do to our relationship to the Qur'an? What would that do to our relationship to God? Could we go on as Muslims? Could we continue to be feminists? (Hidayatullah 2014: 147)

Again, I flag the theological language here and the employment of a set of constructive concerns that invoke the categories of critical scholarship. However, despite her concerns, Hidayatullah, as both a Muslim and a feminist, must try to reconcile these difficulties that she recounts in the aforementioned paragraph. Although the Qur'an "takes remarkable steps toward equality as defined by our contemporary standards" (Hidayatullah 2014: 152), she acknowledges that its message may not fully reconcile with these standards. As a result, Hidayatullah proposes to move "beyond" the quranic text:

> It is important to clarify that in calling for us to be honest about the Qur'anic text, I do not "surrender" the Qur'an to patriarchy and sexism. I do not seek to replace a view of the egalitarian "core" of the Qur'an with a view of the gender-hierarchical "core" of the Qur'an. Rather, I present what I feel to be a more forthright view of the possible existence of both kinds of impulses within the Qur'an ... There are still plenty of good arguments to be made about the Qur'an's indications of dignity, respect, and care for women—but we can no longer make those arguments as definitely as we once did. (Hidayatullah 2014: 172)

She continues by arguing that Muslim feminists need to capitalize on the those quranic verses that support equality, but also look outside of the text, something that for her means taking "full ownership of our interpretive interventions" (Hidayatullah 2014: 173). For her this seems to mean, invoking typical Muslim theological language, the existence of a divine text behind the actual text.[20] Here, I submit, she differs little from those other Muslim feminists of which she is critical. "We will need to pursue," she concludes, "a vision of the Qur'an as a divine text that allows us to imagine justice outside the text's limited pronouncements" (Hidayatullah 2014: 173).

Another example comes from a recent work by Jamillah Karim (Spelman College), an African-American, a Muslim, and a scholar of Islamic religious studies. In her *American Muslim Women* published by NYU Press, she speaks of "the diversity of American Muslims and the connection of our common ideals and pursuits shaping a cross-ethnic community" (Karim 2008: 1) published by the University of North Carolina Press. She, thus, opens her book with the assumption that there is a universal and timeless Islamic message that is not to be questioned or queried, but accepted as the metaphysical glue that unites a universal Muslim sisterhood. When problems of race emerge, this has nothing to do with Islam— something she says is committed to spiritual and universal "ummah ideals" (Karim 2008: 7)—but to inequalities endemic to American culture. Karim, then, reads herself into her narrative:

> My personal story illustrates how race consciousness has shaped my Muslim identity as well as the lens through which I see and often make judgments about others who share my identity as a Muslim. In other words, religion is the lens through which I imagine our sameness, but race is the lens through which I construct our difference. But in addition, as my narrative shows, our ethnic struggles make us different. (Karim 2008: 9)

Muslimness, according to Karim, is assumed to be stable. It unites Muslims across time and geography, whereas race—presumably an American problem— is what divides them. The trope of Islam as eternal and problems as somehow "cultural" or "political" is, as I noted earlier, an age-old trope in speaking about religion. Islam unifies, culture divides, as it were. If properly understood, she implies, Islam can heal the racial wounds of America. Her goal in writing is to help American Muslims "better reach their *ummah* ideals," which are "inspired by Islamic sacred teachings" (Karim 2008: 235). Furthermore:

> Certainly, we Muslims are connected through a common belief system and set of practices, and as the *hadith* implies, we are linked to the extent that our diverse struggles affect others in this shared community. But our struggles and concerns are as distinct as are the parts of the body. Throughout this book, we have seen difference emerge as an undeniable characteristic of the *ummah*. The complex lives of American Muslims challenge ideologies that attempt to imagine the *ummah* as fixed. Representing one kind of location, one kind of Muslim, one kind of struggle (*jihad*), or one kind of activism. Instead the *ummah* represents different loyalties, different geographical spaces, and different understandings and cultural representations of Islam. (Karim 2008: 235-6)

Once again, Islam is a monolith that somehow exists outside of or beyond "cultural representation." Once we are able to realize this, we might be able to work, Karim implies, to make the world a better place. She says as much in the conclusion to the work, "by acknowledging and respecting difference within the *ummah*, American Muslims will be able to better build bridges across difference" (Karim 2008: 236).

It is difficult to argue with this. To do so is to be accused of racism or sexism, or to engage in trying to undermine a personal narrative. What one can do, however, is show how Karim's analysis is based on a set of rhetorical moves that seek to create an authentic and real Islam, an Islam that preaches racial and sexual harmony. It also shows, moreover, how "critical theory" is used in Islamic religious studies and how this usage differs from that found in other disciplines. In Islamic religious studies, theory is not used to critique, but to engage in constructive theological work:

> Fellowship with the purpose of understanding one another, which includes learning about the historical struggles, cultural norms, and sensitivities of different ethnic communities, is essential to crossing ethnic lines in the American *ummah* … Given that many African Americans view race as the dominant power dynamic in their social relations, immigrant Muslims should recognize this tendency in their interactions with them, which certainly means listening to African American Muslims when they talk about racism in the *ummah*, or accepting the fact that a friendship with an African American Muslim might require sensitivity to her feelings about racism. (Karim 2008: 237–8)

Note that race or gender is never queried, but reified. There is a lot of talk about identity, the author's own identity, but nothing on how identity is constructed or manipulated. Instead, what we are offered is sensitivity training for non-black Muslim women. To repeat, if in fact it needs repeating, the conclusion is intimately personal. As a second-generation Muslim woman herself, she writes that "second generation Muslim women must navigate cultural gender norms in both public and private spaces as they form cross-ethnic friendships on college campuses" (Karim 2008: 234). Karim's scholarship essentially amounts to her life story. It is biography in the guise of scholarship. This is something that we shall see time and again in the work associated with Islamic religious studies.

Karim picks this up in a later article that appears in *Rethinking Islamic Studies*, a volume edited by Carl Ernst (University of North Carolina) and Richard Martin (Emory University) and which I have already mentioned at several junctures. Karim's essay in this volume is entitled "Can We Define 'True' Islam?: African American Muslim Women Respond to Transnational Muslim Identities," and its goal is to show how African American Muslim women resist immigrant Islam by referring to it as immigrant or "cultural" Islam as opposed to "true" Islam, which they perceive themselves to practice (Karim 2010: 115). In itself this is certainly an interesting argument and it does seem that Karim is now beginning to relativize terms like "true" Islam. However, as in her previous work, her goal is again to try and arrive at some sort of transcultural and religious Muslim sisterhood that transcends local—be it immigrant or African American—Islam and is instead grounded in authoritative Muslim sources. She writes, for example, that

> As immigrant Muslim women reassess and modify gender norms related to mosque attendance, dress, and work, and as African American Muslim women respond to this repositioning, both groups of women create important Islamic feminist discourse seeking gender justice and women's agency based on the Islamic sources of the Qur'an, the Hadith, and *fiqh* (Islamic jurisprudence). These feminist discourse also contest "the nature of 'real' Islam" as they project the interpretive voices of Muslim women, both immigrant and African American. For both groups "real" Islam is understood as one that advances women's rights, whereas cultural Islam is widely accepted as one that harms women. (Karim 2010: 117)

In this passage Karim acknowledges, and I think correctly, that Muslim identity is in a flux, responsive to a host of variables. These variables can be signified as both "religious" and "nonreligious." Despite this, however, she speaks of *the* Islamic sources as if they are somehow normative. This means that rather than contest the difference between "true" and "cultural" Islam, Karim ultimately ends up reifying them. Women's religious practices—and here she is doing something that is remarkably similar to what Chaudhry and Hidayatullah are doing—remain hidden in the Qur'an, where they remain waiting to be uncovered by the feminist interpreter. "As South Asian women begin to learn Islam in the formal setting of the mosque," she writes, "they witness imams and scholars drawing from the Qur'an, Hadith, and *fiqh* manuals. This new access to the epistemological methods of Islamic practice enables women to engage gender norms and introduce new practices" (Karim 2010: 119). The result, it seems, is that Muslim women from a variety of *cultures* are able to learn the *religious* techniques that will enable them to understand the tradition properly, that is, in a way that corresponds with concepts such as equality and gender justice.

Although Karim is interested in identity and she claims that it is neither static nor monolithic, Islam seems to remain so for her. In speaking of the veil (*hijab*), for example, she writes, "Immigrant women incorporate new knowledge about the *hijab* into their South Asian identities. For example, many wear what I refer to as the *dopatta hijab*, a distinctly South Asian *hijab* style. The *dopatta* is a long, rectangular, almost sheer scarf that South Asian women often wear across the shoulder or neck" (Karim 2010: 120). Other than the fact that she claims that authentic Muslim practice involves women covering their heads, I also note the problematic way she uses the generic term "South Asian," especially given the fact that she has spent so much time trying to tell the reader that identity is complex and not a monolith. For all their talk about difference, they ultimately end up reifying and flattening real historical differences.

Conclusions

Let me move to conclude this chapter by way of another example, this time from a book entitled *Progressive Muslims*, which was published in the immediate aftermath of 9/11. In his Introduction to the edited volume, Omid Safi (Duke University) writes that he and his fellow liberal Muslim academics must

> start swimming in these turbulent waters, to save both ourselves and the vibrancy of the Islamic tradition. It may not be an exaggeration to state that unless we succeed in doing so, the humanity of Muslims will be fully reduced to correspond to the caricature of violent zealots painted by fanatics from both inside and outside the Muslim community. (Safi 2003: 1–2)

While his intentions are certainly noble, to return to the essay by J. Z. Smith that I mentioned in the Preface, the word choice is problematic. First, there is the assumption that there exists a monolithic "*the* Islamic tradition" that can somehow be accessed by him and his colleagues. This monolithic Islamic message is then put in stark counterpoint with the "caricature" presented by "fanatics" and "zealots." The former Islam (i.e., that presented by Safi and his colleagues in Islamic religious studies) is signified as authentic, and the latter as somehow inauthentic. Safi claims that this activity is not apologetical (e.g., 2003: 20–21); however, to equate the tradition's essence with gender justice and pluralism surely reeks of apologetics. In their desire to define and articulate this authentic Islam, these progressive Muslims—most of whom, incidentally are scholars of Islam in departments of religious studies—make a series of moves that are anything but scholarly.

Once again, we witness constructive theology masquerade as critical scholarship. In all of the above examples, we witness attempts to "theorize" Islam by making it compatible with what is believed to be the complexity of racial, religious, or ethnic identity. However, in these cases there is no discussion of the instability, the social-constructedness, of identity—all identity. Islam is constructed, performed, and patrolled by social actors. It does not exist out in the ether waiting to be brought down to earth. Theory is alluded to. The name Edward Said is usually invoked. But then we are told what Islam really means. It is perhaps worth noting here that Said would never go so far as to define, essentially, a tradition; his goal was to point out the political acts of scholarship.

Identity politics not infrequently replaces scholarship with various mythologies of dispossession. These mythologies, not surprisingly, all seem to revolve around the customary "-isms" (colonialism, racism, sexism, and so on). This is certainly not to take a neoconservative line and argue that these "-isms" simply exist in the minds of the interpreter. However, it is to make the claim that, with interpretive legerdemain, it can become possible to insert oneself and all of one's socioeconomic privilege onto the very real suffering of others. Those now on the receiving end of such injustice, whether or not they were affected by it is irrelevant, proclaim their identity to be "complex," and accuse their critics of buying into more simplistic notions (Ahmad 1992: 122; Turner 1994: 11–22). A white "Westerner" or "European" cannot possibly understand the pain of those that Western scholarship has represented over the years.[21] The best that one can do, presumably, is to join those of privilege who have created narratives for themselves based on dispossession and disenfranchisement in their long litany of complaints about the West and its scholarly canons.

The neo-Saidian approaches witnessed in this chapter are not particularly interested in scholarship, at least of the traditional variety, which can be neatly marginalized with claims as "Eurocentric" or "Orientalist." As I tried to show, however, both of these terms, especially the former, function as straw men or red herrings that are never really engaged but simply function as code or metonyms. Such labels also function as convenient Others that enable scholars of Islamic religious studies to carve out a niche for themselves. The result is that many of these scholars are seemingly uninterested in understanding Islam in its historical and contemporary complexity. There is, for them, a true meaning of the Qur'an that medieval and modern fundamentalists ignore; there are good types of Islam (e.g., Muhammad's original version, Sufism, their own) and bad types. Their goal, simply stated, is to understand their own experiences in the tradition and to carve out the epistemological space for themselves in the contemporary academy. "Westerners," at least those who have not converted or who are unsympathetic, unfortunately have little role in Islamic religious studies.

The techniques of identity production—the social and rhetorical techniques that make claims to identity possible—have real social pay-offs for doing Islamic studies. The strategies of identification that scholars employ are certainly not value neutral, and here I agree with many of those involved in Islamic religious studies. Rather, these strategies function as a set of active and ongoing processes of signification that can be made to draw neat and tidy borders that can subsequently define who is in and who is out. The claim, something that one now hears frequently in academic circles, especially those associated with religious and Islamic studies, that we are all "embodied" becomes little more that the product of our liberal multiculturalism. Race, ethnicity, religion, gender, and other such categories afford us a "concession" that presumably permits us to critique the status quo, but they frequently do so only in a manner that reproduces these very concepts. Identity, social legitimacy, and rank are not simply thrust upon us or of our own creation, but are active and ongoing collaborations among all members of a group. Our goal as scholars should be to identify and analyze the social processes that make such claims possible as opposed to reify them.

To be in the "in-crowd" in Islamic religious studies' circles one has to engage in the authoritative rhetoric that its audience judges to be right and proper. At the current moment, this means that one talks about what Islam means, always in a positive fashion, to "me." What, for instance, have been the *personal* struggles of an African-American Muslim woman? What is the real teaching of Islam on gender justice? How can a gay convert to Islam advance an interpretation of the Qur'an in order to create a "gay-affirming" Islam? This is certainly not to imply that issues of race or sexuality are somehow unimportant in contemporary scholarship. One need look no further than the work of Joan Wallach Scott or Judith Butler. When done well and not in such overtly and simplistic terms, it can offer tremendous insights into the construction of identity formations. However, when done theologically as is so often the case in Islamic religious studies, it has very little to offer the academic study of religion in particular and the broader entrenched disciplines associated with the humanities and social sciences (e.g., history, sociology, anthropology) in general.

Notes

1. I discuss some of this in greater detail in Hughes (2012d: 1–6, 118–32). Within that context, I try to differentiate and juxtapose this term with what I call "new Islamic studies" that is less apologetical and more critical.
2. I refer specifically and chronologically to studies such as Proudfoot (1985), Preus (1987), King (1999), Lincoln (1999), McCutcheon (1999), Wiebe (1999), Fitzgerald (2000), Dubuisson (2003), Lincoln (2003), McCutcheon (2003), Masuzawa (2005), Chidester (1996), Hughes (2012a), C. Martin (2012), L. Martin and Wiebe (2012), Arnal and McCutcheon (2013), Nongbri (2013), Chidester (2014), and Schilbrack (2014).
3. Witness, for example, Associate Justice Tom Clark's comments in his writing the opinion of the Supreme Court in the case of *Abington School District v. Schempp*: "We agree that of course that the State may not establish a 'religion of secularism' in the sense of affirmatively opposing or showing hostility to religion.... *It might well be said that one's education is not complete without a study of comparative religion or the history of religion and its relationship to the advancement of civilization.* It certainly may be said that the Bible is worthy of study for its literary and historic qualities. *Nothing we have said here indicates that such study of the Bible or of religion, when presented objectively as part of a secular program of education, may not be effected consistently with the First Amendment.*" His comments may be found in full at https://www.law.cornell.edu/supremecourt/text/374/203.
4. This approach is best articulated by the late Mircea Eliade (e.g., [1957]1987), who was responsible for training an entire generation of scholars of religion in the 1970s and 1980s at the Divinity School at the University of Chicago. Eliade was perhaps best known for his unsupported and unsupportable claim of the "irreducibility of the sacred" and the so-called "morphology of the sacred." For a critique of this approach, see Strenski (1987), McCutcheon (1999: 74–100), and Dubuisson ([1993]2006: 189–208).
5. I certainly do not want to claim that *certain strands* of Orientalism are innocent of unfair or gross characterizations of the Other. However, I also do not want to make Orientalism into a straw man that can be criticized simply as a way to score a political point for one's own ideological portraits. I will discuss this at greater length in the following chapter.
6. The perfect example of this is the work of Abraham Geiger ([1835]1970) or Shlomo Dov Goitein ([1955]1974), both of whom among other things assume that Judaism in sixth-century Arabia is something stable, already articulated, and well defined. It is always assumed that Jews helped shape Islam, that the Qur'an recycles Jewish literature of late antiquity (e.g., midrashim), and that influence moves in one direction. But that was in the late nineteenth and early twentieth centuries. Why do we have to assume that such studies into the formation of Islam are embedded in such assumptions today? What is preventing research into such topics, especially as they relate to identity formation, within Islamic religious studies?
7. See, for example my attempts to explore and analyze this concept in greater detail in my introductory textbook (Hughes 2013a: 17–40).
8. I discuss concrete examples of this tendency, and seek to offer an alternative in Hughes (2012c: 34–60).
9. A generation ago, at the height of the Cold War, the regional or area study in vogue was Russia; in the coming years, it will undoubtedly be China and Chinese studies, which are already beginning to receive increased financial support from the United States government.

10. As I write in Hughes (2012c: 319n5), "Depending upon how one counts these jobs (whether with AOE or AOS) I count—certainly anecdotally and unofficially—6 positions advertised in Islam in October of 2000; in October of 2001, 10; in 2002, 21; in 2003, 22; in 2004, 30; in 2005, 35, in 2006, 34; in 2007, 25, and in 2008, 35."
11. From the IslamAAR listserv, which is the discussion site for scholars of Islamic religious studies, we read the following: "As scholars of religious traditions, we observe that religious symbols are used for political motives all over the world in Hindu, Christian, Jewish, and Muslim traditions. However, we must critically distinguish between politically motivated deployment of religious symbols and the highest ideals that these traditions embody. Just as most would regard bombers of abortion clinics to be outside the pale of Christianity, so the actions of these terrorists should not be accepted as representing Islam in any way" (online at http://groups.colgate.edu/aarislam/sois.htm).
12. See, for example, the list of contributors to Martin (1985) and then compare it with the contributors in Ernst and R. Martin (2010). The difference between these two sets of contributors really encapsulates the sea-change that has occurred in Islamic religious studies over a generation. If Martin (1985) was predominantly white and male, Ernst and R. Martin (2010) is both male and female and overwhelmingly Muslim.
13. In the editorial introduction to their *Rethinking Islamic Studies*, Ernst and R. Martin write that it is "important to examine the implications of both area studies and religious studies, including critiques emerging within these fields, if scholars are to deal effectively with issues relating to Islam in the global political culture that is being formed today" (Ernst and R. Martin 2010: 2). However, as I have argued elsewhere, there is no such engagement with critical discourses of religion in any of the essays that comprise this volume (Hughes 2012c: 100–117).
14. See for example the account of the twelfth-century Ghazali in Moosa (2005).
15. For very poor and historically light attempts to do this in Islamic religious studies, see Afsaruddin (2008), Ramadan (2007), and Safi (2009). For an assessment of these and other works, see my comments in Hughes (2012b: 10–33).
16. To the reader who has no knowledge of these sources: We know next to nothing about early Islam because all of our sources (including the Qur'an) come from subsequent centuries. Every reading of these sources, Afsaruddin's included, must by necessity be tendentious. For a thorough discussion of the terms of the debates, and their methodological shortcomings, see Berg (2000: 6–64).
17. For a sustained critique of this genre in Islamic religious studies, one with numerous examples, see Hughes (2012b: 10–33).
18. On the latter, see my studies in Hughes (2013b, 2014a).
19. This comment, however, does not endorse the practice of Ingrid Mattson, who teaches courses on *dawa* (i.e., proselytization) that is open to Muslim students only at Huron College at the University of Western Ontario in Canada. I shall discuss Mattson in greater detail in Chapter 4 below.
20. By traditional Muslim theology, I refer specifically to the Mutazalites, a school popular in the eighth century CE, that posited the existence of an uncreated Qur'an that was coeval with God. See Martin, Woodward, and Atmaja (1997: 1–18).
21. Aijaz Ahmad, the Marxist literary theorist and political commentator, writes eloquently of the invented nostalgia of these individuals, many of whom come from elite backgrounds and not, as they would have us believe, fractured existences associated with colonialism. The model here is Edward Said, who receives the status of a demigod. The "most passionate following" for this nostalgia, Ahmad writes, "is within those

sectors of the university intelligentsia which either originate in the ethnic minorities or affiliate themselves ideologically with the academic sections of those minorities ... These [immigrants] who came as graduate students and then joined the faculties, especially in the Humanities and Social Sciences, tended to come from upper classes in their home countries. In the process of relocating themselves in the metropolitan countries they needed documents of their assertion, proof that they had always been oppressed ... What the upwardly mobile professionals in this new immigration needed were narratives of oppression that would get them preferential treatment, reserved jobs, higher salaries in the social position they already occupied: namely as middle-class professionals, mostly male" (Ahmad 1992: 195–6).

— 2 —

Prisoners of Said

In the late 1990s and early 2000s, Donald S. Lopez, Jr. and Robert Thurman, two American scholars of religion, engaged in a particularly charged debate over the proper representation of Tibet and Tibetan Buddhism. Lopez's primary interest was in showing how the Western fascination with Tibet, both scholarly and non-scholarly, was based less on history than on a wistful romanticism that sought to connect that country with the font of some pure form of spirituality. This representation, Lopez argued, actually threatened to distort and undermine the complex realities of Tibetan politics, history, and religion. Lopez was particularly critical of Robert Thurman—a close friend of the Dalai Lama, a convert to Buddhism, professor of Buddhism at Columbia University in New York City, and the President of Tibet House US, a non-profit organization in that city dedicated to the preservation and renaissance of Tibetan civilization. In his *Prisoners of Shangri-La*, Lopez contends that Thurman lets his political agenda dictate his scholarly persona. The latter could, for example, enable him to misrepresent Tibetan Buddhist texts, such as the *Tibetan Book of the Dead*. Lopez writes:

> Precisely because he is not Tibetan, he was not born into the lineage that naturally bestows authenticity but must derive his authenticity from other sources. These include his scholarly credentials, his ordination in 1964 (since lapsed) as the first American to become a Tibetan Buddhist monk, his description of himself as a "lay Buddhist," his characterization by journalists as America's leading Buddhist, his occasional role as unofficial spokesperson for the Dalai Lama ... and his position as the Jey Tsong Khapa Professor of Buddhist Studies at Columbia University. Taken together his credentials accord him an official status, a certain orthodoxy ... His active role in the Tibetan independence movement is a further impetus for his identification with a central tenet of Tibet's endangered civilization. (Lopez 1998: 83)

These credentials provide Thurman with the ability to portray himself as an authentic Tibetan voice, one that—as Lopez would subsequently argue—allows Thurman to misrepresent classical Tibetan literature, depending upon his needs, either as science or as offering a blueprint for world peace (Lopez 1998: 147). In a review symposium devoted to Lopez's book published in the pages of the *Journal of the American Academy of Religion*, Thurman reacted with the claim that

38 • *Islam and the Tyranny of Authenticity*

Lopez's book was "self-righteous," based on "polemics," "mere assertions paraded as evidence," and "confused distortions" (Thurman 2001: 191). All of this, writes Thurman, translates into what he considers to be Lopez's "resentment of the Tibetan people that leaps from every page" (Thurman 2001: 191). Rather than engage in a review of the book that shows Lopez's theoretical and methodological shortcomings, Thurman opts to make their scholarly disagreement both personal and political:

> Taking a quick reality check, obviously the theme of imprisonment applies realistically only to the Tibetan people—no informed person denies that they are suffering a real and bitter imprisonment. They are the prisoners who matter, in the live context in which this book was written. Who is it that holds the Tibetan people prisoner? Is it the "forces of Shangri-La"? Where are such forces? When we look at Tibet today, we notice that there are between two and three million Chinese colonists and numerous detachments of the Chinese army, around half a million strong, including special forces, in the so-called Tibet Autonomous Region (TAR) alone, home to only around two million Tibetans. Two-thirds of geographic and "ethnic" Tibet, the three-mile-high plateau three times larger than the TAR that Tibetans have called home for over one millennium, have been split off by annexation to Chinese provinces, the four million Tibetans in those areas also being surrounded by more than one million People's Liberation Army and Public Security Bureau troops and more than five million Chinese colonists. The Chinese soldiers in Tibet do maintain some border posts against the Indians, but they mainly man internal garrisons against the Tibetans themselves. It is very clear when we look at the real situation of the Tibetan people that they are *prisoners of China, not prisoners of Shangri-La*. (Thurman 2001: 192–3; his italics)

For Thurman here the goal of scholarship is not to engage in historical or metahistorical study, but to show real political injustices in the present. Presumably this means, if necessary, adjusting or manipulating the historical and textual record to make one's point.[1] Because Lopez refuses to use scholarship to show the injustices against the Tibetan people, Thurman accuses him of "muddled thinking" (2001: 194). "Sadly," according to Thurman, "we go ahead and read through Lopez's whole book, and we do not find a single thing in it that strengthens any case against China swallowing Tibet or even makes any such case" (Thurman 2001: 196). In response to Thurman's diatribe, Lopez accuses Thurman's "scholarly" critique as little more than an extension of Thurman's larger "crusade" of saving the Tibetan people from Chinese aggression (Lopez 2001: 205). "If I interpret his comments correctly," Lopez continues,

> [Thurman] seems to object not so much to the contents of the book but to its very existence. He seems to argue that *Prisoners of Shangri-La* should not have been written, that, indeed, no book that is not devoted unequivocally and uncritically to the promotion of Tibetan independence should be written until that independence is won. Again, I continue to wonder how relevant *Prisoners of Shangri-La* is to this question. (Lopez 2001: 206–7)

At stake in the debate between Lopez and Thurman is how to represent both Tibet and Tibetan Buddhism. For Thurman, every act of scholarship is a political act. The Tibetans suffer under the weight of Chinese occupation and the majority of scholarly activity on Tibet should go into, presumably, calling attention to this political fact. Because Lopez does not deal directly with the contemporary political reality and instead focuses on the "prisoners of shangri-la" as opposed to the "prisoners of the Chinese," he is perceived to somehow make light of the Tibetans and their problems. For Lopez, on the contrary, every scholarly activity or imagining need not reduce to political expediency. If it did, scholarship would function as little more than advocacy. Rather than focus on actual Tibetan Buddhists except to correct romanticized portayals of them, Lopez has chosen to examine the Western fascination with Tibet and Tibetans. Romanticizing Tibet, especially the Tibet prior to the Chinese Occupation of 1950, does not make Tibetans more real, he argues, but actually less real, fetishistic parodies of themselves who end up being little more than stereotypes with little or no autonomous agency.

I have used this example from the subfield of Buddhism because it shows that the sides, terms, and stakes of the debate in the academic study of Islam are not unprecedented. Far from it, they emerge in virtually all of the subfields of religious studies. What is the "right" way to study religion? Who possesses the authority to study it? Must scholarship always be used in the service of extra-intellectual and political endeavors? Those of whom I am critical in this study want to operate within a vacuum and in such a manner that their presentations of Islam are simply correct and uncontestable, and not part of a larger conversation. The study of Islam, on my reading, has much to learn from and teach the larger field of religious studies.

* * *

Scholarship is by nature a political activity. Because of this it must be inherently and faultlessly self-conscious to avoid cooption. How we bring our data into existence, the rhetorical moves we make to re/present it are not, simply put, natural acts.[2] These are the disciplinary lies, the noble lies, that we must be upfront about. This is why we, as scholars of religion, have an obligation to, to put it mildly, not make stuff up. We have to be self-reflexive and self-critical, consistently asking ourselves "why 'this' rather than 'that' was chosen as an exemplum" (J. Z. Smith 1982: xi). Words, categories, and narratives simultaneously privilege and deny, while they also create and destroy. Certainly there is a political and ideological edge to scholarship, but this does not mean that scholarship's primary purpose is to engage in lobbying. Every scholarly act need *not* be in the service of some larger political project (e.g., defending Tibet against Chinese aggression or countering Islamophobia by creating an imagined Islam that is perceived to be in sync with an imagined pristine Quranico-Islamic polity in the distant past). On the contrary, we need to ask ourselves both constantly and consistently: What data am I using and why? How does my rhetoric help shape that which I purport to study? Does my language unduly influence or presuppose my argument? What does my narrative privilege and deny?

Applying the debate between Lopez and Thurman to the present study, I would like to argue that the majority of scholars under the canopy of Islamic religious studies have convinced themselves that it is their duty to produce "good" Islam as opposed to studying the manifold Islams, including the so-called "meta" acts that have conjured them into existence in the first place, that exist both in the past and in the present. The aim, as we saw in the previous chapter, is to normalize a very particular type of Islam within American culture by holding themselves up as the standard bearers or data of an Islam that they have universally hailed as "true" and "authentic." The problem, of course, is that they primarily misrepresent the tradition precisely because the "tradition" is always invented or manufactured in the service of a particular political or ideological end. Certainly there are streams of Islam, like any religious tradition, that are peaceful and have potential for egalitarianism; however, there are also currents that do not.

The conceptual modeling that these scholars use is deeply flawed. In fact, there is very little theory; in its place is a set of largely presentist concerns that are subsequently projected back on to the Islamic past to show what "authentic" Islam is and how it differs from all of its uncultured despisers. Since many in Islamic religious studies believe—and I do think that "believe" is a better term or descriptor than "argue"—that this "real" Islam is predicated on love, gender justice, democracy, liberalism, and so on, they must argue that those movements, texts, and individuals where these virtues are not found are somehow less than real or less than authentic. Witness, for example, Scott Kugle's claim that when the early Muslims "became strong enough to impose their will on others, they all too often lost sight of their Prophet's teaching of empathy, compassion, and justice" (Kugle 2014: vii); or Beverly Aminah McCloud's problematic contention that "While the Qur'an's emphasis is on the beliefs and actions of believers ... justice and compassion are all but erased by [later] interpreters" (McCloud 2006: 40). We will see this hermeneutic resurface time and again in subsequent chapters. It is a hermeneutic, moreover, that as I argued in the Introduction seriously prevents Islamic religious studies from successfully integrating with other humanities-based disciplines. The repercussions of such a hermeneutic are staggering, essentially moving beyond the pale all those Islams that confront, undermine, or differ from their own construction. If "authentic" Islam is about gender justice, for example, then Saudi Arabia—a country that does not allow women to drive cars or appear in public without a male chaperone—has somehow either corrupted Islam's originary message or has strayed so far from its course that it ceases to be called "Islamic" in the first place.

And this, to me, is the problem. We have scholars of Islam that inhabit departments of religious studies who are completely uninterested in the larger set of critical discourses in that larger discipline. Much like Thurman, they see their primary goal as engaging in acts of what they consider to be proper political representation of their data. To this end, they conflate the personal, the political, and the scholarly. The present chapter seeks to examine this conflation in greater detail among scholars of Islamic religious studies. It argues, among other things, that much of the fault for this lies with the late Edward W. Said, someone who remains, close to 40 years after the publication of his *magnum opus*, *Orientalism*, the major theorist in Islamic religious studies in the present. There are real problems in conflating Said's politico-literary argument with a historico-scholarly one, and in remaining beholden to a work published so long ago.

The Politics of Representation

The act of representation is, by nature, political. It is premised on the selection of criteria that are believed to coincide with preconceived notions of what is "right" and "proper" on the one hand, and what is "wrong" and "improper" on the other. The latter are marginalized, while the former traits are emphasized as somehow being essential to the representative act. This is why identity politics, ontological essentialism, and "correct" representation seem to go in tandem with one another. The important thing to note is that the binaries of right–wrong and proper–improper are relative, not surprisingly reflecting the needs and desires of those doing the representing. The result is an intricate network of stereotypes predicated on apologetics, memory, and distortion. Within this self-constructed pathway, one's vision is obscured with a vista of one's making, little more than what Baudrillard calls a simulacrum, that is, a representation *imagined* as veritable, *de rigueur*, and authentic (Jameson 1991, 15–22; Baudrillard [1981]1994). This creates the epistemological problem that all such representations have a simulacrum quality, actually representing nothing instead of something. The experiences to which perceived representations point, in the words of Arnal and McCutcheon, whose analysis I am influenced by here, are "nonentities or, instead, point to given sets of representations rather than to the (in fact, nonexistent) entities those representations allegedly represent" (Arnal and McCutcheon 2013: 64). The result is nothing less than the erosion of reality, denying value while simultaneously trying to uphold it (Baudrillard [1981]1994: 199).

When we bring this discussion into Islamic religious studies, it translates, in the most simple terms, into the notion that we cannot say anything negative about the type of Islam that scholars have created largely in their own image. This is primarily because this Islam does not, cannot, exist anywhere in reality. Rather than situate these constructions against the backdrop of postindustrial capitalism, of the paradox of globalization that simultaneously feeds off of and creates sociopolitical tribalism (Harvey 1990: 290–95; Arnal and McCutcheon 2013: 66–8), we instead are invited to treat these representations, these simulacra, as reality. These representations as a product of the modern West, perhaps not surprisingly, reflect the consumer-oriented tendency that manufactures identities in ways that resemble the creation and marketing of products. This is why discourses of identity become so important for the creation of an inner core of "identity," a core that is found hidden in the Qur'an and, not surprisingly, in the interpreter. The result is a fetishized Islam, a cultural value, a commodity that, like all commodities, can be presented as authentic, a panacea for modern ills, and subsequently bought and sold in the marketplace of ideas.

There are real repercussions for such acts of (mis)representation. Those who engage in such liberal theologizing claim to be engaged in an accurate representation of Muslims subjects that they hold up as countering centuries of Orientalist presentations. Like those they criticize, however, they do little more than create a set of stereotypes, which with sufficient repetition risk being mistaken for essential traits thought to be immune from intellectual and historical scrutiny (see my comments in Hughes 2012c: 6-7). So rather than portray Muslims "accurately," such liberal theological representations actually have the opposite effect: they deny real Muslims their agency in favor of some ideologically imagined notion of what real Muslims either are or should be.

Shadow Boxing with Said

In the remainder of this chapter, I would like to focus on some of Said's assumptions, which I believe have had an undue influence on the field of which I have been so critical. Although I am critical of Said here, it is important to note that his use and deployment on the part of scholars of Islamic religious studies might actually be a misreading of what he was trying to do. They use his trenchant critique of a particular way of writing about Islam in particular and the Orient in general, for example, but then they engage in a further rhetorical move by creating their own, equally reified and equally essentialized, concept. This latter move, I like to think, is something of which Said would have been exceedingly skeptical.

Regardless, Said's *Orientalism* was an important (but by no means sui generis) book that in 1978 made numerous constituencies within the Academy rethink the ways in which the "Orient" had been traditionally portrayed.[3] Using the theoretical model supplied by Michel Foucault, Said argued that knowledge of a subject was tantamount to power over it. His argument, distilled to its simplest form, is that "the West" has used the "the Orient," a self-constructed Other, to think about and understand itself. Said set out to show that the language and categories supplied by *all* nineteenth and early twentieth-century literature, scholarship, and art dealing with the Orient was an attempt on the part of Europe to articulate and better define itself and its values in the light of this perceived Other (e.g., Said 1978: 15-20). He writes that "Orientalism" is a

> style of thought based upon an ontological and epistemological distinction made between "the Orient" and (most of the time) "the Occident." Thus a very large mass of writers, among whom are poets, novelists, philosophers, political theorists, economists, and imperial administrators, have accepted the basic distinction between East and West as the starting point for elaborate theories, epics, novels, and political accounts concerning the Orient, its peoples, customs, "mind," destiny, and so on. (Said 1978: 2-3)

Most likely owing to the fact that Said was not a historian, but a literary theorist, he was able to frame this knowledge/power dynamic in a manner that many in several disciplines both appreciated and understood. My goal is certainly not to minimize his achievement or the impact of *Orientalism*. Virtually overnight, Orientalism, rightly or wrongly is not my concern at the moment, became a dirty word and pretty much every single department of Oriental studies changed its name. This, not surprisingly, created major shifts in the ways that Islam was not only taught, as I shall examine shortly, but also in its institutional location within the contemporary university.

As I have argued elsewhere (Hughes 2006: 24-5), Said succeeded in helping us attune ourselves to the language and categories we use to represent other cultures. This goes a long way, for example, to explaining the debate between Lopez and Thurman with which I began this chapter. The language of representation, as their debate so forcefully demonstrates, is not simply innocuous or scholarly, but embedded in complex political and ideological webs from which it is impossible to escape. What can we legitimately say about another culture, religion, or region? What gives those doing the representing the authority to make such claims in the first place? Said called for us to be self-reflective and self-conscious of the language we use. I have no problems with any of this especially since I have also argued for the importance of self-reflexivity and self-consciousness in the professional religionist's conceptual toolbox.[4]

However, Said was not as honest as he claimed. His survey of European Orientalism ignored the country that produced the most original and important work on Islam and the Middle East, to wit, Germany. He reasons that

> I believe that the sheer quality, consistency, and mass of British, French, and American writing on the Orient lifts it above the doubtless crucial work done in Germany, Italy, Russia, and elsewhere. But I think it is also true that the major steps in Oriental scholarship were first taken in either Britain or France, and then elaborated upon by Germans. (Said 1978: 17-18)

Yet, if, as Said had argued, knowledge is tantamount to power, why would he not only ignore German scholarship on the Orient, but also lump it in with the Italians and the Russians, two countries that produced relatively little scholarship in this area? It was the Germans, after all, who were, in the words of Suzanne Marchand, the pacesetters "in virtually every field of oriental studies between about 1830 and 1930" (2009: xviii). It was German Orientalists, moreover, who were responsible for the production of some of the most important and non-ideologically motivated scholarship on Islam. Said subsequently admits this when he claims that "Any work that seeks to provide an understanding of *academic* Orientalism and pays little attention to scholars like Steinthal, Müller, Becker, Goldziher, Brockelmann, Nöldeke—to mention only a handful—needs to be reproached, and I fully reproach myself" (1978: 18; my italics).

Here, very significantly, Said intimates that his main interest is not in providing an analysis of *academic* Orientalism, but it would now seem something entirely different. Despite what appears to be his own self-criticism, Said maintains that "what German Oriental scholarship did was to refine and elaborate certain techniques whose application was to texts, myths, ideas, and languages almost literally gathered from the Orient by imperial Britain and France" (Said 1978: 19).

But this is inaccurate. As Nina Berman has forcefully agued, there were many actual encounters between Germans and the Orient that ought to force us to rethink the claims put forth by Said and many others in his wake that seek to exclude the Germans from historiographies of European Orientalism (N. Berman 2004, 2013). Indeed, as others (historians, not literary critics) have argued, the Germans did indeed have "a very long and important relationship with both the Holy Land and the Ottoman Empire and the Wilhelmine Empire did have colonial interests, and even colonial territories (Qingdao and Samoa, for example) in the East" (Marchand 2009: xix; see further the work of Steinmetz 2007).

So what do we make of Said's glaring omission of the German Orientalists? For one thing, and by his own admission, he states that his goal is not academic Orientalism. His interest is in discussing the more madcap and idiosyncratic writings of French Orientalists, such as Ernest Renan, whose work on race was quite quickly dismissed even by his own contemporaries (see Conrad 1999: 145–8). For Said, it was the English and the French who were largely responsible for the monolithic treatment of the Orient from "the late 1840s to the present in the United States" (1978: 17–18). This work, produced I might add during the so-called "high imperial age," enabled him to conclude that Orientalism was simply and monolithically a product of Empire (Marchand 2009: xix). The German material, however, because it was sober and academic and produced by an imperial force, did not fit into his analytical framework so he seems to have been content to ignore it altogether.

Another, more nefarious, reason that Said might have ignored the Germans is that many of them—such as Goldziher, Geiger, Weil, Hirschfeld, Horovitz, Speyer, and Schapiro, to name but a few—who were interested in the historical and linguistic presentation of Islam (the Qur'an, development of hadith literature, law, and so on), were Jewish. While this may simply be a coincidence, it strikes me as not insignificant that this is the case. Said, on this reading, becomes uncannily similar to Hans Heinrich Speyer, who, despite claims to objectivity, did not mention one single German-Jewish scholar in his history of German Orientalism, published not surprisingly in 1940.[5] It is unfortunate that today so many take Said's ideologically driven literary argument for an objective historiography of the field. Indeed, despite all the problems associated with Said's arguments, *Orientalism* continues to structure our understanding of the European encounter with the East, even when Germans are included.[6] In revisiting this criticism I am certainly not arguing that we return to a pre-Saidian way of writing about the Orient. But surely we need some other way to think through this morass of complicated issues so that we may begin to unravel, contextualize, and historicize its various strands. To quote the work of Marchand:

> We need, instead, a synthetic and critical history, one that assesses oriental scholarship's contributions to imperialism, racism, and modern anti-Semitism, but one that also shows how modern orientalism has furnished at least some of the tools necessary for constructing the post-imperialist worldviews we cultivate today. (Marchand 2009: xx)

I would now like to return to Said's comments about Islam, which is my concern in this study. For him, traditional attempts to understand Islam on historical grounds amount to little more than a politically motivated attempt to undermine the tradition. Although Said's larger point was with Orientalism, he really focused the force of his attacks on the representation of Islam in the West. In the contemporary world, Said reserves his harshest criticism for Bernard Lewis, someone who, for Said, symbolizes all that is wrong with scholarship on Islam. Lewis, according to Said, writes in bad faith:

> One would find this kind of procedure less objectionable as political propaganda—which is what it is, of course—were it not accompanied by sermons on the objectivity, the fairness, the impartiality of a real historian, the implication always being that Muslims and Arabs cannot be objective but that Orientalists like Lewis writing about Muslims and Arabs are, by definition, by training, by the mere fact of their Westernness. (Said 1978: 319)[7]

Here Said argues that by virtue of their "Westernness," Lewis—and by extension others—are simultaneously unable or unwilling to engage in "accurate" or "objective" presentations in their portrayal of Arabs and Muslims. Whether they know it or not, or whether they acknowledge it or not, Western scholars by the very nature of their enterprise are hostile to the Arab world. Orientalism, for Said and for so many of those who follow in his wake, is about the political act of representation. Among the many questions that Said has raised, the one that is most pertinent to the focus of this book is, Who is in the best position to write about the "Orient"? Unfortunately, the answer to this question has been interpreted by those in Islamic religious studies as being only those who are Muslims (whether by birth or conversion) or those sufficiently sympathetic to their representations. If Said could at least admit that traditionally trained Orientalists could break out of their "ideological straitjackets," his acolytes have taken this to mean that the only way one can be a non-Muslim and study Islam is to assume a highly apologetic position that acknowledges the suffering of Muslims subjects at the hands of "the West."

The results of Said's critique are not difficult to witness. The entire scholarly apparatus used to study Islam has now become suspect because of its assumed links to imperialism and colonialism. It has now become impolitic for non-Muslims to study Islam, given their investiture in non-Muslim and Eurocentric categories. We must remember, however, that Said was writing as an outsider to the field that he claimed to critique. He was, by training, a scholar of English literature. He was *not* a scholar of Islam, nor was he anyone who had any of the historical and linguistic training necessary for the study of this tradition. The main thing that he had going for him was that he was a Palestinian Arab (a Christian, not a Muslim) and his experiences as such. That Said could not read classical Arabic or that he had no training in the field that he attacked has mattered little. Instead, with one fell swoop his *Orientalism* destroyed an entire field, that is, Oriental Studies, and ushered in a new experiential-based paradigm of dealing with Arabs, Islam, and the Middle East. Reading texts in original languages is no longer important, dealing with historical problems are now irrelevant, and the examination of thorny issues in early Islam (e.g., the redaction of the Qur'an or the quest for the historical Muhammad) becomes discouraged, if not actually forbidden, the stuff of the old "Orientalism."

Criticizing Said, however, is difficult to do in a field that now holds him up as its exemplar. Although his book was published close to 40 years ago, many scholars of Islam continue to read *Orientalism* as if it were cutting edge scholarship. The larger field, however, has changed. Oriental studies for the most part no longer exists, at least in its classic form. This is another way of saying that the overwhelming majority of scholars no longer speaks or writes in the terms that Said was so critical of, though scholars of Islamic religious studies still pretend they do.[8] The result is that "Said" has become code for a collective defensive posture that defines who can and who cannot portray Islam "accurately." Though many in Islamic religious studies favorably remember Said as a critic of tyranny and power, they have paradoxically been content to set up their own control of their chosen field in Said's name.

Certainly Said was an important thinker, someone who changed the shape of the field of representing Islam, the Middle East, and Arabs in general and Palestinians in particular. None of this is the problem. The problem occurs when scholars of Islam take a particular perspective away from something that Said wrote close to 40 years ago and believe that it is still operative today. We have yet to recover from Said's critique, and the postcolonial studies paradigm that became fashionable in its wake. To engage in research into the sources of the Qur'an or hadith, to try and recreate the early Muslim polity in seventh century Arabia now becomes intertwined with "empire maintenance" and not allowing the other "the integrity that is their due." The result is that Islamic religious studies has largely become a closed club wherein born Muslims, converts to Islam, and those non-Muslims who function as their enablers set the parameters of the discourses of what gets to count as "legitimate" scholarship and what does not. This is why we see panels at the Annual Meeting of the American Academy of Religion devoted to topics such as " Putting the Prophet to Work: Social, Political, and Religious Dimensions of Literary Depictions of Muhammad" as opposed "Problems in Reconstructing the Historical Muhammad"; or "Cutting Edges in Islamic Feminism" as opposed to "Islam and Sexual Repression or Oppression."[9]

What do we learn from this discussion? For one thing, it shows the genealogy of why scholars of Islamic religious studies are so bothered with "Orientalism." Although Orientalism has ceased to exist, especially the way Said problematically portrayed it, the trope of "Orientalism" allows these scholars to do something very similar to that which Said accused the Orientalists of doing, of using a reified and essentialized construction to define who they are and what it is they are both doing and not doing. None of them ever actually critiques a real, living Orientalist because I doubt they know any, just as I doubt there are any of the pre-Saidian variety of which he was so critical. Instead the tropes of "Orientalism" or "Orientalist" allows for the pernicious creation of a primordial distinction between "Europe" and the "the Orient." But who are these "Europeans"? What are their identities? The way to understand Orientalism, writes Suzanne Marchand, is neither to make it into a critique of ideology nor a hermeneutical defense of scholarly progress (2009: xxii).

We need to understand and contextualize this writing about Islam and the Orient in terms of its institutional settings and the *serious* study that was performed in the service of studying the languages, histories, and cultures of the Orient. Instead of writing all this off *tout court*, we need to examine, critique, and modify its practices. Without doing this, we have nothing to build on. Rather than make Orientalism into the inverse of what it is that we perceive ourselves to be doing, surely we need to return and revisit some of its first principles, allowing us to use what we can and discard that which we deem to be unuseful.

If Said and his acolytes among scholars of Islamic religious studies accuse Orientalism of reifying Islam (or, alternatively, "the East") based on their own fantasies, it is surely worth pointing out that they do something similar. They look for, and not surprisingly find, a host of values—egalitarianism, pluralism, gender justice—that have derived from their own epistemological coordinates in the "West" and transferred them onto the "Orient" (e.g., the Qur'an). As Partha Chatterjee notes, however, the division of a Western material world with an Eastern spiritual one has both driven and reproduced itself in a host of anticolonial nationalisms. These nationalisms buy into the former (with its technology, science, politics), even though they regard the material as structurally inessential, all the while insisting the core identities occur in its own spiritual and immaterial world (Chatterjee 1993: 5–7). The critique of the West and the simultaneous desire to find its values in the East (i.e., Islam) is a central component of the identity formation of Islamic religious studies.

In all of these conversations, what counts as knowledge, to invoke the specter of Said for my own purposes, is not value neutral, but based on those who have power, for example, over what gets to count as valid scholarly topics in an institution. Today, as the AAR clearly shows us, this involves creating and disseminating a liberal form of Islam to counter the version of the tradition that encouraged terrorism. The personal narratives of liberal Muslim scholars now litter the field, and those critical of this project can be written off as hostile to Islam. Are we any better off in understanding the complexity of traditions that go by the collective name "Islam"? I would argue that we are not.

"Critical" Theory

I know of no other discipline wherein one can say "we do not want to use the disciplinary tools bequeathed to us and instead we wish to replace them with some sort of vague, inner-focused and apologetic-driven hermeneutic." If one wants to write a history of, say, the Jews in America in the early twentieth century or the emergence of Pakistan at the time of Partition, one must use the tools of the discipline of history and apply them to the particular data (e.g., the Jews of America in the early twentieth century or the emergence of Pakistan in 1947). If one wants to write a sociological study of Lebanese migrants to Dearborn,

Michigan in the 1920s, one must apply sociological method to one's data (to wit, the Lebanese migration to the Detroit area). One cannot get around the fact that there exists disciplinary questions and method on the one hand, and data that one interprets on the other. If one confuses discipline and data, conflates how one studies with what one studies, the result is intellectual bedlam.

Theory and method are so important to this enterprise because they function as the tools that scholars use to analyze their data, in addition to functioning as the means whereby data are brought into existence in the first place. This is certainly not meant as an argument for methodological purity; however, it is to make, and underscore, the important point that we cannot make intellectual disciplines into whatever we want them to be because it happens to suit us. One cannot engage in a sociological study and call it English literature, just as one cannot engage in a historical study and call it philosophy. Certainly there can exist studies that blur these lines (e.g., the sociology of reading or intellectual history), but they do so only if they have clear ideas of what constitute disciplinarity.

The problem with Islamic religious studies, like many other subfields that populate departments of religious studies, is that there is absolutely no concern for such questions of disciplinarity. I am not sure, for example, how many scholars of Islam are familiar with the terms of the debate, let alone the actual debate, between Lopez and Thurman or, say, the debate engendered by Sam Gill, who argued that the concept of "Mother Earth" in first nations' traditions is of recent provenance and, in part, a scholarly invention (Gill 1987). This is as much a failure on the part of Islamic religious studies as it is on that of the parent field of religious studies. Part of this has to do with the unsavory history of the discipline that has seen (and indeed continues to see) numerous variations on the theme of the confusion of theology and social science (for a critique of which see, e.g., Wiebe 1984, 2006). And part of this problem also has to do with the fact that religion matters to a lot of people, and that religious studies, rather than interpret its topic of study culturally, socially or biologically, simply repeats this importance and does so, moreover, with appeals to amorphous concepts such as experience or sacrality by pretending that they are analytic markers. In addition, religious studies has notoriously created a situation wherein those who are religious, the putative subject of the discipline, have largely set the terms for their own study. The result is that *critical* theoretical and methodological concerns have traditionally been marginalized in the academic study of religion.

This lack of critical scholarship in the parent discipline might well explain the inherently apologetical impulse within Islamic religious studies. When we factor into this the soft discourse of postcolonialsm—that is, those discourses that seek to bypass rather than query traditional categories of scholarship (including identity)—we encounter the current malaise. Rather than undermine the problems of disciplinarity *on intellectual grounds*, there is the tendency to ignore such problems by focusing on the personal and political grievances of the interpreter.

A case in point is the edited collection entitled *Rethinking Islamic Studies* (Ernst and R. Martin 2010), a work that I have already touched on briefly.[10] I now wish to focus on this work because of its bold claim that the authors seek to "rethink" the field by ostensibly bringing it into line with critical scholarship in the humanities. Recent years, the coeditors inform us, have "encouraged scholars to rethink how to theorize and problematize the textual and social data of Islam and how to adjust their investigations to methodologies that address the urgencies of Islamic studies in the twenty-first century" (Ernst and R. Martin 2010: 2). As it quickly becomes apparent, however, the editors are less interested in *critical* scholarship in the humanities, something that should in theory include religious studies, than they are in *post-critical* study, which refers to some vague and amorphous state where we have transcended traditional historical, political, and theoretical categories in favor of some sort of relativistic posture to what we study (see Foster 2012: 3–8). Criticism can now be neatly sidestepped as "cynical," or "Eurocentric," or even "old fashioned." However, when we loosen the bonds of criticism, when we engage in mutual congratulations without the risk of offence, we risk a return to the problem of fetishization, in which the object emerges as a quasi-subject. This, to quote the art critic and historian Hal Foster, "takes thoughts and feelings, processes them as images and effects, and delivers them back to us for our appreciative amazement" (Foster 2012: 7).

In their opening chapter to *Rethinking Islamic Studies*, Ernst and Martin—two of the most senior scholars in the field and who have trained many of the younger scholars examined in my study—spend considerable time showing the growth of Islamic studies within the American Academy of Religion. However, at no point do they actually engage with the *critical* categories supplied by the academic study of religion (i.e., my conversation partners in this study). This, to me, is symbolic of the status of Islamic religious studies in the field more generally: there is a desire and a willingness to attach its apologetic and fetishistic discourses to the field of religion without really engaging the premises of the field. Let me be absolutely clear here: I am not saying that Islamic religious studies must conform itself to this discipline, but at the very least it must critique this critical study of religion if for no other reason than to show what exactly is the problem with its regnant discourses. Unfortunately, the tendency today, as I have showed, is simply to ignore these categories either by pretending that they do not exist or by associating them with some vague notion of postcolonial inheritance. Either way, the end result is the same: these categories do not have to be engaged with seriously.

This is ludicrous, however. Recent theorists have shown precisely how religious studies has been invested in Empire maintenance, but they have done so moreover in ways that seek to rehabilitate certain critical discourses (see, for example, Chidester 1996, 2014). My sense is that because so much of Islamic religious studies confuses subject and object, the best that it can do is engage in a fetishistic slippage in which scholars celebrate themselves through their objects of study, which function as little more than metonyms of themselves. In their Introduction to the aforementioned volume, the editors try to get at a new vision of Islamic studies by critiquing the work of Charles Adams, who argued that scholarship must engage in traditional textual study.[11] Adams, they argue, makes no mention of the reactions of Muslims to Euro-American scholarship ... or, to their participation in it. His discussion of Islamic studies does not consider the impact of having Muslim students in the classroom. Nor is there any reflection on the scholar's own precommitments. He does not discuss the massive stereotypes of Islam relating to terrorism, violence, oppression of women, and so forth. He makes little mention of recent history, particularly European colonialism, modernity, and fundamentalism. Furthermore, he does not refer at all to the role of the media and popular culture presentations in establishing the image of Islam today. (Ernst and R. Martin 2010: 5–6)

The "new" Islamic studies, in sum, is apologetic, presentist, and based on countering hostile portrayals in the media. It is not, by definition, critical. In fact, given their description above it cannot be critical because "criticism" (e.g., of gender, violence) is what those hostile to Islam engage in. Instead, there is a movement to what I have called "post-criticism," but which the authors included in the volume refer to by the name "cosmopolitanism." The latter, based on the work of Kwame Anthony Appiah (2006), is not based on criticism, but rests upon the three pillars of tolerance, pluralism, and global harmony. Ernst and Martin inform us that there is now a difference between the way Islam is examined in religious studies departments and in Near or Middle Eastern studies programs. They write,

> Today foundational questions in the study of Islam, such as the origin of the Qur'anic text or the development of exegetical genres, usually take place in area studies or Near or Middle Eastern studies programs, whereas the anthropological inquiry of Islamic ritual, such as the performance of pilgrimage or the performance of religious identity, for that matter, are often also explored in religious studies departments. (Ernst and R. Martin 2010: 7)

This disciplinary balkanization ostensibly keeps Islamic religious studies free from "Orientalist"-type questions. Presumably, Ernst and Martin mean that textual and philological work occurs in disciplinary amorphous programs (e.g., Middle Eastern Studies, Near Eastern Languages and Culture), but that anthropological work occurs in religious studies. The conflation of anthropology and religious studies again shows the categorical errors of Islamic religious studies. Why engage in anthropological study in religious studies as opposed to departments of anthropology? The reason, I have been suggesting throughout this study, is that one can use other disciplines in religious studies only in so far as it does not get in the way of asking hard questions of one's material. One can, for example, look at the way African American converts to Islam wear the hijab and how this empowers them racially and religiously (Karim 2008; Grewal 2014), but one should never engage in examining the creation of "Islamic" identity at the time of Muhammad. The latter is the stuff of Orientalism, presumably because it implies that the Qur'an might not actually be the product of divine revelation, but the former is okay because presumably no Muslims are offended in the process.

Rather than use, employ, or critique categories from the academic study of religion, the contributors to *Rethinking Islamic Studies* use post-critical theorists, like Appiah, or completely defang other theorists if they believe that they can support their readings. When these latter are invoked, the best example being Talal Asad, they are done so subversively and in ways that further reify identity and related concepts (e.g., race, gender, ethnicity). Ernst and Martin, for example, invoke Asad, but reduce his complex work to the claim that his major contribution is "that Muslim societies must be understood on their own terms and not a superimposed model" (Ernst and R. Martin 2010: 9). No mention of the subjective processes related to embodiment and discipline; or no emphasis on how Asad tried to get us to appreciate how the objective conditions in which subjects find themselves enable them to decide what they must think and how they live. It seems to be enough that Asad speaks from a position of marginality or has some sort of subaltern identity (even though he was trained at Oxford University and occupies a distinguished chair at the Graduate Center in New York City), and that his work as a critical theorist can be boiled down to the simplistic notion that, like Said, Muslims must study and represent themselves, as opposed to being represented by others.

Let me now spend a few pages discussing the work of Talal Asad with the aim of showing just how problematic he is for the type of scholarship that many in Islamic religious studies are doing, especially when they invoke the term "religion" as if it were a non-problematic category. Rather than assume that "religion" has any content, Asad argues that the term is not universal and that both in the past and in the non-West, it would have operated in ways that we today do not define as "religion" or "religious." Religion, for him, is a by-product of the unique historical and political circumstances of modern Western modernity (Asad 1993: 39–43). He writes that

> Several times before the Reformation, the boundary between the religious and the secular was redrawn, but always the formal authority of the Church remained preeminent. In later centuries, with the triumphant rise of modern science, modern production, and the modern state, the churches would also be clear about the need to distinguish the religious from the secular, shifting, as they did so, the weight of religion more and more onto the moods and motivations of the individual believer. Discipline (intellectual and social) would, in this period, gradually abandon religious space, letting "belief," "conscience," and "sensibility" take its place. (Asad 1993: 39)

The concept of religion, for Asad, serves a variety of modern political ends. "It converges," he writes, "with the liberal demand in our time that it be kept quite separate from politics, law, and science" (1993: 28). Religion, as a human phenomenon, has no privileged sphere even though many want to give it such a sphere. On the contrary, as Arnal and McCutcheon argue, "religion" becomes the space in which and by which "collective goals (salvation, righteousness, judgment, condemnation, etc.) are individualized and made into a question of personal preference, commitment, or morality" (Arnal and McCutcheon 2013: 29). As Arnal and McCutcheon recognize, Asad was one of the earliest theorists of religion to call for the historicization of the very idea of religion in the first place—how its study is, in effect, the study of the modern state.

But note what Asad is not saying. He is not saying that Islam simply needs to be studied on "its own terms." Rather, he argues that we need to be aware of the very preconditions for non-hegemonic analyses of the variety of practices and beliefs that we moderns problematically designate with the term "religion." Also note that Asad is not saying that it is okay, or even acceptable, for scholars of Islam to manufacture an identity for themselves that buys into the same categories of which he is so critical above. He is, moreover, not saying that we should engage in the practice of creating an essentialized or reified Islam that exists independently from the political and anthropological spheres that paradoxically seek to make "religion" into a privileged sphere. Indeed, for Asad, this view of religion—as interiorized and personal—is a direct outgrowth of the modern invention of the secular state. Indeed, Asad represents the exact type of critical theory in the academic study of religion that scholars of Islamic religious studies seek to avoid. So why do so many invoke him? Perhaps because of his call to do away with a reified notion of "Islam" and instead study Muslims on the ground or in the street, as it were. However, when scholars of Islamic religious studies still have predetermined notions of what Islam is and, therefore, what Muslims to study, they make a mockery of Asad's theoretical point that "there is no single, privileged narrative in the modern world" (1993: 9–10).

In his *Formations of the Secular*, Asad further expands on these notions. His interest is less in secularism than in the very idea of secularism, arguing that there is a tendency in much contemporary scholarship to use terms without thinking through both their meanings and deployment (Asad 2003: 10). The idea of secularism, he argues, does not make the world a better place, but simply rearranges the rules of the game: "A secular state does not guarantee toleration; it puts into play different structures of ambition and fear. The law never seeks to eliminate violence since its objective is always to *regulate* violence" (Asad 2003: 8). Moreover, he writes that

> "the secular" should not be thought of as the space in which real human life gradually emancipates itself from the controlling power of "religion" and thus achieves the latter's relocation. It is this assumption that allows us to think of religion as "infecting" the secular domain or as replicating within it the structure of theological concepts. ... Secularism doesn't simply insist that religious practice and belief be confined to a space where they cannot threaten political stability or the liberties of "free-thinking" citizens. Secularism builds on a particular conception of the world. (Asad 2003: 191)

This means that, for Asad, we must not simply redeploy traditional categories, but, once again, reflect on and ultimately change their meaning. Politics, ethics, religion, among other such categories now become, as they had in his earlier work, sites of redescription that undermine triumphalist narratives of either the Western or Islamic variety.

In fact, if anything, the likes of Asad and Said, especially when the latter is read through a particular lens, actually warn us of the dangers of precisely the type of empiricism practiced by scholars of Islamic religious studies. According to

Asad, following on the heels of what I discussed above, the hermeneutical circle that ethnographers can fall into is to think that they can simply reproduce their own personal experiences and the experiences of their like-minded colleagues because they, and they alone, have a proper understanding of some amorphously constructed "experience" based on their religious beliefs and/or disbeliefs (Asad 2003: 9–10). They do so, moreover, in such a manner that makes their own set of experiences homogeneous, complete and consistent, and in such a manner that their own "form of life" represents an indisputable reality as opposed to an internally ambiguous interpretation. Their own ordinary language, again invoking Asad, is now signified as somehow more authentic than the language of the theological texts in whose name they purport to speak.[12]

In addition to appropriating and misunderstanding those like Asad, there is also an overwhelming tendency in Islamic religious studies circles to deny what many theorists in religion call the social construction of religion (e.g. McCutcheon 1997; Lincoln 2003; Arnal and McCutcheon 2013), a genealogy into which we must certainly insert Asad's pioneering *Genealogies of Religion* (1993). It is unclear why these scholars are not addressed more—perhaps there is an assumption that their criticisms are somehow embedded in or beholden to "Eurocentric" modes of analysis. This, as but the briefest and most cursory of perusals of their work will reveal, is ludicrous. The criticisms leveled against such scholars, or just the plain ignorance of their work, enables Islamic religious studies to hold out for some vague and reconstructed "liberal religion" rooted in the idea of private belief. Rather than query "religion" as a category or a trope, the product of the very West of which they are so critical, scholars of Islamic religious studies reinforce it by clinging to the notion that "religion" must have an essence that is, *inter alia*, good, sacred, and spiritual.

The result is that the manner in which scholars of Islamic religious studies think about religion is out of sync with the ways that critical scholars of religion (including Asad) attune us to think about this problematic category. The way the latter think about religion and related categories, in other words, is not all that different from the way Asad does. In fact, they build upon his critique. The question, then, is why Asad, but why not Lincoln or McCutcheon? The solution, as I have suggested above, is that Asad presumably has a *personal* narrative grounded in postcolonial dislocation. Those with names like Lincoln, Smith, or McCutcheon lack such credentials and, because of their names and not the force of their criticism, can be safely ignored.

Conclusions

When theory is invoked to study Islam, it is usually not done so using the critical discourses found in religious studies, its parent discipline. The latter—perhaps best exemplified in the writings of those like Bruce Lincoln, Jonathan Z. Smith, Daniel Dubuisson, Timothy Fitzgerald, Russell McCutcheon, not to mention Talal Asad—seeks to undermine the category "religion" showing how rather than study the timeless and eternal experiences of religious actors, we should shift our focus to study how "religion" is produced and manipulated by social actors in history. Such critiques have largely gone unnoticed among Islamicists. Instead, focus has shifted to what I have elsewhere called "soft" or "light" postcolonialism (Hughes 2012a: 321–3). Basically, this means that we have to be aware of the philosophic and methodological presuppositions of our Eurocentric mindset and in such a way that it "is time to accord the 'other'—be it a person or a religion—the integrity that is their due in an age when it is becoming increasingly difficult to do so" (see, e.g., Joy 2001: 192). This usually translates into the idea that we have to let others represent themselves on their own terms, whatever those may consist of. In terms of the critical study of religion, this creates numerous problems: What does it mean to "accord the 'other' the integrity that is their due"? Is every act of redescription a hostile act founded in the violence of colonialism?

The movement from Oriental studies to Islamic religious studies has come with a cost. No longer are scholars interested in language work, history, or philology. Indeed, given the topics that people work on now, such as race and gender in contemporary America, I am not convinced that many scholars have competence in Arabic and other relevant Islamicate languages. All of the major issues that had interested Islamicists for most of the past 150 years—the redaction of the Qur'an, the development of the hadith and local contexts, the development of Islamic law, research into the Greek sources of Islamic philosophy, medieval literature, poetry and other narrative—have largely fallen away to be replaced by feminist- and gay-friendly interpretations of the Qur'an. The Qur'an is never the problem for homophobia or sexism, but traditional male and heterosexual commentators are. Perceived to exist outside of time, modern-day Muslim activist-scholars seek to make the Qur'an, and by extension Islam, compatible with the West. This is not scholarship, however, but theological advocacy.

One way out of this abyss, suggested by Ruth Mas, is to acknowledge that criticism need not be "reduced to the simple and thoughtless act of finding fault" (Mas 2012: 390). "Critique," she argues is not necessarily the same thing as "criticism," and that we must differentiate between these two acts as they have come down to us through the modernist project. This is certainly fair enough, but, once again, I am left wondering, where does this leave us? This is, perhaps, the largest impasse currently facing the academic study of religion today. Unlike Mas, I have no problem with finding fault, since I would like to think that this is the way that disciplines and fields sharpen their modes of analysis. In the following two chapters I shall further engage in this act of criticism.

Notes

1. Lopez, for example, accuses Thurman of transmogrifying Tibetan Buddhism into science, and of reading Nyingma texts (that are more interested in magic) as if they actually came out of the Geluk sect (i.e., that of the Dalai Lama) of Tibetan Buddhism (Lopez 1998: 83).
2. This, of course, is the point that J. Z. Smith made over 30 years ago in the oft-quoted statement that *"there is no data for religion*. Religion is solely the creation of the

scholar's study. It is created for the scholar's analytical purpose by his imaginative acts of comparison and generalization" (1982: xi; his italics).
3. Earlier such arguments may be found, for example, in Owen (1973), Asad (1973), and Laroui (1976).
4. Parts of this and the following paragraph rework and build upon Hughes (2006: 24–16).
5. An important corrective to which is Fück (1955).
6. For more balanced and historically minded treatments of knowledge and the East, see R. Berman (1998), Prakash (1999), Bayly (2000), and Steinmetz (2007).
7. I also note that it would not be inaccurate if we reversed the protagonists and antagonists in this quotation.
8. Certainly Bernard Lewis does (e.g., Lewis 2003). But he most certainly is an anomaly and an exception that justifies the rule.
9. Study of Islam and related panels from the 2014 Annual Meeting in San Diego are: Islam and the Anthropocene: Biosphere and Climate; Religion, the State, and Islamic Institutions of Higher Education: Authorizing Authority; Looking Back, Looking Forward: A Conversation about the Past and Future of Islam, Liberation and Gender Justice with Amina Wadud and Farid Esack; Making Muslim American Musics; Devotional Objects and Embodiment in Islamic Traditions; Discourses by/on Muslims in Minority Contexts; Texts, Contexts, and Interpretations; Political Authority and Theology. The online program book may be found at https://papers.aarweb.org/program_book?page=2&keys=Study%20of%20Islam&field_session_slot_nid=All.
10. I have also examined this work in considerable detail in Hughes (2012d: 100–117). My examination here, however, is considerably different.
11. For my critique of Adams, albeit on radically different grounds from Ernst and Martin, see Hughes 2006: 74–79.
12. My ideas here are inspired by Craig Martin's interview with Asad in Martin (2014).

— 3 —

Insiders, Outsiders, and the Path Between

Mohammad Alexander Russell Webb was the official Muslim delegate to the famed World Parliament of Religions held in Chicago in 1893. While certainly not the first American convert to Islam, he counts among the first to promote this almost completely foreign religion in such a public way among American audiences. In addition, he was also the leader of the earliest Islamic movement on American soil: a mission to propagate his new faith by creating a network of study circles that would take their names from the cities in which he started them and which, among other things, would read his works. Webb had been strongly involved with the Theosophical Society in St Louis before President Cleveland appointed him to be the American Consul in the Philippines (Abd-Allah 2006: 5). As a Theosophist, Webb naturally looked to the Orient as the romantic embodiment of exotic spiritual and religious truths. Webb undoubtedly believed that his new position as the American Consul would provide him direct and unmediated access to these spiritual truths. Although brought up Presbyterian, he dabbled in Buddhism, before deciding to convert to Islam without ever having met a single Muslim. He finally converted in 1888, after he encountered several prominent Muslim modernists associated with the Aligarh Movement in India.[1]

Webb subsequently resigned his consular post, and began a speaking tour throughout India before traveling to Egypt and the Middle East to learn more about his newly adopted religion. When he returned to the United States he went about setting up a mission in New York City with the aim of propagating Islam among Americans. His conversion and the opening of his mission attracted significant attention, including front-page headlines in the *New York Times*.[2] When Webb stood up to address the World's Parliament on September 20, 1893, a cold and early fall morning, many gathered to hear a figure that the local press had referred to as "the Yankee Mohammedan" (Abd-Allah 2006: 1). In his first speech to the delegates, entitled "the Spirit of Islam," Webb talked about his initial ignorance and antipathy towards Islam, his spiritual quest, and the subsequent embrace of his new way of life. He remarked, "But when I came to go beneath the surface, to know what Islam really is, to know who and what the prophet of Arabia was, I changed my belief very materially, and I am proud to say that I am now a Mussulman" (quoted in Abd-Allah 2006: 240).

© Equinox Publishing Ltd. 2015

Webb's spiritual journey to Islam was intensely personal; however, his desire to represent Islam in the marketplace of ideas at the Parliament of World Religions was very much a public act. His goal was nothing less than to show Americans that Islam was both a beautiful religion, compatible with values that Americans held dear, and to justify why he had decided to convert to this little understood religion in the first place. His life goal came to be to explain Islam, and its teachings to Americans. He writes, for example, that

> It is not an exaggeration to say that there is not more than one Church-Christian in half a million who has any just and proper conception of the Islamic system of religion or knows how and when and where the Mussulman prays; what his prayer means, what his daily religious practices are or how the system he follows is arranged. In writing this book I have had two objects in view. The first, is to supply American and English converts to Islam with a complete and explicit guide to prayer; the second, is to educate honest, fair-minded, thoughtful people to a better knowledge and appreciation of the leading doctrine, or cornerstone of the Islamic system. (Quoted in Abd-Allah 2006: 202)

The expository speeches that he gave in front of his audiences, both in public and in print, comprised an admixture of personal devotion and religious zeal on the one hand, and the latest scholarship on the other. Frequently it is difficult to decide where the personal narrative ended and the scholarly one began, and vice versa. Although Webb did not have a PhD in Islamic or religious studies, he nonetheless published numerous books on the topic of Islam (e.g., Webb 1892, 1893), including how to propagate the faith throughout the United States (Singleton 2007). As was in keeping with the general mandate of the Parliament, the various lectures from the various participant-believers were designed to foster a global dialogue of faiths for the coming millennium.[3]

While things have changed dramatically since the time of Mohammad Webb, the desire remains—as witnessed in previous chapters—on the part of many American-Muslim academics to show the correspondences between so-called "American" values (e.g., liberty, democracy, equality) and Islam, and how the latter presupposed or anticipated them. The result is that Islam still is conceptualized apologetically and in a constructive theological manner. Certainly the way that scholars of Islamic religious studies today disseminate their vision of Islam must be situated, indeed as it was in the days of Webb, against a broader context of fear, hatred, and ignorance. However, we must always keep in mind that this representation is not acknowledged as *a* representation, one representation among many, but as the truth. The methodological moves and techniques used to uncover this essence make me, as a scholar of religion, extremely uncomfortable. It is one thing to try and dispel prejudice about a religion, but quite another thing to convince oneself as a scholar that these representations are based on anything other than a set of imaginative acts derived from the privileging and denial of data.

I am also interested in the fact that Mohammad Webb was a convert to Islam. While his spiritual journey is certainly interesting, I am less interested in that than I am in his public declarations about Islam after his conversion. Much of this seems to have been motivated by the ignorance of, and even hostility towards, Islam among his contemporaries. Islam now became for him everything that Christianity was not. It became the most rational religion, the most spiritual, and the one that was best fitted for contemporary life. All these claims, of course, are subjective and certainly ones that a recent convert must inevitably make in order to justify his or her conversion process. The intersection between the *apologia pro vita sua* and scholarship is as fine as it is fascinating, and surely it problematizes the traditional insider/outside debate in the academic study of religion.

What does it mean for a scholar of a particular religion to convert to what one studies? Obviously, it means, for one thing, that the individual has found some sort of religious or spiritual connection with what he or she studies, something that is more than just academic. Yet, in converting, I would hope that one would be aware, acutely aware, of one's new scholarly voice. One cannot just pass over this in silence or pretend that it is neither unimportant nor insignificant.

If one is not a "native-born" scholar of the particular religion that one studies, there exist several ways to establish one's bona fides among those that are. Jewish and First Nations studies perhaps set up the biggest hurdle between insider and outsider. In the latter, one must speak reverentially (e.g., Ruml 2006), and in the former one must practice dissimulation. In East Asian religions, it is not uncommon to try and maneuver the gap by means of endogamy or exogamy; and in South Asian religions, one can try to negotiate this through yogic and/or tantric devotion. In Islam, as we shall see below, one of the primary ways to do this is through conversion. All seem to represent established techniques of acquiring authenticity, providing the way that "outsiders" can signal to others that they are now somehow "insiders."

The present chapter explores how the insider/outside debate plays out specifically in Islamic religious studies. Given what we saw in previous chapters—the role of identity politics, the inattention to critical theory on religion (despite appeals to the contrary), and the reification of an essentialized Islam defined by liberal values—the question now arises, who has the authority to produce this Islam? How is this authority maintained and patrolled? Framed in terms of the subject matter of the present chapter, what constitutes insidership and, its obverse, outsidership? To do this, the present chapter focuses on the traditionally untheorized, though generally well acknowledged, concept of the convert and his or her place in Islamic religious studies.[4]

The Insider/Outsider Debate

The insider/outsider debate is certainly one of the major issues in the humanities and is by no means confined to the academic study of religion. Russell McCutcheon defines the magnitude of the problem in the following terms:

> Whether, and to what extent, someone can study, understand, or explain the beliefs, words, or actions of another. In other words, to what degree, if any,

> are the motives and meanings of human behaviors and beliefs accessible to
> the researcher who may not necessarily share these beliefs and who does not
> necessarily participate in these practices? (McCutcheon 1999: 2)

At stake is how can anyone get at, let alone examine and analyze, the experiences and practices of another, whether diachronically or synchronically? It is worth noting that this is not just about whether or not a Muslim can or should be able to study Islam more accurately or sympathetically than a non-Muslim. Rather, taken to its logical conclusion, it calls into question the very ability of any interpreter to understand the moods, motivations, and beliefs of any social actor. Framed somewhat differently, can a Muslim understand the experiences or intentions of another Muslim, especially in different times and geographical locations? Does a contemporary Muslim scholar of Islamic religious studies, for example, have more insight into the mind or even religious practices of a ninth century quranic exegete than a non-Muslim scholar?

Those who believe that the so-called "insider" has more authority in studying their own tradition in the academic study of religion want to contend that a special set of interpretive tools must be used that permit some sort of unmediated access to the deep meaning of religious acts and symbols. These tools, it is assumed, are somehow different in type or kind from how we study other mundane aspects of human culture (McCutcheon 1999: 27–34). Yet, whenever any domain of human production is protected, put outside the boundaries of scholarship (which, as we saw in the previous chapter, can be written off as "Orientalist"), a specific set of practical, social, and political implications ensue.

In terms of the academic study of religion, the insider/outsider debate usually revolves around the notion that either insiders (i.e., religious practitioners) have a lot invested in their own religious lives and traditions, and that, as a result, they may be either unwilling or unable to study their own beliefs and practices "objectively." Or, that the insider actually possesses an intimate knowledge of the tradition that puts him or her in the best possible position to study and appreciate his or her own religion. The insider might even go so far as to say that the goal of religious studies is neither criticism nor reductive interpretation, but to foster appreciation and understanding. Needless to say, it is an intractable debate. When translated into the register of Islam, insidership further lends to the assumption, already broached in the previous chapter, that only Muslims truly understand what it means to experience Islam, only they can teach about it sensitively, and, thus, engage in its "accurate" portrayal. Yet, as I tried to argue in that chapter, this point can be made only because *the* Islam being articulated and disseminated is largely the Islam of liberal or "progressive" Muslim scholars of Islamic religious studies and is, thus, largely of their own creation. This means that these scholars have positioned themselves as the only valid "insiders," the only ones who can legitimately talk about, write about, and teach about what they consider to be authentic Islam.

What, then, is the role of the outsider? Given the characterization in the previous paragraph, it would seem very minimal. In the final of his "Theses on

Method," which I have quoted in another context in my Introduction, Bruce Lincoln argues that

> When one permits those whom one studies to define the terms in which they will be understood, suspends one's interest in the temporal and contingent, or fails to distinguish between "truths," "truth-claims," and "regimes of truth," one has ceased to function as historian or scholar. In that moment, a variety of roles are available: some perfectly respectable (amanuensis, collector, friend and advocate), and some less appealing (cheerleader, voyeur, retailer of import goods). None, however, should be confused with scholarship. (Lincoln 1996: 227)

Without wanting to make the claim that every insider is automatically rendered apologetic or struck dumb when it comes to talking about his or her religion, we must also be conscious of the fact that many so-called "outsiders" adopt the language of insidership and speak about religions that are not their own in ways that strike us as too reverential. This is done, presumably, so as not to offend religious practitioners of that specific religion or religious practitioners in general regardless of their particular affiliation. Or, it is done on account of some deep-seated sense of ecumenicism: all religions are ultimately the same because they all share a common essence in the "sacred"; therefore, to appreciate one (e.g., my own) means that I necessarily have to appreciate them all (i.e., those that are not my own). However, I think we need to pay close attention to Lincoln's warning about what happens when scholars move beyond the "temporal and contingent." In effect, once this happens, we see a shift in discourse to the timeless and the revelatory. Temporal vis-à-vis timeless, contingency vis-à-vis revelation, signal two radically opposed methods of understanding phenomena constructed as "religious." Once we speak of the "real" or the "authentic," as opposed to how the real is imagined and constructed or the rhetoric of authenticity, we have largely moved beyond the pale of scholarship and into the domain of apologetics. If one is not a Muslim, returning to the frame of Islamic religious studies, possible options include—as the quotation from Lincoln makes clear—friend, advocate, cheerleader, or voyeur. If one does not engage in these activities, one risks marginalization as either an "Orientalist" or an "Islamophobe."

Another possible option is conversion. And many scholars of Islamic religious studies have certainly taken this path. The difficulty in discussing this topic within the academic study of religion, however, should be readily apparent. How is it possible to theorize the modern conversion of scholars of Islamic religious studies (or any other subfield of religious studies)? I certainly realize that there are all sorts of personal reasons for conversion, ones that I would neither deny nor contest. However, I raise the issue, in part, because of the slippage between scholarship and advocacy in the field and, in part, because of the sheer numbers of self-confessed converts.[5] People such as Kecia Ali (Boston University), Vincent Cornell (Emory), Beverley Amina McCloud (University of Florida), Juliane Hammer (UNC-Chapel Hill), Amina Wadud (University of Louisville), Jonathan Brown (Georgetown), Scott Kugle (Emory), and Ingrid Mattson (University of Western Ontario) are all Muslims and all engage, in varying degrees, in the type of essentializing Islamic discourses of which I have been critical in the previous chapters. Without getting into the details of their personal journeys to and within Islam—which I respect and are not my concern—I wish to examine their *academic* writings in this and subsequent chapters with an eye to understanding further the complex relationship between "insider" and "outsider" within Islamic religious studies.

The Role of Scholar-Converts

To proceed with my analysis, I wish to examine a topic that is rarely addressed in the scholarly literature, that of the scholar-convert. It may well be a cliché to speak of "the zeal of the convert," but, like all clichés, there is certainly a modicum of truth to it.[6] The convert is someone who perceives his or her identity in terms of the new religious community that they have joined. Their personal identity now becomes, for a variety of reasons, bound up with their new religious commitment, their new religious selves, and their new religious communities.

If we opt to study all religious acts as political and social ones, it is necessary to examine the effects and consequences of what happens when a scholar, qua social actor, converts to the religion that he or she studies. In his study of conversion to Islam in the Middle Ages, the historian Richard Bulliet argues that "it may be proposed as an axiom of religious conversion that the convert's expectations of his new religion will parallel his expectations of his old religion" (Bulliet 1979: 35). Presumably, he means by this that the new religion will provide the convert with some of the answers to questions that were originally broached in the old religion but found unsatisfactory. While it is important to note that Bulliet's analysis remains confined to the medieval period, some of his generalizations might well prove useful in thinking about conversion more generally. Of particular relevance is his insistence that when one converts to a new religion, one imagines oneself as entering a new social world with increased opportunities (Bulliet 1979: 37).

It is certainly difficult, if not impossible, to speculate as to why one converts to a new religion in the modern period. Presumably the old religion is seen as either a problem or as irrelevant to one's new expression. This tension between "old" and "new" can certainly be exacerbated in the academic setting of religious studies. The "old" religion can be and often is associated with negative experiences from childhood, perhaps with being intellectually stagnant; whereas the "new" religion is often encountered in an intellectually vibrant and personally liberating manner. It also depends with whom one studies. As we saw in the previous chapter, for example, Gwendolah Zoharah Simmons credits her shaykh with introducing her to "an Islam of justice, truth, beauty, and grace" (2003: 238). Simmons, not unlike Amina Wadud, and other African American converts to Islam, thus, see in their version of Islam a system of racial equality—they are both African Americans—that was lacking in their Christian upbringing in America in the 1950s and 1960s.

If many in Islamic religious studies emphasize the personal and how the personal is the political, surely converts who engage in Islamic religious studies must acknowledge the processes behind their conversion. This does not mean personal confessions, but it ought to mean that there be some sort of explicit acknowledgment. As so many theoreticians of religions stress (e.g., Smith, Lincoln, McCutcheon), self-reflexivity is the sine qua non of our field. The scholarly act is ultimately an act of choice, selection, and focus as opposed to discovering the eternal meanings of texts or symbols. Because of this, we cannot just pass over the conversion of scholars in silence or as if it is simply irrelevant to scholarly practices because it involves solely their so-called "spiritual" state. Indeed, given my own methodological take in this study, there can be no pure or proper "spiritual" state since every state is ultimately socially and politically constructed and understandable. The convert-scholar obviously saw something in Islam that his or her old tradition neither had nor could provide. What was it? How, just as importantly, does this presumably spiritual lack in their old religious tradition color their judgment of Islam, on the one hand, and the tradition they left, on the other?

In addition, we also have to be aware that the because many converts to Islam who engage in Islamic religious studies are not up front about their conversion, the reader necessarily has difficulty situating their work. While some scholars, like Amina Wadud, speak about their conversion and what it meant for them to leave one religious tradition and embrace another, many scholars are not so self-reflexive.[7] Yet, I think they have to be because such self-reflexivity will help us as readers contextualize their scholarship—why, how, and whence they write—in a more honest manner. I neither know nor care why or from what they converted. But, as newly constituted insiders, they and we need to acknowledge the baggage that they have carried with them to their new religious lives. Are they simply using scholarship to justify and legitimate their new selves? Can one be critical of a tradition to which one has just converted? There are, in other words, many different types of insiders. Everyone writes from within somewhere, some community, and there are rules and local knowledges that necessarily govern what one can and cannot say. Yet, at the same time, we must remember that the imaginative acts that make scholarship possible are not, contrary to opinion, either straightforward or simplistic. Can one write like an "insider," when for most of one's adult life one has existed as an "outsider"? We may try to justify this using the language of the fluidity of identity, but we also have to be aware that there is potentially much, much more at work.

In what follows I would like to examine some of the writings, and assumptions, of several prominent converts who engage in teaching, research, and dissemination of Islam from within the disciplinary home of Islamic religious studies.

Scott Siraj al-Haqq Kugle

At least Kugle is honest about from what perspective he writes given the fact that he uses his Muslim name—Siraj al-haqq ("the lamp of truth")—in his writings. He does not, however, at least as far as I am aware, write about the reasons behind his conversion.[8] Kugle's life project seems to be in trying to show that Islam, *when properly interpreted*, is tolerant and accepting of gay, lesbian, and transgender

Muslims. Again, this is a very noble project, and I hope that his interpretations of the Qur'an and other authoritative Muslim sources have done some good in creating such an inclusive framework. My concern is solely with the fact that all of his constructive theological and apologetical readings take place within and are sanctioned by the larger project of Islamic religious studies, which claims to be a scholarly and intellectual activity that takes place under the auspices of the *secular* university.

The goal of Kugle, a convert to Islam, is to show the pluralistic and progressive nature of "his" Islam and, in the process, to legitimate his own experiences therein.[9] His 2010 monograph entitled *Homosexuality in Islam: Critical Reflections on Gay, Lesbian, and Transgender Muslims*, is described by the press as "the first book length treatment to offer a detailed analysis of how Islamic scripture, jurisprudence, and Hadith, can not only accommodate a sexually sensitive Islam, but actively endorse it."[10] In the Introduction to the work, he writes that,

> As a Muslim, I assert that [homosexuals]—like all natural phenomena—are caused by divine will, though biological processes or early childhood experiences are important means by which they come into being. Whether the "cause" is God's creation, biological variation, or early childhood experiences, homosexuals have no rational choice in their internal disposition to be attracted to same-sex mates. The Qur'an mentions them obliquely and does not assess them negatively, but it also does not deal with their existence as a social minority group. Instead, the Qur'an address the majority who are oriented toward the other sex, that is heterosexuals whose sexual urge can result in procreation and replication of the social order. Where the Qur'an treats same-sex acts, it condemns them only insofar as they are exploitative or violent. (Kugle 2010: 2)

Here Kugle engages in an interpretive framework that, as we have already seen numerous times, is one of the hallmarks of Islamic religious studies, to wit, a pristine and egalitarian message in the Qur'an is subsequently corrupted by the so-called generic "Islamic tradition" that can be signified, depending on the interpreter, as male, misogynist, homophobic, and/or anti-Sufi. "The question," asks Kugle, "is whether these negative assessments in oral tradition and jurisprudence are in accord with the Qur'an as scripture, and whether these other non-scriptural sources of authority are authentic and reliable for Muslims" (Kugle 2010: 3). The rest of the book involves Kugle going through various Islamic traditions and telling us which ones are "authentic" and which ones are "inauthentic." Not surprisingly, the criteria that he uses, indeed the criteria that so many of these scholars use, for placement under these two rubrics are whether or not these traditions agree with an egalitarian and pluralist reading. However, the goal of the critical scholar of religion should be to tell us how the rhetoric of authenticity functions in a religion, not to engage in further mythopoesis that invokes terms such as "authentic/inauthentic" to get at the *real* message of Islam. I will leave it to others to assess Kugle's essentialist comments that homosexuals behave the way they do because of some innate disposition, but I will point out that his discussion of identity as something real or fixed as opposed to unstable and socially constructed is potentially problematic and certainly controversial to social theorists interested in interrogating identity from a non-essentialist position.

When Kugle writes of the meaning of Islam, it is perhaps not surprisingly governed by the virtue of tolerance:

> The reformist or progressive approach must take into account new possibilities for human fulfillment in increasingly non-patriarchal societies like those evolving under democratic constitutions, where Muslims are living as minority communities and fellow citizens. In these new environments, it is possible for homosexual relations to be based on ethical reciprocity, truth, justice, and love, just as heterosexual relationships ought to be based on these values in the ethical vision of the Qur'an. What matters is not the sex of the partner with whom one forms a partnership, as long as that partnership is contractually on par with legal custom. Rather, what matters is the ethical nature of the relationship one has with the constraints of one's internal disposition, which includes sexual orientation and gender identity. (Kugle 2010: 3

My criticism, to be clear, has nothing to do with Islam's compatibility with justice or truth. It has to do with how this compatibility is manufactured and the institutional (i.e., scholarly) actors that permit it. It is based on a tenuous separation between scholarship and apology, and between analysis and special-pleading. My goal is to sound a warning that without proper deliberation and reflection on the field of Islamic religious studies, it risks becoming lost in a dizzying barrage of political correctness based on manipulation and misrepresentation.

In his *Living Out Islam: Voices of Gay, Lesbian, and Transgender Muslims* (2014), Kugle takes his constructive theological discourse as articulated in his previous work and now turns it into a "scholarly" monograph about identity. For the most part, however, it carries on in the same vein as his theological work. He writes, for instance, that

> Muslims began in their community as vulnerable and despised outsiders. When they became strong enough to impose their will on others, they all too often lost sight of their Prophet's teaching of empathy, compassion, and justice. This book shares the voices of some marginalized within the Muslim community who call out to be recognized as fellow believers—sisters and brothers—who are worthy of respect, who deserve protection, and who demand justice. (Kugle 2014: vii)

In this passage we see the pretty standard claim of progressive Muslims more generally, namely, that there was a pristine and egalitarian message preached by Muhammad that was somehow corrupted by later generations. The key to a progressive Islam in the present is to somehow get back to the pristine message found in this Ur-Islam. This is, of course, theological and ahistorical in the extreme. It is also circular: the end is the beginning and vice versa. There is no interest in the historical Muhammad or in the problems associated with reconstructing early Islam. Instead, we are presented with a timeless, though threatened, meaning that is accessible to anyone with the sympathy to hear it.

I certainly have no problem with the fact that Kugle offers a liberal reading of Islam or that he is trying to make space within the Islamic tradition for those who are gay, lesbian or transgendered. My objection is that this approach masquerades as scholarship and that a university press (NYU) publishes it (as opposed, say, to an Islamic theological press). The argument of the book is that "gay, lesbian, and transgender Muslims can reconcile their sexual orientation and gender identity with Islam. But this reconciliation requires active struggle, struggle that is sustained only by camaraderie with like-minded individuals and the solidarity of support groups" (Kugle 2014: 2). While Kugle acknowledges the importance of gender identity, the above quotation implies that Islam is somehow static or eternal, and that one must simply get others to appreciate how egalitarian Islam can be, *if properly interpreted.*

This is certainly in keeping with Kugle's earlier work discussed above, wherein he sought to show how Islam, especially that associated with Sufism or Islamic mysticism, speaks with sophistication about the value of love, regardless of the gender or sexual orientation of the beloved.[11] In the book under discussion now, Kugle again invokes Sufism as the appropriate channel to get back at the early message of egalitarianism preached by Muhammad: "All Muslims together—whatever their sexual orientation or gender identity—must revive the Islamic quest for love that transforms" (2014: 229). This quest, he says, existed at some point in the distant past and the key in the present is to "revive" it.

The problem, though, is that Kugle bases his observations on interviews with 15 activists (four lesbian women, nine gay men, and two transgender persons—one transitioning from female-to-male and one identifying as male-to-female) living in the West. That's it! His sample pool, then, is statistically or sociologically irrelevant. The rest of the volume involves him taking his own theological agenda and intertwining it with those of these 15 individuals. He writes, for example,

> Those who engage with this mode of activism assert their ability to forge ahead beyond the limits of family expectation or religious dogma to search for viable individual identities that will allow them to live fulfilling and creative lives. Islam urges them onward in this search, they argue, even if their fellow Muslims would rather hold them back. Religious solidarity can be compromised or rejected, they feel—especially if their coreligionists do not strive to sincerely understand them and their existential position with regard to sexual orientation and gender identity. In the end, they uphold the teaching that God judges each person as an individual according to his or her intention and action. (Kugle 2014: 218)

Even though it is clear that what is driving Kugle's analysis is his own life story, nowhere does he mention this. He acknowledges in the book's Introduction that he is a Muslim (2014: 8), but nowhere provides the reader with what brought him to this study. It is obvious that the diversity of sexual identity is important to him presumably for both personal reasons and for theological ones, but again he nowhere provides us with what is driving his study. Instead we are presented in his most recent work with a theological treatise that is essentially about 15 interviews with gay, lesbian, and transgendered Muslim activists. Again, we see scholarship in Islamic religious studies on the verge of no longer being concerned about group formation, social categories, or trying to solve textual puzzles; rather, it is in danger of becoming little more than indulging one's personal needs for self-legitimation.

Amina Beverly McCloud

In 2000, Gisela Webb (Seton Hall University), another convert to Islam, edited a volume entitled *Windows of Faith: Muslim Women Scholar-Activists* (published by Syracuse University Press). The goal of the volume, as she says in the Introduction, is to provide a "frontal challenge to the established Muslim cultural patriarchy in its use of the Qur'an, *sunnah* (the example, or tradition, of Muhammad), and *shari`ah* (Islamic law), which these women see as having moved away from the essentially egalitarian thrust of the Qur'an and the model of participation of women in the public sphere set during the early Islamic period" (Webb 2000: xiii). Once again, we see the trope of a pristine *religious* message undermined by subsequent *cultural* and *ideological* practice. The volume itself is divided into 10 chapters, four of which are written by other converts to Islam. In her essay, "The Scholar and the Fatwa," Aminah Beverly McCloud (DePaul University) writes of the role of the scholar,

> The scholar of Islam trained in an American university will ostensibly give the broadest view possible, taking in all of the twists and turns of history and its testimony to the perennial relationship of power and knowledge. Scholars of Islam know what a *fatwa* (legal opinion) is and who is qualified to give one. They also know that the class of "learned men" has often suffered from corruption and that their *fatawa* (pl. *fatwa*) have sometimes reflected a concern for patronage. U.S. court officers, guidance counselors, lawyers, and mediators seek information that they can use and that has been reasoned with an understanding of U.S. law. The scholar knowingly, or unknowingly, becomes the agent who gives legal advice that, one hopes, is grounded in Islamic knowledge. (McCloud 2000: 137-8)

The job of the scholar of Islam trained at a secular American university, according to McCloud, is to talk about Islam "as it really is." Such a scholar, it is implied, knows all about Islam, its historical and textual traditions, and thus is in a position to say who has the authority to speak for the religion. In addition, McCloud argues that this scholar should be "grounded in Islamic knowledge," although she never mentions what that should or might consist of. Nor does she tell us what is the role of the non-Muslim scholar of Islam in all of this. She does claim, however, without a shred of evidence, that because of Orientalism's traditional stranglehold on the study of Islam, "scholars in these fields do not understand the worldview of Islam, and their perspectives on the religion are often rigid and narrow" (McCloud 2000: 139).

In her 2006 monograph *Transnational Muslims in American Society* (University Press of Florida), McCloud picks up on this theme of the importance of the scholar of Islam's knowledge. It is the role of this scholar she writes in the Introduction to correct assumptions about Islam among non-Muslims and to help Muslims understand the *correct* meaning of Islam (McCloud 2006: 4-6). She writes, for instance, that there is a fundamental difference between "culture" and the "religious guidance" presented in the Qur'an. The latter is positive, something that can cure the ailments of society; whereas the former is that which is responsible for a variety of social ills and the undermining of originary Islam's egalitarian message. For her, "economic disparity, mistreatment of women, misinterpretation of the Qur'anic exhortations and admonitions by those in leadership, those cultures that adopted Islam did so without much change in fundamental cultural values, though if the Qur'anic guidance had been implemented, many of those cultural mores would have been extinguished" (McCloud 2006: 39). She elaborates:

> While the methods of jurisprudence are unique and exceptional in quality, the law's partial reliance on the narrations of the sayings and actions of the Prophet (pbuh[12]) have been most challenging to women, the poor, and the concerns of social development. While the Qur'an's emphasis is on the beliefs and actions of believers (men and women; women and men), justice and compassion are all but erased by its interpreters. Largely due to cultural norms, emphasis is placed on maintaining a curious patriarchal suppression of women and other family patterns, unjust relations with the poor, and maintaining great disparities in wealth. Qur'anic guidance on the structure of relationships between believers, husbands and wives, or neighbors is articulated but rarely practiced. (McCloud 2006: 40)

Much like Kugle, McCloud here buys into a pristine and originary message that emerges from the Qur'an and that later interpreters have somehow bastardized. It is presumably this original and originary message, provided by spiritual teachers, that provided the means for converting to Islam in the first place. Much of their scholarly lives are then subsequently involved in the attempt to articulate and disseminate this originary message.

Whereas Kugle seeks solace in the more open society of the democratic West for gay, lesbian, and transgendered Muslims, McCloud, an African American, seems to blame colonialism and the West for Islam's ills. "The West," though she never defines the term, "desires to replicate itself, turning every country into both a puppet state and a market economy" (McCloud 2006: 40). The result is that

> Simultaneously, colonialism and then neocolonialism devastated almost every society in the Muslim world. As the wealth potentials of the already rich and the new classes of wealth created by colonial powers grew, the misery of the masses naturally increased. In almost every Muslim country this misery was met with oppression. Explanation for societal chaos was sought in Qur'anic guidance. One problem that seems to have occurred here is that an extreme problem was answered by extremes. (McCloud 2006: 40)

Not only does McCloud envisage a pristine and originary Islamic message in the ether—or, more precisely, hidden in the Qur'an—she blames medieval men and the modern West with covering it up. It is the goal of the progressive Muslim convert to try to liberate it.

Juliane Hammer

In her *American Muslim Women, Religious Authority, and Activism: More Than a Prayer* (2012), Juliane Hammer also writes from an insider perspective, though she never tells the reader why or how this came to be the case. Instead she informs the reader that the progressive theological texts produced by scholars of Islamic religious studies are "as much invested in the triangle of faith, community, and representation as the texts and authors analyzed here" (Hammer 2012: 5). But we have no idea from where she writes? Does she write as Muslim female reformer? If so, why not tell the reader? Does she write from the perspective of a non-Muslim feminist, then again this is surely of interest to the reader. If the postmodern turn is about, among other things, situating authors in perspectivalism, whence does Hammer write?

Much of the subsequent volume is concerned, in Hammer's own words, with how the work of Muslim women academics, like herself,

> demonstrate the investment of their authors in a triangle of self- understandings and textual production: they write for the sake of formulating, negotiating, and sometimes saving their faith and religious identities as Muslim women; they address intra-Muslim and communal audiences in an attempt to generate discussions about gender discourses, attitudes, and practices in those communities; and they are acutely aware of and directly involved in media representations of Muslims and Islam and/or the dynamics of authority and scholarship in the secular American academy. (Hammer 2012: 3)

This passage epitomizes what I believe to be everything that is the matter with Islamic religious studies at the current moment. First of all, as she makes clear, so many of these scholars are involved in their own "self-understanding," so much so that historical and textual problems of the tradition largely fall to the wayside. Their goal is "to save their faith and religious identities as Muslim women," they are involved in "media representations of Muslims and Islam," all the while professing these concerns and representations in the context of the "secular American academy."

This is surprising because in the conclusion to the book, Hammer seems sensitive to the insider/outsider problem (2012: 200–201). She writes, for example, that most female Muslim scholars of Islam "have not problematized their Muslim identities, however differently they may understand them to be constituted, but they debate internally and in their writings the possibility of using the label 'feminist'" (2012: 201). Yet later she switches pronouns from "they" to "we": "As Muslim scholars and Muslim women scholars we urgently need to carry out our own work, exegetical and otherwise, while more intentionally reflecting on methodology, politics of representation and identity, and our equally important activist commitments" (2012: 202–3).

Gwendolyn Zoharah Simmons

Gwendolyn Zoharah Simmons is another African-American convert to Islam. As we saw in the previous chapter, she credits her conversion to her shaykh, who showed her "an Islam of justice, truth, beauty, and grace" (Simmons 2003: 238). In her chapter for the aforementioned Webb volume (2000), she writes how this individual taught her "true Islam." This meant not "returning his disciples to a culturally Arab seventh-century Islam. His was a twentieth-century Islam that adhered to the foundations and to the eternal and universal principles of the religion" (Simmons 2000: 202–3). Simmons seeks to connect her work within the Civil Rights Movement in the American South with her conversion to Islam:

> Conservative interpretations [of Islam] defy what I, and many other progressive Muslims, see as the essentially egalitarian message of the Holy Qur'an and of the early Islamic community. These conservative views deeply offend my notion of what is just. Furthermore, given the historical role that African American women have played in women's struggle for justice, it is unbelievable that African American male Muslim leaders seek to marginalize women in the Islamic community, attempting to relegate them solely to domestic and silent roles. In my opinion, such practices will only accelerate the growing decline in impoverished African American communities at a time when it needs its best religious minds (male and female) engaged in the project to rebuild inner city communities and to rescue large numbers of children from crime, drugs, and despair. (Simmons 2000: 203–4)

Simmons here puts tremendous weight on the scholar of Islamic religious studies' shoulders. Like the others in this chapter, she perceives (or is told by others to perceive) the original message of her newfound faith and it is something that seems to fit with what had been missing in her previous existence. Her jeremiad continues along these lines, surveying briefly, the role and place of women in a variety of Muslim contexts. She concludes with the statement that I think is telling of convert scholar-activists, "I long to see the promotion of an egalitarian, compassionate, merciful, and peaceful Islam where male and female believers grow in the *three thousand gracious qualities and ninety-nine attributes* of the living God. I hope to engage in whatever work I can to promote a universalist, egalitarian, and pluralist Islam" (Simmons 2000: 225).

Vincent J. Cornell

Another scholar-activist and convert to Islam is Vincent J. Cornell, who describes himself as a "critical traditionalist." Once again, like those mentioned above, Cornell's intentions are certainly noble. His desire is to help create and articulate a more pluralistic version of Islam with an eye to the past and its sources. One of his major goals is to address contemporary problems of fundamentalism and its unwillingness to adapt to modern realities. He reasons that the Muslim who views the world from a narrow, fideistic perspective can only perceive God through his or her personal experiences. How God is to be conceived and what His commands entail are questions whose answers are constrained by the limitations of one's understanding of self and others. The sectarian interpretations that the believer gives the commands of God may be justified in a qualified sense, but they are likely to lead to injustice if they are applied universally and uncritically. This is because human understanding of the divine command reflects one's own biased perspective more than it reflects a theological or philosophical understanding of God as God truly is. (Cornell 2004)[13]

To a scholar of religion, who argues that religion is a social fact and must be studied using non-theological language and categories, statements such as these (and those found in many of the writings of those "convert-scholar-activists" mentioned above) are difficult to understand. Cornell writes as a Muslim believer, not as a scholar of religion. This causes all sorts of dissonance in the reader, not to mention the student, who thinks that he or she is reading or being taught the tradition in a non-theological and non-partisan manner. For Cornell, Sufism represents true Islam and that those, mainly "fundamentalist" or Salafi, critiques of it are wrong. In fact, it is easier to claim that Sufism, writes Cornell, "not Salafism, is the more authentic, because its traditions are more consistent with the historical contours of Islamic thought" (Cornell 2004).

In a subsequent essay, entitled "Reasons Public and Divine: Liberal Democracy, Shari`a Fundamentalism, and the Epistemological Crisis of Islam," Cornell seeks to show how Sunni Islam has failed to make progress according to its own standards of rationality (2010: 29). Once again, writing as a Muslim theologian, Cornell's desire is not to point this out academically, but to try and resolve the crisis in a theological manner. He writes that

> The key to resolving an epistemological crisis is to develop new resources and frameworks for the tradition under pressure. Such resources, however, cannot be created merely by grafting elements of an alien tradition onto the original. To be acceptable ... [they] must be seen as authentic: they must exhibit continuity with the worldview that defined the original tradition in the first place. In addition the new resources of the tradition must constitute a tradition of their own. They must provide a systematic and coherent solution to problems that have so far proven intractable. Finally the revision of tradition must be critical. It must provide an explanation of what it was that rendered the original tradition, before acquiring the new resources, sterile or incoherent or both. (Cornell 2010: 30)

Rather than discuss the rhetoric of authenticity, Cornell is intimately involved in its production. His goal is to find an "authentic starting point" that will permit Muslim reformers to use "modern political theory to engage the future without abandoning the past" (Cornell 2010: 30). This offers Cornell, in addition to others, a way to show how and why the likes of Osama bin Laden and Sayyid Qutb went wrong in their interpretations of Islam and Islamic law. And why, of course, his own interpretation is the correct one. The issue is not the contextualization of the various Islams that skirmish under the larger and monolithic canopy of Islam, but in working out the ills that currently confront Islamic jurisprudence.

Cornell's essay, it should be noted, does not occur in one of the many volumes devoted to progressive Islam, but rather in a collection of scholarly essays by leading scholars in Islamic religious studies that seek to show new approaches to Islamic studies (Ernst and R. Martin 2010) within the larger discipline of religious studies. This is telling and, I would hope, further supports my main contention in this study, namely, that the primary goal of Islamic religious studies is the articulation of liberal Muslim theology. As such it has very little room for non-Muslims or even critical scholarship, both of which can be neatly written off as "Orientalist." There are, instead, two ways that non-Muslims can enter the field: either to be cheerleaders or to convert to the tradition.

I could go on, but will end this discussion here. I will, however, pick it up again in the following chapter where I wish to examine the writings of several scholars, virtually all of whom are converts, and whom others have described favorably as being able to "move back and forth between their work at the academy and their function in the community and/or public intellectual activity" and as "models ... to be emulated by the current and future generation of Islamic studies" (Safi 2014).

Conclusions

All of the individuals surveyed in this chapter are converts to Islam who problematize the insider/outsider debate that is a perennial part of the academic study of religion. Every single one of these scholars propagates the myth of a pristine and egalitarian Islam that has subsequently been corrupted by later male elites. This pristine and originary Islam is universally signified, as we have seen so many times, as egalitarian and pluralistic (although, of course, these scholars never produce any credible historical evidence to back up their claims). Some talk about their conversions and what this meant to them personally; others do not. Regardless, the overwhelming majority write from a position of extreme reverence for their new religious tradition. This reverence is reserved for the Qur'an and earliest Islam. Their goal in the present is to somehow showcase and liberate this Islam from those Muslims who seek to cover up its foundations.

Those examined in this chapter are not content to write as scholars (e.g., historians, philologists) of Islam, but as constructive theologians. I certainly do not mean to imply by this that one cannot be a convert to Islam and engage in academically neutral activity; only that in Islamic religious studies this tends not to be the norm. There is a desire, in other words, of these scholar-convert-activists to join the swelling ranks of Islamic religious studies and to engage in further mythopoesis. The result is that Islam is not studied as a historical or social phenomenon, but as something eternal and timeless that can be corrupted in the hands of the wrong people.

So what do we do with the academic study of Islam at the current moment? The discipline is currently at a crossroads. Either it can go down what I consider to be the unhealthy path of identity politics—and note that this identity is often assumed at conversion—or it can retreat and choose one of mutually profitable engagement with other disciplines. The former is that of "insidership," a path that revels in the personal narratives of perceived dispossession and disenfranchisement, a path of mirrors wherein the political refracts the personal and vice versa. The latter path, on the contrary, is one where scholars—both Muslim and non-Muslim—engage in serious scholarship on issues that transcend such personal narratives. The following two chapters will chart, in greater detail, the two paths and their ramifications.

Notes

1. For a full-length study of this interesting individual, his journey to Islam and subsequent adventures after the Parliament, see Abd-Allah (2006).
2. The *New York Times* described him in the following terms: "A person of dignified though gracious bearing. His skin is tanned, and there is about him, especially in his movements, an Oriental air. He has large brown eyes and a dark brown beard of moderate length. He speaks easily and with directness and earnestness. He is of average height, and just a trifle stout. There is a suggestion of suppleness rather than briskness in his gait. His face is almost dark enough for him to be mistaken for a light Hindu, and he talks with a slight foreign accent. With a fez he would easily pass for a Mohammedan" (quoted in Abd-Allah 2006: 28–9).
3. On the Parliament, more generally, see the study found in Hughes Seager (1995). A more thorough treatment of the Parliament is surely a scholarly desideratum.
4. One of the few attempts to do this is the stimulating article in Tourage (2013). I build on his comments here and try to take some of his conclusions and apply them to the world of academia.
5. Of course, they do not use the term "convert" to describe themselves, but simply "Muslims."
6. See, for example, the Pew Research forum at http://www.pewforum.org/2009/10/28/the-zeal-of-the-convert-is-it-the-real-deal.
7. I do not discuss Wadud in this chapter, but will do so in Chapter 4. My reason for doing this is that my goal in that chapter is to survey the writings of a group of scholars, virtually all of whom are converts, that have been described as "models" for the future of Islamic religious studies.
8. In the Acknowledgments to Kugle (2010: ix), he writes "I give a quiet word of thanks to my *murshid*, my spiritual guide, who upholds the spiritual path of those who hold the Prophet Muhammad's most important teaching to be, 'All people are God's family, and God loves those most who do the most good for God's family,' despite our division into nations, tribes, and factions."
9. In an interview with Susan Henking, he says that in writing his essay entitled "Sexuality, Diversity and Ethics in the Agenda of Progressive Muslims" (for Safi 2003) he "was basically 'coming out' twice. I was coming out as a Muslim believer to my Academic colleagues. I was coming out as a gay man to my Muslim fellows. Neither position was very comfortable. So to do both at once was very foolish. Yet, I never regret it." The interview, "Coming Out Twice: Sexuality and Gender in Islam," may be found at http://religiondispatches.org/coming-out-twice-sexuality-and-gender-in-islam/.
10. Online at https://www.oneworld-publications.com/books/scott-siraj-al-haqq-kugle/homosexuality-in-islam.

11. See, for example, my criticism in Hughes (2012c: 114–15).
12. "Pbuh" = "peace be upon him," a customary phrase that a Muslim says after invoking the term "the prophet" or his name Muhammad.
13. This is an online article and, as such, has no page numbers.

— 4 —

Business as Usual

The previous chapters have, I trust, shown the problems associated with Islamic religious studies. I am not sure if these are the result of growing pains, the taking over of the field by constructive theologians, the desire on the part of the dominant players to engage in identity politics and the concomitant notion of political correctness, or indeed various permutations of all the above. Within Islamic religious studies there are things that one can legitimately say about Islam (e.g., that it is, at bottom, about pluralism and justice) and that one cannot say (e.g., the bellicose side of early Islam) for fear of disciplinary censure. This situation is the result, I suggested in Chapter 2, of what we might call a Saidian impasse. Since there is a history of Western polemics against Islam that date to the religion's foundation in seventh century CE,[1] contemporary scholarly criticism of progressive Islam, as I am engaged in here, can unfortunately be situated and subsequently dismissed by some in the same light. Just as Muhammad was said to have created a fair and just polity in seventh-century Arabia in the face of ignorance and hostility, these scholars imagine themselves to be doing something similar today, moving as it were from ignorance (*al-jahaliyya*) to truth. The result of all this is that too much work is invested in the claim, as we have seen, that Islam is a just tradition. If one wants to engage in historical or critical topics some argue that such treatments ought to be "safely buried in obscure academic journals" (Ernst 2003: 97), or be written off as "improbable and idiosyncratic" (Afsaruddin 2008: xix).

This results, however, in a skewed understanding of the manifold traditions that go by the generic name "Islam." We cannot lie to ourselves and to others, according to J. Z. Smith, simply because we want to tell a good story, from which all unpalatable details have been neatly expurgated or safely ignored. Nor ought we to bend the truth to counter the many ideologically motivated attacks against Islam that circulate in the right-wing and neoconservative media.[2] We would do well to remember that Islam, like all religions, is a messy tradition that includes within itself the ugly and the beautiful, and the murderous and the peaceful. To ignore the former of these binaries at the expense of the latter is both wrong and manipulative. Yet, in their desire to create their own version of Islam, many in Islamic religious studies want to minimize other Islams, and this, to reiterate, is why their project is theological as opposed to academic and, to go even further, intellectually dishonest.

The question, of course, is why are we allowed or sanctioned to put peace or pluralism and Islam together, but not, say, jihad or misogyny and Islam? Every book published on Judaism and Christianity in departments of religious studies does not have to take an apologetical line and claim, for example, that Judaism is fundamentally about peace, or Christianity created a just and equitable society at the time of Jesus until corrupted by crafty priests.[3] So why do we have to listen incessantly to such claims from scholars of Islamic religious studies? If we are allowed to talk about jihad, to use an example, why must it be of the inner or spiritual variety as opposed to the external kind?[4] We have to recognize claims like these for what they are: "noble lies" that mask political half-truths. Such issues get to the heart of how fields and/or disciplines envisage their origins, construct their narratives, and police their borders. At stake, as witnessed in the previous chapters, is the representation of Islam. Who is allowed to engage in it and for what purposes?

Keep on Keepin' on

In 2014, Omid Safi, one of the leading figures in the progressive Islam movement, published a short essay offering his opinion on the current state of affairs in Islamic religious studies and how it had been "successfully" folded into the larger organization known as the American Academy of Religion (2014).[5] Cognizant of the fact that the field had hit a critical crossroads, he was aware of the contentious issue of theory and method in Islamic religious studies. "It pains me today," he writes, "to see scholars of Islamic studies—in this case I am mostly referring to Muslim scholars of Islamic studies—who move through the discussions of normative/descriptive approaches to religion without an awareness of how much effort has gone into working out the uneasy compromises in the religion academy." I take it that by "normative/descriptive" Safi means approaches to Islam that are quick to define what constitutes real Islam or Islam-ness. He further argues that "it is still far too frequent to hear Muslim academics dismiss Shi'a, Sufis, philosophers, or feminists, as being fundamentally deluded Muslims or even beyond the sphere marked 'proper' Orthodox Islam." The problem with this statement, of course, and as we have seen countless times in the previous three chapters, is that Safi and his colleagues in Islamic religious studies are all too quick to make such "normative/descriptive" statements themselves. The result is that the field of Islamic religious studies becomes less about intellectual or historical integrity and more about theological turf wars between rival Islams that use the quasi-academic jargon of religious studies.

Like so many in the field, Safi concurs that the events of 9/11 were the "game changer" for the field. "In the aftermath of those events," he writes, "the overwhelming majority of American universities and colleges suddenly found themselves without the necessary faculty to 'explain' the event to their students, to serve as a spokesperson in engagement with local communities, and to interact with the media." Unlike my comments in the previous chapters, Safi puts a greater emphasis than me on scholars serving as spokespeople and media talking heads. Whereas he sees it as something positive, I tend to regard these public discourses as extremely problematic and claim that they have actually succeeded in creating a set of intractable intellectual problems. Indeed, as I have argued elsewhere (Hughes 2006: 90–96), most scholars are not cut out for these roles, which can, in fact, both take away from and impede critical scholarship. I say this because scholars must take valuable time away from original and presumably critical research in order to provide sugar-coated presentations to various community groups, in addition to engaging in the same sort of apologetical work for the media. Not only this, but the extra-curricular work, rather than remain something scholars of Islamic religious studies do in their "free" time, has instead bled over into their academic work and to such an extent that it becomes difficult to know where the one begins and the other ends. The result is the predicament wherein Islamic religious studies currently finds itself.

Safi presents a much more sanguine portrait of the field, it seems to me, because he gives the American Academy of Religion—today the locus of Islamic religious studies—a much more charitable reading than I do. Safi believes that the raison d'être of the AAR, unlike, say, the Middle Eastern Studies Association (MESA), is its commitment to theoretical and methodological concerns. For him, the AAR takes "very seriously ... not only the post-colonial and feminist critiques, but also the anthropological insights, the work being done in different realms of 'theory,' the Said and post-Said critique, and more." This, as we have seen repeatedly, is as far as many in Islamic religious studies want to go. Very few, however, are interested in challenging the axiom that "religion" is, at bottom, a theological category, one with a great deal of baggage that travels in its wake and that has the potential to obscure the various mundane and human practices that go under that name.

It thus dawned on me that what counts for "theory" for one person or group might not count as "theory" for another. For those in Islamic religious studies, the AAR provides the ideal forum in which to discuss issues of gender and post-colonial theory inspired by the writings of Edward Said. Safi further comments that "the AAR itself had undergone a remarkable range of discussions about how one could be a scholar of a religious tradition (or more than one) and participate (or not) in that tradition in a whole spectrum of sympathetic and critical fashions."

Others, however, myself included, have real difficulties with what passes as theorizing at the AAR. Rather than engage in reifying or essentializing gender, race or religion when it suits us, the goal of theory ought to be to undermine such claims and show their investment in a host of political and ideological processes. Rather than describe "sacred" texts, we ought to engage in an analysis that includes, among other things, demystifying and removing unhelpful and loaded terms such as "the sacred."[6] "Theory," in other words, is an equivocal term. When one engages in its practices, it is sophisticated; when those with whom one disagrees with do so, it is naïve. The theory debates, as we shall see in greater detail in the final chapter of this study, revolve around what one realistically wants, and expects, theory to perform. For some, theory is a way of maintaining the status quo and of further buttressing truth claims; for others, theory is about dismantling that which we hold dear. The former, as we have seen, can certainly invoke theoreticians (e.g., Asad, Butler), but, as I argued in Chapter 2 above, their ideas are rarely engaged with in a serious manner because, if they were, radically different conclusions would be arrived at.

A subdiscipline's theoretical first principles are only as good as those provided by the parent discipline. Since I have already examined in detail many of the theoretical shortcomings of Islamic religious studies, I wish here instead to instead focus on one of the final paragraphs from Safi's essay on the state of the field.[7] Near the end of his essay, he writes,

> Lastly, we now see a number of Muslim scholars of Islamic studies who move back and forth between their work at the academy and their function in the community and/or public intellectual activity. In fact, many Muslim scholars expect that they should be able to undertake this dance as part of their multi-faceted identity. We see scholars like Sherman Jackson, Amina Wadud, Jonathan Brown, Kecia Ali, Ingrid Mattson, and others who have mastered this negotiation in remarkable ways, and one hopes that these models continue to be emulated by the current and future generation of Islamic studies. (Safi 2014)

Since most if not all of the scholars that Safi mentions here as role-models are converts to Islam, I thought that this would provide a convenient opportunity to continue the discussion begun in the previous chapter on insiders, outsiders, and those who transgress this porous boundary. I note that these "models" for emulation are all Muslim scholar-activists. Not one of them is a non-Muslim. I am not sure if Safi holds them up as models because of their scholarship or because they have all embraced Islam and now, for the most part, write about it with a zeal and a passion that transcends traditional scholarly categories. The question then arises, something I have broached several times already in this study, is what place does this leave for the non-Muslim who wants to engage in historical or literary scholarship (without the activism or the apologetics)? In what follows, I wish to examine in greater detail the work of these scholars with an eye towards examining their assumptions and first principles that determine how they speak about Islam.

The problems that I have with Islamic religious studies, as Safi's comments reveal in considerable detail, has nothing to do with Islam per se, but with the larger field of which we all inhabit—religious studies. I contend that the pseudo-theological language of religious studies, with its emphases on the experiential and the spiritual as opposed to the political and the social, facilitates the types of discourses within Islamic religious studies of which I have been so critical. Both the dominant strain of religious studies and of Islamic religious studies are not interested in querying or interrogating the very term "religion." I find this particularly curious in the case of the latter on account of the insistence of Islamic religious studies to constantly stress the Saidian critique of Western scholarship. Rather than envisage "religion" as a Western category that sidelines or distorts local traditions in the service of Western state and economy, scholars of Islamic religious studies are for some reason content to reproduce it.[8] This must be on account of the fact that the theological propensity within the larger field of religious studies to produce good religion trumps the actual interrogation and problematization of the term "religion." Islamic religious studies, then, ends up in the curious predicament of critiquing the Western categories of "Orientalism" while simultaneously buying into the equally Eurocentric language associated with religion.

It is for this reason, *pace* Safi, that I find the American Academy of Religion not helpful but actually pernicious to critical scholarship in religion in general and Islam in particular. In order to show the difference between the vision of Omid Safi, which I take to be the mainstream in Islamic religious studies, and my own, this and the following chapter will outline this difference in considerable detail. The present chapter will explore the theoretical work of those scholars/converts listed by Safi as models for the Islamic religious studies of the future. This will be followed, in the next chapter, by a rather different and more critical path.

Sherman Jackson

In 2005, Sherman Jackson, holder of the King Faisal Chair in Islamic Thought and Culture at the University of Southern California, published an important book entitled *Islam and the Blackamerican: Looking Towards the Third Resurrection* (Jackson 2005).[9] In the book, Jackson argues that Blackamerican Islam owes its genesis not to a religious expression that dates to the late antique Middle East, but to a distinctively American idiom that he refers to as "Black Religion," which is defined by a God-centred holy protest against anti-black racism. The origins of Islam in Black America, then, originated primarily as a communal search for tools and narratives with which to combat racism and redefine American blackness. All of this would change in 1965, however, with the repeal of the National Origins Quota System, which meant that there suddenly appeared on the shores of the United States a massive number of Muslims from, among other places, the Arab World and South Asia. Many of these immigrant Muslims, given their sheer numbers, now began to exercise a virtual monopoly over the definition of what constituted Islamic life and its political concerns in America. For these Muslims, the nemesis was not white supremacy, but "the West," and Islam now came to be defined as an antidote to a civilizational as opposed to a racial threat (Jackson 2005: 10–15).

The focus of Jackson's study, however, is on the latter, and he tries to show how, in the past, Blackamerican Islam had been rooted in both the agenda and sensibilities of Black religion, and that its future must be tied to Blackamerican Muslims aligning themselves with the intellectual legacy of classical Sunni Islam.[10] Jackson is interested neither in Shi`ism nor Sufism, but only in orthodox Sunnism, his own religion. Jackson's goal is to "position Blackamerican Muslims as active agents, as opposed to passive recipients" so that they recognize a "fundamental difference between bona fide Islamic thought on the one hand and ideas and propositions whose proponents simply happen to bear Muslim names on the other" (Jackson 2009: 4). For Jackson, then, the classic Sunni tradition—as opposed to say the Nation of Islam—contains within itself the resources to reconcile blackness, Americanness, and adherence to Islam. Buying into the rhetoric of authenticity, Jackson maintains that this reified Islam—one devoid of cultural or political baggage—offers the lifeline to save people from contemporary problems. However, Jackson also posits that it is essential to preserve within Islam the legitimate aspects of "Black Religion" in order to avoid the domestication of religion, by which he seems to mean that a "domesticated" Islam would be rendered incapable of responding to or resisting the (non-Muslim) state and its dominant (white) culture.

My interest in the comments that follow is less on what he has to say about Blackamericans than about how Jackson sets up the US Constitution as an obstacle or stumbling block that gets in the way of Muslim Americans' full acceptance of the US political system (Jackson 2005: 145). It seems that it is within the latter context, at least as far as I can tell, that Safi seems to hold Jackson up as a model for emulation. Yet, as I hope to show, there are real problems with the type of argument that Jackson wants to make. For Jackson, Muslims must question the Constitution not only because it separates church and state (something that his version of Islam opposes) but, even more significantly, because it is a document that is inferior to God-given Muslim law (*sharia*), something that is grounded in authoritative Muslim sources. He writes,

> In my approach the U.S. Constitution is no more binding on the Muslim-American moral/religious conscience than was, say, tribalism or agrarianism on that of the early Muslim-Arabian community. But, as the constitution is for Muslim-Americans as intractable a reality as were tribalism and agrarianism for the early community, the Constitution cannot be viewed as being any less relevant to constructions of normative Islam in America than were tribalism and agrarianism to earlier constructions in Arabia and elsewhere. (Jackson 2005: 145–6)

This is an extremely problematic statement. I take it to mean that, for Jackson, the American Constitution, not unlike the agrarian culture of Muhammad's day, is the product of an age that is counterproductive to Islam. It is perhaps no coincidence that the tribal culture of Muhammad's day was and still is referred to as "the age of ignorance" (*al-jahaliyya*). By implication, Jackson would seem to claim that the American Constitution emerges out of an era that is tantamount to the polytheistic culture of seventh-century Arabia. The sharia, as God given, is superior, on his reading, both to the *jahaliyya*-culture of the early Muslim polity and, by extension, to the political framework of the American Republic. The American Constitution, Jackson points out, "was the result of an agreement among a group of *non-Muslims* about how to distribute political rights and powers within a non-Muslim polity" (Jackson 2005: 146; his italics). The problem for Jackson is how to be a Muslim on the one hand and live within a political culture of ignorance on the other.

Jackson boxes himself into a very difficult situation. The problem, he argues, facing the majority of Muslims in America is the liberal and open nature of the Constitution:

> The issue, to be more precise, is not whether Muslims can support a system that protects their rights to be Muslims. The issue is, instead, whether they can support a system that protects the rights of gays, atheists, and witches to be gays, atheists, and witches. This is an enormous challenge for Muslim-Americans, indeed, to many a mortal flaw in the liberal-pluralist vision. (Jackson 2005: 140)

For Jackson, too many modern Muslims base their model for the ideal legal code on the Islamic State (not to be confused with the group that currently goes by this name in Iraq and Syria today) as opposed to "what the Prophet Muhammad established in Arabia [and on] the system subsequently endorsed by the classical Tradition" (Jackson 2005: 140). Whereas the latter two are authentic for him, the former, the Islamic State, is a relatively modern construct "inspired in large measure by the European concept of the nation-state" (2005: 140). Whereas the latter can be quite intolerant of the rights of non-Muslims, he contends that the former protected such rights. It is the Prophet and the premodern tradition that Jackson holds up as the ideal for Muslims in the modern world or, at least, Muslims in America: "both the examples of the Prophet and Muslim Tradition allow for if not encourage a political culture according to which Muslims pursue political arrangements that directly serve their interests even as they indirectly serve the interests of those whose actions may contravene the rules and values of Islam" (2005: 141).

Within the present context, I would also like to flag just how different Jackson's vision is from Scott Siraj al-Haqq Kugle's, whose work I discussed in the previous chapter. Kugle, it will be recalled, had tried to argue that "true" and "authentic" Islam was necessarily gay-friendly or gay-tolerant. Jackson, in marked contrast, implies that orthodox Islam (= Sunnism) is necessarily opposed to granting equality to gays, whether Muslim or otherwise. Again, we see competing exemplars of what Islam is or is supposed to be. Whereas Kugle's is progressive and seems to be the freest in the West—that is, outside of patriarchal Islamic countries—Jackson's is inherently conservative and works best when it runs against the grain of contemporary American democracy.

It is clear from passages such as these that Jackson firmly believes that the sharia, as divinely inspired or God-given, must take precedence over the Constitution, which is little more than a product of local custom (*'urf*). It is his belief, quoted earlier, that the Constitution was an agreement among non-Muslims within a non-Muslim polity; however, he completely overlooks the fact that this Constitution was, in theory if not in practice, meant for all—Christian, Jew, Muslim, and all others. Instead, Jackson sets up the Constitution in direct opposition to the sharia. He writes:

> American custom (*'urf*) must be recognized as a legally valid consideration in areas where Islamic law admits reliance on custom. Once these compatibilities and benefits have been clearly laid out, there should be no constitutional impediments preventing a representative from bringing to the floor of the state or the federal legislature proposals that are grounded in the vision and values of Islam. (Jackson 2005: 150)

Note that nowhere does Jackson mention, though of course we can imagine, what happens where the Constitution and sharia are incompatible.

Like so many discussed in this chapter, it is unclear in what capacity Jackson is writing. Scholarship and theology intermingle uncomfortably. What begins as a fascinating historical and analytical study on the history of Blackamericans and Islam ends with proscriptive statements about how Muslims, presumably of any racial or ethnic background, should behave within the democratic political framework of the United States. While trained secularly as a scholar of the history of Islamic law, Jackson's work morphs into, for me at least, an uncomfortable situation wherein he seems to tell Muslims what to do ("Muslims must guard against ..."; "American Muslims must ..."). I am not sure if this amounts to activism, nor am I sure that this should be, *pace* Safi, a desideratum for the future state of Islamic studies.

Amina Wadud

Amina Wadud, until recently a professor of religious studies at Virginia Commonwealth University, is a *cause célèbre* within the progressive Muslim movement. In 1994, she became one of the first females to deliver a Friday sermon (*khutbah*) in a mosque, and in 2005 she led Friday prayers at a congregation in the United States, breaking with Islamic tradition, which has allowed only males to be prayer leaders (*imams*) in mixed-gender congregations. She is, by all accounts, a brave woman and precisely the type of strong and committed individual that is needed if there is to be a "reformation" within Islam. My interest in her, however, is not in her activism, but the type of scholarship that drives her activism.

Unlike many other converts to Islam, Wadud speaks at length about her decision to embrace Islam:

> My life experiences as a believing Muslim woman, and Islamic studies professor, have been intimately connected with Islamic reforms. As a participant in these reforms, I struggle to knit together intellectual discourse, strategic activism, and holistic spirituality. I did not enter Islam with my eyes closed against structures and personal experiences of injustice that continue to exist. In my "personal transition," most often called conversion, however, I focused with hope and idealism to find greater access to Allah as *al-Wadud*, the Loving God of Justice. (Wadud 2006: 2)

Wadud tells us unabashedly that her *Inside the Gender Jihad: Women's Reform in Islam* (Wadud 2006) is written from an insider perspective. I appreciate this confession and it is this type of clarity and self-reflexivity that I think is necessary in a field wherein constructive theological work masquerades as objective scholarship. Nevertheless it was treated like a work of critical scholarship and was reviewed in major scholarly journals. So, even though it is a theological work that is written from an insider position, Wadud is treated as a disinterested scholar of religion. Wadud also informs us of why she became a Muslim, "I entered Islam with a heart and mind trusting that divine justice could be achieved on the planet and throughout the universe" (2006: 2). For Wadud, then, Islam offers a universal message of justice and salvation that transcended her own upbringing as an African-American Methodist woman.

Despite being a scholar of Islamic religious studies, we should not be surprised to learn that her work is heavily motivated by theological claims. In the Introduction to her earlier *Quran and Women* (Wadud 1998), for example, she writes:

> One objective behind my research was to establish a definitive criteria for evaluating the extent to which the position of women in Muslim cultures accurately portrays the intention of Islam for women in society. It was easy to designate the Qur'an as the ultimate criteria available within the Islamic intellectual legacy, as well as its most authoritative reference point, because it enjoys an overwhelming consensus among Muslims—however variously understood—as the word of Allah, revealed to the Prophet Muhammad for the purpose of guidance to all humanity. Hence, it could be used as criteria for checking if the status of women in actual Muslim societies could be defined as Islamic. (Wadud 1998: ix)

Wadud, like many religious feminists, seeks to go back to the tradition's foundational text (Hebrew Bible in the case of Jewish feminists like Judith Plaskow; or the New Testament in the case of Christian feminists like Rosemary Radford Ruether).[11] For her, the Qur'an becomes the only "definitive criteria" to ascertain whether or not women in Muslim societies are accurately treated in the way that they *should* be. If they are not, it is because the original text has been corrupted at the hands of subsequent male interpreters:

> Mercifully, the more research I did into the Qur'an, unfettered by centuries of historical and androcentric reading and Arabo-Islamic cultural predilections, the more affirmed I was that in Islam a female person was intended to be primordially, cosmologically, eschatologically, spiritually, and morally a full human being, equal to all who accepted Allah as Lord, Muhammad as prophet, and Islam as din. (Wadud 1998: x)

For Wadud, like so many scholars of Islamic religious studies we have witnessed in previous chapters, centuries of interpretations (often associated with patriarchy, homophobia, and so) can be effortlessly peeled away to arrive at some pristine message that is unfettered by either culture or politics. She "assumes the basis of knowledge to be the one established in the Qur'an" (1998: xi), and that "it is unfathomable that the Lord of all the worlds is not potentially multilingual" (1998: xii). Wadud, it would seem, is determined to get behind the historical, political, linguistic, and cultural patina of the text in order to arrive at pure unadulterated and divine meaning. The problem with this, however, is that once we strip a text of all these features we arrive at a mirror, in which we see nothing but our own reflection.

Wadud's work, needless to say, was criticized from conservative Muslim scholars who claimed she lacked the proper madrasa or seminary training to make such pronouncements. Perhaps to answer this charge, she makes clear how her work differs from "classical and neo-Orientalists," again invoking the straw man of

Islamic religious studies (Wadud 1998: xvii). She even goes so far as to claim that for these Orientalists (no names are given) "no constraint or motivation of belief exists" (1998: xvii). Unlike them, she refers to her own position as "pro-belief": "As a believer, I accept certain aspects of Islam as sacred: the Qur'an is the work of Allah, and the Prophet(s) Muhammad, to whom this message was conveyed, has established his *sunnah* as normative behavior for believers" (1998: xvii).

Again we see how scholarship is done in the name of internal reform of the tradition. Islam, unlike the traditions into which many converts were born, seems to offer some sort of message that is found lacking in their previous religious traditions. Beyond this, I do not think it fair to speculate. I do want to reiterate, though, that Wadud, like so many other converts to Islam who are engaged in scholarship associated with Islamic religious studies, found their own religious lives unfulfilling (or else they would not have converted in the first place), discovered something compelling in Islam, accepted it as their own tradition, and now write forcefully in a manner that their roles as religious believers and as scholars blur to the point of disappearing.

Ingrid Mattson

Ingrid Mattson holds the London and Windsor Community Chair in Islamic Studies at Huron University College located within the University of Western Ontario, in London, Canada. Previously she was the Director of the Duncan Black Macdonald Center for the Study of Islam and Christian-Muslim Relations at Hartford Seminary in Hartford, CT. From 2006 to 2010, Mattson served as President of the Islamic Society of North America (ISNA)—an umbrella group that includes, among other things, the Muslim Students Association (MSA), and which is often described as the largest Muslim organization in North America. She was both the first woman and the first convert to Islam to hold that position. Needless to say, her high-profile position in the Islamic community in North America has necessarily made her the target of numerous right-wing attacks that have accused her of being everything from a Wahhabi (code for a Saudi-backed fundamentalist) to a sympathizer of extremist groups such as the Egyptian Brotherhood and Hamas in Palestine. These charges, however, are certainly incongruous with the work that Mattson has done in the pursuit of interfaith work, serving, for example, on the Interfaith Task force of the White House Office of Faith-Based and Neighborhood Partnerships (2009–10) and as a Member of the Faith-Based Advisory Council of the US Department of Homeland Security (2012). As president of ISNA, she, among other things, invited the President of the Union of Reform Judaism to address ISNA's annual convention.

Mattson, like pretty much everyone discussed in this chapter and many others that I have been critical of in this study, is truly committed to interfaith work, and engaging in active and important work with those in other religions. None of this is my concern as I do not think that interfaith dialogue ought to be a necessary component within the critical academic study of religion. I am interested solely in her academic work, and am motivated neither by personal grudge nor neo-conservative critique. It is important to say this because the Saidian paradigm that governs Islamic religious studies might intimate otherwise, namely, that my critique is somehow inspired by political ideology, which of course is one of my problems with that paradigm. My critique of Mattson concerns what happens when interfaith work takes on the garb of scholarship or when constructive theology is presented as if it is somehow value neutral and critical.

Before I examine some of Mattson's work, I wish first to mention that she teaches for-credit courses at Huron College in which only Muslims are allowed to enroll. Mattson, for example, has offered a course at Huron entitled "The Muslim Voice: Islamic Preaching, Public Speaking and Worship," which is ostensibly devoted to the topic of getting Muslim students to learn about and engage in the practice of *dawa* ("proselytization") among non-Muslims. It made the news in Canada recently because a non-Muslim student was allowed to audit it, but was subsequently told several weeks into the course that he could no longer do so. The excuse was that too many other students, all of whom were Muslim, had subsequently signed up for the course for credit.[12] Before we condemn this practice, however, I think it important to note that this was taking place in Canada (which does not have the same strict separation between Church and State as the United States) and in a religiously affiliated college (Huron College is affiliated with the Anglican Church of Canada), which are found with some regularity on Canadian campuses (in this case the University of Western Ontario). My problem is less with Muslims (or Jews) doing what Christians do in these religious colleges than with the confusion of purpose. To offer a course on *dawa* or proselytization of any sort and to claim to be a professor of religious studies, where one presumably teaches the *academic*, that is, neutral and social-scientific study of religion, is problematic.

I also think that this issue is worth mentioning because, as we saw at the beginning of this chapter, some want to hold Mattson up as a role model for Islamic religious studies. I have, however, a real problem with this and it is a problem that revolves around boundaries. Certainly Mattson has done much in her leadership roles in the Muslim community of North America; however, this should not be mistaken for giving her the intellectual wherewithal to be a scholar of Islam. Certainly she has a PhD (from the University of Chicago in Near Eastern Studies), yet a quick perusal at her online curriculum vitae shows very few peer-reviewed publications in the field.[13] Her one book, to be discussed shortly, is an introductory treatment of the Qur'an in Muslim life and praxis. It is not clear for Mattson, as indeed it is for so many of the scholars discussed in this chapter, just where faith ends and scholarship begins and, of course, vice versa.

Mattson's *The Story of the Qur'an*, which is meant for North American undergraduates with little or no experience with Islam, is written from "the perspective of a Western academic who is also trying to live as a faithful Muslim" (Mattson 2013: xi). Mattson's subsequent narrative is what we might call historical- or critical-light. There is no mention, for example, of source or redactional criticism of the Qur'an—that is, where it came from or how it came to be edited into the version we now possess. Such questions, it is worth noting, are largely anathema to Muslims because it is traditionally assumed that the Qur'an was simply given to Muhammad as an oral teaching via the archangel Gabriel and that it was subsequently written down with no human mediation. Instead, Mattson informs us that the "Quranic revelation, although transmitted through the Prophet, is not a response to his concerns alone" (2013: 3), and, again on the same page we read that, taken together, "these legal judgment, prayers, and narrative passages form a unity by virtue of their status as God's words, revealed to the Prophet Muhammad" (2013: 3). Much of the rest of her narrative carries on in such a reverential and historically inaccurate manner.[14] What follows reads like it is right out of the earliest hagiographic literature on Muhammad, where fiction takes on the guise of historical work. She is, for example, very quick to make sure that the persona of Muhammad is no way incriminated in the Qur'an's production. It is a divine text, the product of divine revelation, and that is all that a non-Muslim undergraduate who wants to learn about the Qur'an, in a secular setting, needs to know. And this is a real problem, as far as I am concerned. A student who takes a course on the Hebrew Bible/Old Testament or the New Testament at a secular university will learn that these texts did not simply fall from heaven, but were the product of real human communities with pressing social interests and issues. A similar student taking a course on the Qur'an will not learn about such social contexts, but will instead be subjected to a series of faith-based sermons that parrot back what the earliest Islamic narratives say about the Qur'an, that is, that it is a product of divine revelation as opposed to human formation. To understand it "correctly," moreover, we are encouraged to "use all the intellectual resources God has given us to attempt to understand the true meaning of the Qur'an" (Mattson 2013: 26).

Muhammad and the Qur'an are simply presented back to us as if the sources that speak about them, all of which date to the period roughly two hundred years after the fact, are works of history with no interest in ideological or political perspectives. The result is that the reader, far from learning a value-neutral or historical perspective of Muhammad and the Qur'an, is presented instead with myth and further mythmaking. At the end of her book, we are told that to understand the Qur'an truly we must open our hearts to it and its inner meaning. Mattson continues:

> The second necessary condition for understanding revelation is the proper intention—to sincerely wish to be guided by God. This does not mean that non-Muslims and even atheists cannot contribute to the factual body of knowledge useful to contextualizing the Qur'an; but you cannot attain what you do not set out to find. The meaning of the revelation can only be accessed by those who believe the ultimate meaning is beyond the limited understanding of any human being and who sincerely turn to the Qur'an for the purpose of finding meaning. However, attaining the state of humility that is characteristic of a sincere intention is not easy. How many individuals are confident of the purity of their intentions and the soundness of their hearts, yet clearly are deceiving themselves? (Mattson 2013: 262)

Here Mattson seems to intimate that the best a non-Muslim historian can do is contextualize the Qur'an for us, but he or she can never get at the meaning behind the page of the text. Only Muslims with the requisite purity of heart and proper intentions can do this. Experience, as we have seen many times in this study, trumps scholarship when it comes to Islamic religious studies. While "outsiders" may learn Arabic and contribute to historical understanding, they will never appreciate or understand the Qur'an, and by extension Islam, as an "insider." Mattson's comment that "you cannot attain what you do not set out to find" is indeed the mantra of Islamic religious studies. Many of these scholars know their conclusions before they even begin their analyses.

Kecia Ali

Kecia Ali, associate professor of religious studies at Boston University, specializes in the role and portrayal of women in both classical and contemporary Muslim discourses. In her acclaimed *Sexual Ethics and Islam* (Ali 2006), she notes that her approach is not as theological as other Muslim feminists (e.g., Amina Wadud and Leila Ahmed). Unlike these scholars, who focus virtually solely on the Qur'an in order to uncover its inherent egalitarianism, Ali instead expands her textual horizons to examine and take more seriously post-quranic portrayals of women and Islam. Distinguishing between "Qur'an-only feminists" (such as Wadud) on the one hand and "pro-hadith Salafis" (code for fundamentalists) on the other, she seeks "a critical and constructive engagement with the Islamic intellectual heritage" to provide "a framework for renewed and invigorated Muslim ethical thought" (Ali 2006: 20). Because she moves beyond the textual horizon of the Qur'an, she claims that she is unwilling to regard it as a pristine space that represents "true" or "authentic" Islam. This does not stop her, however, from trying to get at authoritative Muslim teaching. She writes, for example, that

> Careful investigation of the legal tradition, for instance, demonstrates the
> ways in which authorities have, from the earliest years of Islam, used their
> own judgment and customs of their societies to adapt Qur'anic and prophetic
> dictates to changed circumstances. It illustrates that some of the doctrines taken
> for granted as "Islamic" emerged at a particular time and place as the result of
> human interpretive endeavor and need not be binding for all time. Furthermore,
> the precedent of earlier jurists can authorize a similar interpretive and adaptive
> process for Muslims today, including bypassing (through a variety of interpretive
> devices) even seemingly clear Qur'anic statements. (2006: xx–xxi)

Although she claims to move beyond the Qur'an, it appears that she will ultimately end up with conclusions that are remarkably similar to Wadud's, namely, that the Qur'an is the source of authentic and originary teaching that has subsequently been corrupted by later cultural contexts. Although she claims to move beyond the Qur'an to examine the subsequent "Islamic intellectual heritage," she nonetheless assumes that the former uniquely provides authentic Islamic teaching whereas the latter can be mistaken or taken for granted—presumably by male elites trying to justify or legitimate their power over others—as "Islamic." Ali also implies that only "some of these doctrines" from this amorphously constructed "Islamic intellectual heritage" can be assumed to be "Islamic." But why not all? What criteria does she use to judge? Coincidence with her own ideas of what constitutes gender justice? What scholar of religion is in a position to say or judge which interpretation is proper, and thus "Islamic," and which improper? Once again, we are brought to the precipice of liberal Muslim theology, whereupon the scholar of Islamic religious studies will inform us what constitutes veritable Islam. Despite the fact that Ali claims to have deep respect for the Islamic legal tradition, she ends this above quotation with the claim that later jurists might actually have misinterpreted "even seemingly clear Qur'anic statements." The question again surfaces: Who gets to decide what constitutes a "seemingly clear" verse? My training in *critical* religious studies has taught me that scholars of religion should avoid such normative judgments and instead look at how various human communities understand texts in light of themselves and vice versa. On this reading there can be neither a proper reading nor an improper one. All there is, in other words, is interpretations, not right ones or wrong ones.

Ali's comments imply not only that the Qur'an, or at least part of it, is at all times and at all places clear for Muslims, but also that we can from the vantage point of the liberal Western academy neatly ascertain this clear meaning. As a result, Ali is quick to tell the reader what constitutes a clear statement and what does not. Those statements that agree with her reading, not surprisingly, are clear and correct; and those that do not, are opaque and must be interpreted away or excised so that they fall in line with her initial intent. Her role as a scholar of Islamic religious studies, she informs us, is what provides her with the credentials and intellectual ability that enables her to avoid "confusion over the issue [that] arises in part because of the unfamiliarity of lay Muslims with the basic concepts structuring Islamic notions of lawful sex" (Ali 2006: xxv). It is presumed that the secular-trained scholar-activist knows better than either lay Muslim or traditionally trained Muslim scholars who issue rulings that are considered insufficiently "egalitarian."

It soon becomes quite obvious that these "seemingly clear Qur'anic statements" are interpreted through the prism of a set of values that she, as a progressive Muslim scholar/theologian, holds dear. In her Introduction to the work, she writes,

> It is an obvious point, but it bears stating directly: in making value judgments, people are influenced not only by religious texts and teachings but also by their own social, cultural, and religious backgrounds. The early jurists were no exception to this rule; like contemporary Muslim thinkers, they could not help but be influenced by their own sense of what was right and wrong, natural and unnatural. In engaging with Muslim texts of the past, it is important to consider the ways in which their author's base assumptions differ from those of the present. (Ali 2006: xxvi)

In this passage, Ali seems to be well aware that interpreters in the past were influenced by various external contexts (e.g., religion, class) that necessarily colored or influenced both their ability and desire to interpret the authoritative texts of Islam. However, she herself does not look into this hermeneutical mirror; instead, she—like so many of the progressive theologians that swell the ranks of Islamic religious studies—writes as if unencumbered by her own situatedness, as if she somehow occupies that Archimedean point that enables her to write outside of her own localized context. In dealing with Muhammad's marriage to Aishah at the age of six, and consummation of the marriage at the age of nine, Ali writes that we need to recognize "the circumstances under which this marriage took place were radically different from those of the twenty-first century" (2006: 148). Such verses are, of course, omitted from analysis because of the fallout. As a Muslim scholar-activist, Ali presumably is unable or unwilling to make secular or scholarly critiques of the Islamic tradition.

Instead of critique, she offers "reinterpretation," something that presumably provides the scholar of Islamic religious studies the ability to transform the past into a modern tradition that is grounded in a set of liberal traits that include pluralism, democracy, and, of course, gender justice. Ali writes that

> Reinterpretation is not only an individual project, for application in personal lives; it must also be a collective enterprise of scholars thinking, talking, and writing jointly and in counter-point. Muslim feminists have become part of the Islamic intellectual tradition and, in so doing, have begun to push at its boundaries and reshape its contours ... as we expose reductive and misogynist understandings of the Qur'an and hadith, refusing to see medieval understanding as coextensive with revelation, we must not arrogate to our own readings the same absolutist conviction we criticize in others. We must accept responsibility for making particular choices—and must acknowledge that they *are* interpretive choices, not merely straightforward reiterations of "what Islam says." (Ali 2006: 153)

Here, and this should now be unsurprising to the reader, we witness constructive theology in the guise of objective scholarship. An interested student or reader who wants to learn about "sexual ethics and Islam" will instead find in this work a progressive feminist theology that runs roughshod over the past by selecting what fits and marginalizing as inauthentic or a later interpretation all that does not. My objection to this type of project is that it blurs the line between neutral scholarship and constructive theology. Where does the one end, and the other begin? Why will the author not tell us, the readers, about what she is up to?

I am also uncertain as to Ali's claims that Muslim feminists are now part of some amorphous "Islamic intellectual tradition." There are certainly feminists—like Ali and like others examined in the pages above—that write eloquently about feminist interpretations of Islam; however, it seems to me that they essentially write for one another in the disciplinary field known as Islamic religious studies. No traditionally trained *faqih* will take them seriously, and this is not only because they are women but because they have absolutely no training in traditional Islamic jurisprudence (*fiqh*). All they possess are PhDs from American universities. Moreover, as I have tried to make clear throughout this study, it makes it extremely difficult for non-Muslim scholars who want to engage in critical scholarship to enter this field. The non-Muslim scholar of Islamic religious studies must essentially act as a cheerleader to these theological discourses. The only type of critical scholarship that is done is sorting through earlier sources and deciding which to keep and which to reject. Those that are kept align with the type of Islam that these scholars want to create in their own images; those rejected are done so because they stray from the spirit of Islam and are little more than the products of "medieval interpreters."

While Ali certainly seems to be aware that such an approach is potentially "dishonest and ultimately futile" (Ali 2006: 153), she responds that the way to make it more honest is to look at the jurisprudential tradition in Islam to show that the "ways in which jurists have related source texts to social contexts demonstrates that the law they constructed has 'always already' been subjected to acts of interpretation" (2006: 154). Note the tension here: one should use traditional Islamic jurisprudence because it shows how interpretation is historically conditioned; yet, at the same time, one can use the methods of this tradition to get at a truer sense of Islam that avoids the detritus of earlier generations.

One of the ways that Ali and others denigrate the theological positions of those with whom they disagree is to claim that they fail to understand the tradition properly. "It is important to note," she writes, "that many Muslim thinkers and authors who are perceived as authorities, and who write and speak from a position of authenticity, are not themselves fully grounded in the classical tradition; they have a selective and often incoherent relationship to law and scriptural interpretation" (Ali 2006: 155). Once again, then, we see a scholar of Islamic religious studies present herself as a qualified, and presumably thus true and "authentic" interpreter of the tradition.

Jonathan Brown

Jonathan A. C. Brown is currently an Associate Professor of Islamic studies at Georgetown University in Washington, DC. Unlike the others, he is neither trained in religious studies nor does he teach in a religious studies department. His scholarly work is not as apologetic as the others surveyed in this chapter. I mention him here solely because Safi (2014) invokes him, as we saw at the beginning of the chapter, as a "Muslim scholar" who is able to "move back and forth between their work at the academy and their function in the community and/or public intellectual activity," thus, functioning as a role model of sorts for a future generation of scholars of Islamic religious studies. As with all the other individuals examined in this chapter, Brown's approach to Islamic data is held up as a normative model for approaching the academic study of Islam.

In his *Hadith: Muhammad's Legacy in the Medieval and Modern World*, Brown sets out to offer "a 'neutral' or 'objective' tone according to the methods of modern historians of a religious tradition" (Brown 2009: 197). However, when he gets to the chapter describing Western approaches to hadith literature—that is, those sayings of Muhammad that form the centerpiece of the Sunna, which, along with the Qur'an, functions as one of the main sources of Islamic law—he writes, not as a "neutral" or "objective" historian, but as a critic of what he calls Western hegemony that invokes, as all of those examined in this chapter do in one way or another, the specter of Edward Said. After initially praising the Western scholarly tradition of hadith-criticism for "advancing our understanding of Islamic origins," he writes that

> Western criticism of the hadith tradition can be viewed as an act of domination in which one worldview asserts its power over another by dictating the terms by which "knowledge" and "truth" are established. From this perspective, one could ask why the "light" that Western scholars shed on hadiths is necessarily more valuable to "the advancement of human understanding" than what the Muslim hadith tradition has already offered. As the likes of Edward Said have shown, knowledge is power, and studying an object is an act of establishing control over it. (Brown 2009: 198)

These are tricky charges that I have been confronting in one way or another throughout this study. They imply a relativism in that every culture has its way of understanding and classifying the world and the only culture that seems to have a problem with this is the West, which insists on making other cultures conform to its intellectual models. To engage in the practice of redescription, as opposed to just description, is somehow to commit taxonomic violence. On the one hand this is certainly true, the West has forced other cultures to define itself using its concepts, such as religion (see the comments in Fitzgerald 2000 and Dubuisson 2003). However, it is quite another thing entirely to say that the critical method of Western scholarship is either solely reducible to or unable to step out of its investment in imperialism. Brown informs us, for example, that "Western discussion about the reliability of the hadith tradition are thus not neutral, and their influence extends beyond the lofty halls of the academy" (Brown 2009: 198). Here he presumably has Said's critique of Orientalism in mind. However, as we saw in Chapter 2, Said's criticism was itself anything by value neutral, and was instead highly ideologically charged.

Brown's comments here are potentially worrisome because they all but curtail any criticism of Islam. Good criticism, the type that he as an "insider" presumably does, is rooted in the Islamic past, a past that did not have the concept of history or secularism, and Muslim values. Bad criticism, the type that presumably "outsiders" engage in is signified as politically charged and invested in Empire maintenance or, using today parlance, Islamophobia. According to Brown,

> The Authenticity Question is part of a broader debate over the power dynamic between "Religion" and "Modernity," and between "Islam" and the "West." Instead of approaching the Authenticity Question from a teleological perspective, where we assume that the native "Muslim" vision of the hadith tradition is wrong and that Western scholars have awakened it from its millennial slumber and are guiding it gradually forwards, we will assume what I think is a more accurate approach: the hadith tradition is so vast and our attempts to evaluate its authenticity so inevitably limited to small samples, that any attitudes towards its authenticity are necessarily based more on our critical worldviews than on empirical fact. (Brown 2009: 198)

Here Brown seems to imply that we can never get at the truth behind the origins of hadith literature. Although he will subsequently go into considerable detail examining some of the premises behind Western critical scholarship on the hadith—and, by extension, early Islam—Brown is concerned more with undermining critical scholarship ("sometimes doubting these sources obliges us to believe things more fantastical than simply accepting that the sources might be authentic"; Brown 2009: 232) and in upholding traditional (Sunni) Islamic scholarship ("it is possible that it was the prioritization of law over other areas that led to the inclusion of large number of unreliable hadiths in Sunni collections"; Brown 2009: 235).

Conclusions

The individuals examined in this chapter are all critical of the traditional models used to understand Islam in the Western academy, which have largely been shaped, as I argued in Chapter 2, by Said's critique of the field of Orientalism. Although all trained in this academy, these individuals have largely renounced its methods, as either too historical or as too politically tainted, and have instead opted for a vague and, for lack of a better term, "inner focused" hermeneutic. At the same time, however, many have refused to adopt or adapt to a traditional Muslim way of examining the questions in which they are interested. Traditional Islam, the product of male elites who have desired to protect their own entrenched values, they seem to argue is equally pernicious. On the contrary, many of these scholars have tried to walk a difficult middle path between largely uncritical religious studies scholarship on the one hand and a set of values that they deem to be authentically Muslim on the other. This is the real Islam for them. It is the one that Islamic religious studies imagines, creates, and disseminates; it is the Islam that has precipitated their conversions, guides their life principles, and justifies their scholarly projects. Their work, as we have seen in this chapter, occurs at the intersection of constructive theology, apologetical scholarship, and their own journeys to and within Islam.

The following chapter examines another possible model, one that is unlike the one suggested by Safi.

Notes

1. To give but a few examples, see Rodinson (1987), Hoyland (1997), and Tolan (2002).
2. Indeed a real problem is that on occasion critical work on the study of the study of Islam, such as my own, can be picked up by websites such as campuswatch.org, and manipulated in such a manner that is unfortunate and certainly dishonest. This does not mean, however, that we should not engage in the critical endeavor. Nor must it mean that critical work is somehow "anti-Islamic."
3. In the latter case, it would become apparent quite quickly that such an interpretation would be based on Protestant bias, and not particularly scholarly at all.
4. According to David Cook, "In reading Muslim literature—both contemporary and classical—one can see that the evidence for the primacy of spiritual jihad is negligible.

Today it is certain that no Muslim writing in a non-Western language (such as Arabic, Persian, Urdu), would ever make claims that jihad is primarily nonviolent or has been superseded by the spiritual jihad. Such claims are made solely by Western scholars, primarily those who study Sufism and/or work in interfaith dialogue, and by Muslim apologists who are trying to present Islam in the most innocuous manner possible" (Cook 2005: 165–6).

5. Safi's reflections are in an online blog post entitled "Reflections on the State of Islamic Studies" (Safi 2014). This means that they are not supported by footnotes nor do they have page numbers, and hence I provide no page numbers in the quotations. Safi and I got into a public debate over his reflections when I responded to his initial post. See my "Sometimes Bad Scholarship Is Just Bad Scholarship: A Reply to Omid Safi" (Hughes 2014b). My comments here are meant to offer a more substantive and substantial response.
6. I refer to people such as Arnal and McCutcheon (2013); Asad (1993, 2003); Bloch (2005, 2008, 2013); Boyer (1994, 2001); Chidester (1996, 2014); Day (2007, 2010); Dubuisson (2003, [1993]2006); Fitzgerald (2000, 2007a, 2007b), Lincoln (1996, 1999, 2003), Lopez (1998), C. Martin (2010, 2012), L. Martin (1987), L. Martin and Wiebe (2012), Masuzawa (1993, 2005), McCutcheon (1997), Smith (1982, 1990, 2003), Styers (2004), Sullivan (2005), McCauley and Lawson (2002), Wiebe (1984, 1999, 2006), and Yelle (2013a, 2013b).
7. On these theoretical shortcomings, see my comments above, and in Hughes (2006, 2012a, 2012b, 2012c).
8. See, for example, Fitzgerald (2000: 6–9); Dubuisson (2003: 112–15); Asad (2003:181–94), and Arnal and McCutcheon (2013: 102–13).
9. Jackson uses the term "Blackamerican," in his own words, because "to speak simply of 'black Americans' as the counterparts of 'white Americans' is to strengthen the hand of those who wish to deny or hide white privilege. On the other hand, to speak of African Americans is to give short shrift to almost half a millennium of New World history, implying that Blackamericans are African in the same way that Italian Americans or Greek American are Italians or Greek" (Jackson 2005: 17).
10. Jackson goes on to make this point even more explicit in his sequel to the book under discussion here, entitled *Islam and the Problem of Black Suffering* (Jackson 2009). In this latter book, he, among other things, attempts to explain how an all-good God can allow sustained black suffering "in a manner that justifies the effort to overturn this suffering in light of the theological presumption that it could only exist by the power and will of an omnipotent, omnibenevolent God" (2009: 4)
11. This approach, I note, was fairly popular among Jewish and Christian feminist theologians in the 1970s. It is today, however, fairly discredited in the academy, and such feminist thinkers have moved onto other approaches (e.g., theolatry, a-theology, apophasis). Again this coincides with my larger point that much theorizing in Islamic religious studies is stuck in the modalities of the 1970s.
12. See the story in the *National Post*, Canada's national newspaper, at http://news.nationalpost.com/2014/02/11/barbara-kay-huron-college-should-open-up-its-islam-course-or-shut-it-down.
13. This may be found on her personal webpage at http://ingridmattson.org/about/cv/.
14. I have critiqued these approaches elsewhere (Hughes 2012c: 10–33).

—5—

Jacob Neusner Meets Islamic Studies

As with my discussion of the Lopez-Thurman debate, I again look for analogues in other relevant subfields to illumine what I consider to be a major fracture in the study of Islam as currently carried out in departments of religious studies. This means that we do not have to reinvent the wheel in our own subfields, but it does mean that, as scholars of religion, we have to be aware of the larger debates that drive our discipline. In the previous chapter we witnessed one possible model for the academic study of Islam. It is largely the path of present, that is, one that consists of an approach to Islamic data that is crypto-theological at best, outrightly theological at worst, and largely based on showing a set of similarities between modern values and Islam.[1] It is rarely critical, scientific or historical, and is instead based on a set of convergences between a particular author, often a convert to Islam, and his or her need to apologize for the tradition for whatever reason. If this is the future of the academic study of Islam, in which scholars such as those mentioned in the previous chapter are to function as "role models" for the next generation, then it is a future that will be highly apologetic, insular, and, I would argue, largely uninterested in making connections to other disciplines in the humanities or social sciences because it is overwhelmingly concerned with reforming the religion internally. In the place of critical historical and textual study we instead witness the construction of an authentic "Islam"—defined by love, peace, justice, and equality—that reflects more the desires of the interpreters than the historical record.

    I would now like to contrast that endeavor with another scholarly paradigm, borrowed by way of the academic study of Judaism. This is certainly not to imply that Jewish studies is somehow immune from theological explication or identity politics. The role of private money, the intractable debates over Israel, the fact that the overwhelming majority of scholars in the field happen to be Jewish should, at first blush, signal that this field is far from being a bastion of disinterested scholarship.[2] However, rather than focus on Jewish studies writ large, I wish to turn to the pioneering scholarship of one scholar within this subfield in particular, Jacob Neusner, as a way to chart another possible future for the academic study of Islam. Within this context, Neusner has done more than anyone to bring the study of Jewish data into dialogue with the larger academic field of religion. If Jewish studies did not speak to larger disciplines, he reasoned, it would be irrelevant to non-Jews and the academy more generally, and would instead be based solely on some vague and inchoate sense of ethnic pride. Before him, when Judaism was taught it was done so primarily in Israel and, if and when it was taught in the United States, it was done so in seminary settings (e.g., Jewish Theological Seminary of America, Hebrew Union College). In both contexts it was largely theological in orientation, apologetic in intent, and untheoretical in execution. As both a critical scholar of religion (a so-called "outsider") and as an ordained rabbi (a so-called "insider"),[3] Neusner argued that this theological orientation needed to be left behind and that it was important to study Judaism, especially its texts, in a manner that was critical, historical, and systematic.[4] I wish to suggest in this chapter that Neusner can and should function as an exemplar to those in Islamic religious studies that are either unwilling or afraid to engage in any sort of critical work because it might somehow compromise them and their self-perceived roles as "insiders."

The present chapter seeks to provide a basic outline of Neusner's contribution to the study of Judaism, comparing what he found when he first entered the field with what is currently going on in Islamic religious studies. Neusner began to ask a set of unprecedented questions that took many by surprise and that, just by asking them, suddenly opened the field to larger sets of analysis. It was Neusner more than anyone who enabled and facilitated the entry of Jewish studies both into religious studies and into the humanities more generally. He was not an "Orientalist" in any sense of the term, but someone who realized that unless one had mastered the textual tradition of Judaism, one could do very little. His concerns, moreover, were not simply in the late antique period; rather he wrote on all aspects of Judaism. I mention this because it means that Neusner's pronouncements on modern Judaism were not just a matter of personal opinion, but informed by his reading, as we shall see shortly, of *all* of the documents associated with the classical tradition of Judaism.

Rabbinic Judaism, that is the various traditions that emerged from roughly the first to the seventh centuries CE, is often referred to as Judaism in the formative period. This period saw the development of Judaism out of the sources of the Bible, and witnessed, among other things, the codification of the great legal and religious texts of the tradition: the Mishnah, the two Talmuds, to name only a few. It is within this period of formative Judaism that Neusner wrote both copiously and profusely. Unlike those before him, he saw himself as providing a *secular* and scientific methodology for the study and contextualization of these texts. Here it is important to be clear that Neusner wrote elegantly about how an understanding of this literature was not simply an ethnic or a religious duty, but was an activity that could contribute positively to the humanities curriculum of the modern university. In this curriculum, on Neusner's reading, the Mishnah and the Talmuds ought to take up their rightful position next to the writings from Greek and Roman antiquity, Shakespeare, and other classics.

An appreciation of the genius of this literature's system and structure, he maintained, would take it out of the theological world of the seminary and locate it firmly within the humanistic learning of the secular academy. And this is precisely what Neusner, to his credit, did. His critics, however, charged him with imposing a methodological structure on his sources that, while sounding good in theory, did little in the way of helping us to understand the actual texts in question (e.g., Lieberman 1984; Sanders 1990: 309–31). My concern in this chapter is neither to endorse Neusner's method nor to side with his many critics. My goal, rather, is to focus on the novelty of Neusner's approach to rabbinic literature, with the aim of offering it as an alternative model to the theological work that currently passes for critical scholarship in Islamic religious studies.

My aim in this chapter is neither to engage in nor reproduce a Neusnerian analysis of the documents associated with formative Islam. This would take, as his own *oeuvre* shows with respect to classical Judaism, a lifetime. My goal is much more simple and modest in the present context: to make a set of comparisons between Jewish studies prior to Neusner and Islamic religious studies today. This comparison revolves around the problematic use of sources, taking texts to be transcripts as opposed to sites of contention, and a general unwillingness to ask historical or text-critical questions. In so doing, I want to try and prod those already active in Islamic religious studies or, perhaps more hopefully, those about to enter the field to a set of issues that have real potential to help us understand the contexts, past and present, in which Islam has been framed and articulated. These are not "Orientalist" issues, to repeat, but ones that will help us understand how human communities make sense of their complex social worlds.

A New Approach

Behind much of Neusner's work stands the documentary approach as pioneered in biblical studies. The novelty of Neusner was to transfer this method to rabbinic texts. Rather than regard the entire rabbinic corpus, from 200 CE to the early modern period, as presenting a unified system that exists in a timeless bubble, Neusner will only speak of discrete documents (e.g., the Mishnah as opposed to "rabbinic Judaism"), each one of which possesses its own integrity and its own understanding of what Judaism ought to look like. For this reason, Neusner refuses to speak in terms that use "Rabbinic Judaism says x," or "the rabbis believed y." He writes:

> This brings me to the most difficult act of imagination which I must ask readers to perform: a supererogatory work of social imagination. Can we imagine a corner of the modern world in which this state of interpretation—of total confusion, of harmonies, homologies, homogenies, is not found confusing but reassuring? Can we mentally conjure up a social setting for learning in which differentiation is avoided and credulity rewarded? in which analysis is heresy, dismissed as worthless or attacked as "full of mistakes"? Can we conceive of a world in which repetition, in one's words, of what the sources say is labeled scholarship and anthologizing is labeled learning? (Neusner 1995: 11)

Only after each text had been understood on its own terms (what he calls "description") can it be compared to other discrete texts (what he calls "analysis") and then understood to be part of a system as a whole. Then, and only then, would it be possible to speak more generally of something called "rabbinic Judaism" (what he calls "interpretation"). However, one could not start at interpretation and either work backwards or ignore the other two stages altogether.

This leads Neusner to speak not of Judaism in the singular, but of Judaisms in the plural. That is, each document reflects and refracts a particular social and intellectual context, which differentiates it from those that produced other texts. Each text, in other words, envisages a particular "Judaism" that mirrors the interests of those who imagined it. So rather than see texts and the ideas that they contain as disembodied and timeless, all connected to one another through commentary and intertextuality, Neusner goes through the entire rabbinic corpus, text by text, describing the contents, including the system and structure that each reveals. Only after such a process—the understanding of various Judaisms—has been undertaken, does he believe that we can begin to make any sort of meaningful comparative or grandiose claims.

After he graduated from Columbia's Department of Religion in 1960, Neusner published his revised doctoral dissertation as *A Life of Yohanan ben Zakkai* with Brill in 1962. In this work, what he calls his "pre-critical" phase, Neusner sought to create a snapshot of the life of this first-century CE sage by examining and summarizing all the extant sources, both early and late, that mention him, with very little or no interest in where these sources came from, how they were vectored by later texts, or why they were employed in the first place. Although Neusner would eventually repudiate this approach, characterizing it as "gullible" (1995: 13), he remarks in the Preface to the book that his goal at the time was to ascertain who exactly Yohanan ben Zakkai was:

> He was one of the leaders of the Pharisaic communities in Jerusalem before the destruction of the Temple, and afterward he undertook the work of reconstruction. Who he was, what he taught, and how he met the perplexities of religion in his time—all this needs to be recovered from the rather scanty remains of his life, scattered throughout Talmudic and midrashic literature. (Neusner 1962: 2)

Neusner's goal in this very early work, stated differently, is to recover as much of Yohanan ben Zakkai's intellectual biography as he can. This "methodology," he would later remark, differed little from how Jewish texts were studied in medieval seminaries in the sense that both were textual, uncritical, and not interested in being illumined by larger questions. Rather than focus on the forms of the traditions that relate to this rabbinic figure—for example, how, when, and why they took shape and were transmitted—Neusner instead focused on the actual contents of these traditions and assumed that they could tell us something of this first century rabbi's life and times. A few years later, Neusner began to realize just how naïve such an approach to this literature was. In 1970, he published a much more self-critical study of Yohanan ben Zakkai, entitled *Development of a Legend: Studies on the Traditions Concerning Yohanan ben Zakkai*, the same year in which the second edition of his *A Life of Yohanan ben Zakkai* appeared. If the latter described the content of Yohanan ben Zakkai's life, this new work seeks to examine the various traditions that made the formation of this life possible in the first place. In the Preface to the new work, he writes that

> I do not suppose we can come to a final and positive assessment of the historicity of various stories and sayings. We surely cannot declare a narrative to be historically reliable simply because it contains no improbabilities or merely because some details are accurate. We must not confuse verisimilitude with authenticity. At best we may reach a comprehensive and critical estimate of what we know about Yohanan ben Zakkai than was available earlier. (Neusner 1970: xi)

Neusner has in mind the form and redaction criticism found in New Testament scholarship, especially the ways in which such criticism reveals how biographical materials are created, shaped, and manipulated by the needs of subsequent traditions. That is, a particular individual might not actually have said what later tradition ascribes to him. So the question must become why and how was such a phrase put in the mouth of, for example, Yohanan ben Zakkai? In a later volume entitled *Rabbinic Judaism: Structure and System* (1999), Neusner makes clear, in his typical pugnacious manner, to the reader what he thinks is new in his own *oeuvre* beginning with *Development of a Legend*:

> And what if, further, we no longer assume the inerrancy of the oral Torah's writings? In Jerusalem they say we are required to accept as historical fact whatever the stories say, unless we have reason to reject it. In Tel Aviv that attributions are sacrosanct, arguing, "If it were not true, why should the sages have assigned a saying to a given authority?" In Ramat Gan, at Bar Ilan University, professors have been known to argue with a perfectly straight face, "Do you really think our holy rabbis would lie?" So the proposed premise set forth in [my] rubric should be regarded as revolutionary, even though in all other fields of humanistic learning it has lost all novelty. (Neusner 1999: 25)

The novelty of Neusner's approach meant that he was subjected to much vociferous criticism (though he certainly gave as good as he got). These criticisms included the usual: he did not know Hebrew well enough; he had not trained in traditional yeshivas (his rabbinic ordination came from JTS, the Conservative seminary of America), his understanding of the manuscript tradition was insufficient, and, most tellingly, that the questions he asked were irrelevant to understand the Judaism produced by the late antique and medieval rabbis.

These criticisms leveled at Neusner, it seems to me, reflect the larger tension between the academic study of religion and area studies. In his desire to connect rabbinic texts to a larger set of questions supplied by the disciplinary perspective of religious studies, Neusner was destined to step on the toes of those trained within the tradition of rabbinics and who spoke only to other specialists in a narrowly defined field of study, one that tended to be governed primarily by philology as opposed to any other recognizable methodology. The genius of Neusner, as I have reiterated several times already, is that he did not want to join this narrow conversation, but to open up the study of Judaism, specifically rabbinic texts, to a larger intellectual audience who worked with other data but who asked similar questions. Within this context, much of the criticism leveled against Neusner emanates from the seminary approach to these data.

The Documentary Hypothesis

Imagine a situation, Neusner asks us, in which historians of the New Testament ignore that the four Gospels formulated distinctive statements that reflected the discrete communities that produced them, and instead treat them as if they formed an harmonious account of what Jesus really said and did. While such an account may well pose no problem for the religious believer, it flies in the face of what we know historically and stylistically about the Gospels. This, however, is precisely how scholars approach rabbinic texts and, as I have argued in previous chapters, how scholars of Islamic religious studies approach an amorphous set of texts that they vaguely and problematically refer to as "the Islamic tradition." The result is that historical settings and contexts are overlooked, differences are streamlined, and the overwhelming focus is on disembodied ideas that ignore the lives and contexts of those who produced them. Neusner's novelty, to reiterate, was to treat these texts not as "sacred" or "holy," but as human productions. They did not carry the timeless truths of Judaism, but created "truths" that enabled communities to authorize themselves. To understand these texts, he sought to introduce a new method, what he calls the documentary approach, which he learned from scholars of the Bible. This approach has four features and, for Neusner, four distinct advantages:

1. It asks about circumstances, traits, and generative problematic of the several writings, from the Mishnah through the Talmud of Babylonia. In that way, each document is read in it is own terms and settings.

2. The same method simply dismisses as not subject to falsification or verification attribution of sayings to named master.

3. But, treating the document as irrefutable evidence of the viewpoint of those who compiled the document and how they saw matters, the documentary method asks about the context in which a given document's contents found consequence.

4. And the documentary method formulates issues as these are defined by the respective documents: their concerns, their problematic, their categorical structure and system. It further proceeds to the question of how several documents relate to one another.[5]

I think it significant to note here what Neusner is *not* doing. He is decidedly uninterested in finding a liberal Jewish take for modernity or creating a progressive Judaism using the rhetoric of authenticity. He is examining the manifold traditions of Judaism, warts and all. One could argue here that Neusner had an easy task because of the relatively long history of Jews in America, especially when compared, say, to Islam in this country. However, such an argument completely ignores the history of antisemitism in America, especially during the

1940s and 1950s when Neusner both grew up and began to write professionally about Judaism.⁶

For Neusner, each document of rabbinic Judaism—the Mishnah, the *Sifra*, the two *Sifres*, Genesis Rabbah, Leviticus Rabbah, the Babylonian Talmud, the Yerushalmi Talmud, and so forth—clearly differentiate themselves, both stylistically and topically, each from the others. Although certain passages may well exist in different documents, it is clear that the documents in question cannot be confused with or collapsed into one another. There, thus, is no "Jewish tradition," only traditions. Each document is the product of a particular group and, in turn, reflects its unique culture and society. One cannot simply pick and choose from them to fit one's agenda, liberal or otherwise. In order to understand something as mammoth and convoluted as "rabbinic Judaism," Neusner argues that it is first necessary to understand each text as an *autonomous* unit, as possessing its "own framework, exhibiting its own distinctive traits of rhetoric, topic, and logic, as a complete book with a beginning, middle, and end, in preserving that book, the canon presents us with a document on its own and not solely as part of a larger composition or construct" (Neusner 1995: 6). This approach, as mentioned, led Neusner to examine, on its own terms, all of the works that comprise rabbinic Judaism.

Following this descriptive part of the project, the documentary approach then permits Neusner to begin the process of *connecting* the various works. He puts it in the following terms:

> If a document contains materials shared verbatim or in substantial content with other documents of its classification, or if one document refers to the contents of other documents, then the several documents that clearly wish to engage in conversation with one another have to address one another. That is to say, we have to seek for the marks of connectedness, as for the meaning of those connections. (Neusner 1995: 6)

This means that texts do not simply exist in isolation, but actually can and do speak to one another in specific ways. In this regard, all texts that comprise rabbinic literature refer to the same basic writings, the Hebrew Bible, and so they all conjoin in this particular sense. In like manner, later texts build upon and draw upon earlier texts, so that, for example, the rabbis of the Talmuds build upon the writings of, say, the Mishnah. But if we simply start at this later stage we may get an appreciation of the whole, but we will miss out on the ingenuity of all the parts, especially the earlier ones and how they were made to fit together.

Neusner labels the third stage of his methodology *continuity*. By this, he refers to a set of texts that a community, for a variety of reasons, eventually concurs to be authoritative and, thus as constituting a whole or seamless "Torah." Much like the second stage, Neusner maintains that, traditionally, many scholars have been content to begin only here. Again, though, this confuses ends with means. It is only at this third stage in the process, Neusner declares, that we can begin to speak of Judaism's theology, that is provide "a description of how an entire corpus of literature holds together as a coherent, proportioned, and cogent statement" (1999: 26).

Neusner further divides his work on rabbinics into a series of mutually overlapping triptychs. Description, analysis, and interpretation correspond to autonomy, connection, and continuity. That is, each text must be understood as (1) an individual, autonomous unit; (2) how it connects or relates to other texts; and (3) how, taken together, these texts are subsequently seen to provide an interlocking and timeless system. Finally, on the level of the history of religions, he examines the type of Judaism produced by (1) each *text*; (2) the *context* of texts of the same age; and, finally, (3) the matrix or, what he calls, "the system seen whole" (Neusner 1999: 7). In order to undertake a study of rabbinic Judaism's system and structure, Neusner undertook a systematic examination (description, analysis, and interpretation) of *all* the works that are seen as comprising rabbinic Judaism. This monumental undertaking would see Neusner translate, describe, and interpret the entire rabbinic corpus.[7]

No longer, if one agreed with Neusner's systematic approach to this literature, would it be possible to treat the diverse texts that comprise rabbinic literature as a uniform whole. Each document possesses a distinctive set of formal and intellectual attributes. It stands to reason, then, that every text will be in possession of its own attributes, which must be described and analyzed on its own terms. These texts, if one buys Neusner's approach, do not provide a monolithic statement on or for Judaism (i.e., Judaism says "x" on any particular topic). Moreover, such texts cannot be studied theologically as speaking to a set of timeless and disembodied truths or harmoniously as if all these texts can be read as a seamless whole. Neusner's method essentially involves deconstructing centuries of harmonization and construction seen in the texts themselves and reverting them to their constitutive parts in order to contextualize them within their social worlds and to see how they functioned therein. "For in the end," Neusner summarizes, "knowing what people thought, without understanding the world about which they reflected, does not help us either to understand the people who did the thinking or to interpret the results of their reflection" (1995: 19).

In so doing, Neusner single-handedly transformed the study of rabbinic Judaism. The field would never be the same even when, in recent years, it has begun to ask different sets of questions. These new questions, however, would be unthinkable without Neusner's pioneering work into these texts. He originally encountered the study of rabbinic Judaism on a theoretically rudimentary and methodologically unsophisticated level, and he has left the field in a way that no serious or self-respecting critical scholar of Judaism will speak of "the Jewish tradition" or attempt to write a biography/hagiography of an ancient rabbi. The entire cartography of the study of Judaism changed.

The Mishnah

A good example of Neusner's approach may be found in his *Judaism: The Evidence of the Mishnah* (Neusner 1988a), a work that he and others consider to be among his most important. Neusner defines his approach in the work as "radical nominalism," which he later characterizes with the slogan "what we cannot show we do not know" (Neusner 1986c: 42). The scholar, in other words, cannot just make up conclusions that the data cannot or will not support. Scholars of Islamic religious studies would do well to internalize this slogan. In the work, as even critics would note, is the articulation of a fresh vision and a new set of questions applied to the Mishnah and related works. Therein, Neusner sets out to discuss the formation and social meaning of the Mishnah, codified in 200 CE, a work that would eventually go on to form the backbone of all subsequent articulations and iterations of rabbinic Judaism.

Neusner is perhaps the first student of the Mishnah who refuses to regard it as normative in a religious sense of the term. Moreover, he is also original in his unwillingness to go to later rabbinic interpretations of the Mishnah—in, say, the Talmud or midrashic collections—to try and shed light back on it. He dismisses as later reactions all subsequent interpretations and, because they are later, they have no bearing whatsoever on our ability to understand the Mishnah "on its own terms." This forms the bedrock of Neusner's methodological foundation: he is quick to argue that we need to understand the Mishnah not as it was articulated through a later prism, but as a single work that constituted but one version of what its framers thought Judaism should be. If we do not do this, we risk confusing distinct systems. This means that the Mishnah represents *a* type of Judaism in the first century CE, and that we ought to be aware that other types of Judaisms—other types of religious and/or philosophical systems—existed concurrently with it (Neusner 1988a: 3). Each one of these *Judaisms* thought itself to be and described itself as the authentic veritable Judaism. Neusner writes that,

> The testimonies to these other kinds of Judaism are contained not only in parts of the New Testament—for example, Matthew—produced in the later first century. They also persist in those massive and important compilations under the names of Baruch and Ezra. Like the Mishnah, they were prepared in the aftermath of the destruction of the Second Temple and in response to the crisis of the later Israelite spirit precipitated by it. (Neusner 1988a: 3)

The ideas contained within the Mishnah, then, reflect only the worldview of one group among many, which only later would coalesce into a singular Judaism that would go by the name "rabbinic" (what he had earlier called "continuity" or "matrix"). The relationship of these multiple Judaisms to "rabbinic Judaism" is not always easy to ascertain on account of the paucity of evidence available, just as it is difficult to trace how exactly the framers of the Mishnah would form what would later emerge as normative Judaism. Here Neusner is critical of his predecessors—most notably George Foot Moore ([1927]1954) and Ephraim E. Urbach (1975)—both of whom he criticizes as using later normative sources to describe what Judaism (note the singular) would have looked like in the first century. Of Moore's work, Neusner is particular critical, claiming that it is primarily a theological work, all of whose categories derive from theology as opposed to history, and that it "describes many kinds of Judaism as if they formed a single, fully symmetrical construct" (Neusner 1988a: 7). Moore's analysis, in other words, lacks the tripartite schema that Neusner had championed in his use of the documentary approach.

The Mishnah attributes sayings to authorities who are believed to have lived before the work's ultimate redaction in 200 CE, indeed who lived centuries before this time. Rather than take all these sayings at face value, as Moore and so many others had, indeed as Neusner had at the beginning of his career, he developed an elaborate way of subjecting to verification or falsification, or as excluding as not subject to verification or falsification, the attribution of these sayings. He bases his theory on the anteriority and posteriority of sayings and the names in which they appear. To use Neusner's own words:

> Authorities A, B, C, and D always occurred in juxtaposition with sayings of one another, but rarely, if ever, occurred in juxtaposition with sayings in the names of W, X, Y, and Z. Further, as I shall explain, evidence internal to the Mishnah itself, not adduced from other documents, showed that authorities A, B, C, and D generally said things which in logic stood prior to what was placed in the mouths of W, X, Y, and Z. It seemed to me to follow that what I found in the names of authorities A, B, C, and D should tell me conceptions or principles or problems worked out prior to what I found in the names of authorities W, X, Y, and Z.
> The correlation between priority in the period in which an authority lived and anteriority in the logic of what was said by that authority forms the foundation for my claim that the Mishnah tells us something about the world before the period of its own closure, that is, the second half of the second century. (Neusner 1988a: 18)

In a period of chaos ushered in by the wars with Rome, the framers of the Mishnah—unlike the followers of Jesus, and unlike the authors of more apocalyptic works such as 2Baruch or 4Ezra—sought ahistorical stasis grounded in the cult, even if the cult no longer existed.[8] Most of the rest of the book is devoted to a detailed analysis of the contents of the Mishnah before, during, and after the wars that culminated in the destruction of the Second Temple and the Bar Kokhba Revolt. If before and during the wars we encounter "the formation of bits and pieces of the parts" of the Mishnah, by the time the Mishnah has been codified, we need to examine it as a whole, "and not merely as the agglutination of an infinite number of all-too-clearly-differentiated parts" (Neusner 1988a: 124).

I have spent considerable time describing Neusner's project not only because it risks being lost in the sheer magnitude of his scholarly production, but on account of its relevance to Islamic religious studies. Neusner shows us, for example, that one can be an insider and write as an outsider. An insider, in other words, does not de facto have to take up a posture of reverence. On the contrary, insiders—at least, insiders who also happen to be professional scholars of religion—can and indeed should on account of their familiarity with their own tradition be less inclined to sugar coat it or make it into something that is not. The reason that Neusner was so critical of what passed for Jewish studies was because he thought that Jewish texts were more than of just parochial interest. In order to make this case, he had to show how exactly these texts were of significance to those in religious studies but who study other religious traditions. This, I submit, is precisely the type of posture that we must adopt with Islamic data. Our data, in other words, is not important simply because we say it is important. "We cannot know," to paraphrase Neusner's mantra, "what we cannot show."

Jacob Neusner, Meet Islamic Religious Studies; Islamic Religious Studies, Meet Jacob Neusner

Jacob Neusner devoted his academic life to tearing down the yeshiva walls in order to make room for the study of rabbinic texts within the secular context of the modern university. Needless to say, as the reaction to his work from those inside the closed and rarified environment of the yeshiva shows, he met with both considerable and hostile resistance. This resistance was occasioned by two major objections to his project. The first stemmed from the novelty and freshness of his approach to rabbinic texts; the second and related objection emerged from his general unwillingness to treat these texts as intrinsically special or inherently sacrosanct. Rather than regard these latter categories as either descriptive or autochthonous, he made us aware that they are subjective terms applied in retrospect and, because of this, have little or no heuristic value. Description, framed somewhat differently, must ultimately give way to redescription. Neusner's perseverance successfully integrated the study of Jewish data, as even the quickest of glances at any self-respecting department will show, within the larger field of religious studies. This is certainly not to imply that there are not problems associated with this larger field that, as I have argued in previous chapters, have tended to be less interested in asking the types of hard analytic questions that Neusner forced us to ask, and has instead been preoccupied with a host of irenic concerns such as interfaith dialogue.

Because Neusner neither confused nor conflated his data set, that is, rabbinic texts, with his overarching methodological concerns, it stands to reason that his methodology should be repeatable when applied to other data sets. Indeed, were it not repeatable, his approach would simply be unique and sui generis, two terms that his analysis abhors. To make sure that his analysis of rabbinic texts is not confined solely to the formative period of Judaism, the remainder of this chapter takes the type of issues that Neusner had with the then status quo and then applies it to another set of texts from a different religious tradition. My goal, stated simply, is to take the documentary approach and show how it can potentially illumine texts from the formative period of Islam (c. seventh–tenth centuries). My desire in doing this is simultaneously to show the correctness of Neusner's approach and to provoke those in Islamic Studies, one of the self-imposed holdouts of successful integration into departments of religious studies, to consider the critical questions of the sort that Neusner forced us all to confront in Judaism.

There are certainly important differences between the study of the formative periods of these two traditions. Our understanding of the Qur'an, the Sira (biography of Muhammad), the authoritative hadith collections (sayings of Muhammad that comprise the Sunna), the histories of al-Tabari (c. 838–923 CE), and other literature are not even at the stage of analysis that Neusner found rabbinic texts in the 1960s. In addition, despite the fact that some scholars in the mid to late nineteenth century, primarily German-Jews,[9] had undertaken initial forays into critical and historical analyses of such texts, this approach—as we have seen at several point in this study—can be and often is neatly written off using the now pejorative term "Orientalism." In light of Edward Said's critique of this term, the overwhelming tendency, at least in religious studies circles, has been to avoid all critical questions of early Islam owing to its insensitivity to Muslim sensibilities.[10]

Yet, despite such incongruities, I remain convinced that Neusner's pioneering approach to rabbinic texts can be reproduced, with obvious modifications, to the works of early Islam. This may, in part, be related to the fact that Neusner himself adopted and adapted his documentary approach from biblical scholars. Regardless, an intellectual orientation that refuses to buy into the assumptions of later texts and interpreters, and that instead focuses on each text as a discrete document produced by distinct communities offering their own (ideological) reading of events is more than appropriate to import into the study of Islamic origins, a field that, perhaps not surprisingly given the stakes that are involved, is in considerable disarray.[11] My other reason for focusing on the texts of early Islam is potentially to introduce a new data set to other scholars of the late antique period, some of whom will undoubtedly be scholars of rabbinic Judaism. As products of the eastern Mediterranean basin of the late antique period, early Islamic literatures—including the textual problems involved with their study— ought to become of greater interest to them. Indeed, the types of questions that scholars of late antiquity, Jewish and Christian, bring to their data need to be broached in a much more serious fashion by students of early Islam. What better way to do this than to have non-Islamicist scholars of late antiquity begin to approach this material?[12]

Beyond Theology

Neusner, as we have seen in this chapter, refused to let theology or a good story get in the way of solid scholarly investigation into Judaism in particular and religion in general. Academic scholars of religious texts—be it the Bible, the Mishnah, or the Qur'an—ought not to function as custodians of the tradition (for which we already have religious leaders). Before Neusner, *scholars* (not rabbis) of Jewish studies traditionally and habitually approached rabbinic texts as commentators had since the medieval period and were largely uninterested or unmotivated by larger questions that govern the production of scholarship in the humanities more generally. This, I suggest, is not unlike how *scholars* of Islam—not legal and religious authorities (*fuquha*), but secular scholars with secular PhDs from secular universities—treat early Islamic texts. They comment on them, take what is useful, discard what is not, and create an Islam that is in tune with their values. It is not, to reiterate, a scholarly enterprise. Instead it is a grounded in a "method" that uses texts based solely on their utility to a set of presentist arguments. Secular scholarship should be in the business of clarifying these issues, not further contributing to them. Like pre-Neusnerian scholars of Judaism, many scholars of Islamic religious studies continue to overlook historical settings and contexts, and opt instead to focus on disembodied ideas that ignore the lives and contexts of those who produced them. In terms of early Islam, this translates into the notion that we can actually ascertain a "historical" Muhammad from a set of texts that were written as "salvation history" (*not* to be confused with history!) much after the fact and with such distinct ideological claims concerning the legitimacy and authority of particular, and often distinctly partisan, Islams.[13] Following Neusner, rather than assume that all these texts form an interlocking set produced by those who shared a similar or corresponding vision of what Islam is or should be, it might be more useful to begin the process of prying them apart from one another with an eye towards both their specific concerns, in addition to their localized genealogies and contexts.

An important scholarly desideratum is to begin the process of unraveling the texts of formative Islam from one another, of refusing to assume that they all share a coherent and monolithic vision, and of describing the contents—including the system and the structure—of *each text on its own terms*. This will subsequently permit us to envisage both the similarities and differences between these rather diverse groups of texts. One major problem, however, is our ability to date successfully these texts. Even a text such as the Qur'an, which many see as foundational to later texts (though this has been questioned by some), is impossible to date with any degree of certainty. Whereas tradition has it revealed to Muhammad over the course of his life, others see it as a document that was produced or redacted roughly two hundred years after he was purported to have died in order to legitimate the ideology of rulers who now found themselves in charge of a large and growing empire and who wanted to differentiate themselves from Jews and Christians.[14]

The result of all of this is that we have largely failed to understand early Islam on its own terms because we have confused and conflated it with later interpretations of the tradition. And because of this we largely fail to understand the later tradition as well. It seems that when scholars of Islamic religious studies refer to these texts, they rarely specify which texts, each of which has its own unique history, and instead refer to a generic "Islamic tradition." The reorientation of an early movement based on an apocalyptic end-of-the-world message to an imperial religion within a relatively short span of time "provides a very likely context for dramatic revision to its narrative of origins, including especially the life of its founder, Muhammad" (Shoemaker 2012: 195). If we simply start at the later stage we may certainly be privy to an appreciation of the whole, but we will certainly miss out on the ingenuity of all the parts, the original contexts to which they initially spoke, and the ways they were subsequently transformed by the later commentarial traditions.

The result should not be the monolithic Islam of later centuries, but, as with all social formations, a host of Islams that skirmish with one another over the nature of political authority, the inheritance of this authority, and who has (and has not) a rightful claim to it. This may be witnessed in the fact that the quranic text in the years after the death of Muhammad was in an extreme flux and it was only a later Caliph, Abd al-Malik (646–705 CE), who standardized it in the hope of displacing the variant codices in use in different cities in the burgeoning empire.[15] Just as the documentary approach in New Testament Studies and as pioneered by Neusner in rabbinic texts works on the hypothesis that early communities shaped and reshaped—even invented—traditions about the lives of important individuals, we should not assume that the situation was at all different for the early framers of Islam. Unfortunately, however, this type of scholarship has yet to enter into mainstream scholarship in the field and is instead written off as the rantings of a "minority rejectionist camp, which has based its contrarian position on its own rather tendentious readings of the sources and unsubstantiated speculations" (Afsaruddin 2008: xx).[16]

It is high time that such a systematic analysis as undertaken by Neusner for the field of Jewish studies in general and rabbinics in particular be undertaken for the texts that comprise the earliest record of Islam. My goal is not to undertake this here, only to show what such an approach might well change. Although this has been done in a piecemeal fashion in Islamic studies, it is done primarily by non-Muslims and non-Americans. This, it seems to me, is primarily the result of the political implications of such analysis, especially in the aftermath of 9/11. As we shall witness in the following section, a great majority of scholars of Islam see this approach as "insensitive" to the feelings of Muslims and as a politically motivated attempt to undermine the tradition.

Islamic Religious Studies: The Hold Out

The events of 9/11 have made the study of Islam as carried out within departments of religious studies increasingly insular, apologetic, and largely irrelevant. Scholars associated with Islamic religious studies have largely invoked their authority to elevate their particular and idiosyncratic interpretation of Islam (e.g., liberal and egalitarian) over others and, in the process, deemed their version to be somehow more authentic and normative. The scholarship associated with this, as I have argued throughout this study, systematically ignores, at best, or writes off as politically motivated at worst, the types of critical questions and issues raised in the previous section that seek to make sense of a social movement that would eventually become recognized and recognizable as Islam in subsequent centuries. The net result is that we have, in effect, a "yeshiva" mentality in the heart of the secular academy when it comes to the study of Islam.

One of the most disturbing trends about Islamic religious studies is its presentism and its concomitant complete disregard for anything from the premodern world. Such an interest, as we have seen, has been written off as the stuff of Orientalism. In many of the books surveyed in the previous chapters, the overwhelming interest is instead in the modern period, in which the interpreter seeks to situate his or her own personal narrative. Even if the premodern period is examined, it is done so from a presentist angle and in such a manner that modern concerns are read into foundational texts. There is much talk of identity, but in such a manner that identity is not queried or interrogated in the manner that is done in other disciplines in the humanities, social sciences, or even sciences. In the essays collected in *Rethinking Islamic Studies* (Ernst and Martin 2010), which sets as its goal the redefinition of the field, questions of sources—for instance, problems associated with their authenticity, their interconnections, their verifiability—are not asked. Issues of skirmishes around identity formations are not broached (with the possible exception, for example, of African American Muslim women in the contemporary United States). Any topics that deal with Islam as an overlapping set of social and ideological formations are rarely, if ever, entertained.

Neusner and Islamic Texts from the Formative Period

It is at this point in the analysis that I would like to return to the work of Neusner and begin the process of introducing his critical methodology to the study of texts from the formative period of Islam. Before I do, however, it is worth underscoring two facts. First, as mentioned, we know very little, despite the self-assuredness of some, about the historical and sociological formation of the texts in question (e.g., Qur'an, Sunna, hadiths, tafsir collections). Investigation into these texts, in other words, is not nearly at the same level as it is of rabbinic texts. Second, there is a huge discrepancy, and this is part of the problem, between a social scientific approach to these texts and what they mean to believers. This latter point, as witnessed throughout this study, has created a huge impasse, no less significant than the one Neusner encountered in the 1960s. There is, without putting too fine a point on it, no will among those working on Islamic data in departments of religious studies to investigate these matters. There is a tendency to accept what these texts say about themselves at face value.

The first move that Neusner calls for is that we remove all texts from one another and begin the process of seeing them, not as parts of a whole, but as discrete units that only later are brought together in such a manner. In terms of the texts that emerged out of the formative period in Islam this means that we cannot afford simply to lump them together in ways that reflect later theological concerns. Each document, in other words, represents a distinct system that is unique to the discrete community that composed it. Read in this way, we cannot conflate, as is customarily done, the Qur'an with the Sunna, the Qur'an with the Sira, and so on and so forth, as if they provide a seamless and holistic account of the early Islamic polity. We must try to extract historically credible data, in other words, from "contaminated" repositories. This ought to involve using methods that prove capable of identifying different types of bias and that permit us to remove information from these sources in ways that resemble what those techniques used to reconstruct the historical Jesus from the highly theological narratives of the Christian Gospels and in ways that resemble what Neusner has done with rabbinic texts. This means that, at the very beginning, we need critical editions and new translations or even first-time translations of texts as opposed, say, to religious-based translations that are not interested in such questions of method (many of which come from places like Saudi Arabia)

This must involve careful documentation, translation into non-native terms and categories, and comparisons with the various and manifold descriptions that appear in non-Islamic sources of the period in question (e.g., seventh and eight centuries CE).[17] Many of these sources provide us with radically different accounts than those presented in Muslim sources. Most startling, for example, are those reports in non-Muslim sources that make reference to Muhammad as still alive and leading the invasion into the Roman Near East, where Jerusalem was located. Each one of these stories—both written by partisans and critics of Muhammad and his nascent polity—need to be evaluated for their historical significance. For even if Muhammad did not in fact lead the Islamic conquest of Palestine, what might such a tradition—and this type of question is never far from the type that Neusner himself asked of his own data—reveal about the period of formative Islam? Why was it important for later framers of the tradition to have Muhammad die in Mecca as opposed, say, to Jerusalem? Why did some want him to die in Jerusalem?

Robert Hoyland has begun this process, though much work certainly remains to be done. His *Seeing Islam As Others Saw It* provides both an inventory of these non-Muslim sources, and proposes a methodology for evaluating them. Of each of these sources, he encourages us to ask three basic questions: What is the source of a text's observation/s about early Islam? What is the character of the observation? Finally, what is the subject of the observation?[18] All of these questions will ideally enable us to avoid apologetics on either side, and he works on the assumption that simple observations probably have considerable greater historical veracity than more grandiose and theological claims (Hoyland 1997: 592–4).

The second thing that Neusner's documentary approach calls for is not to assume that the texts that are now considered by believers to be normative in the religious sense of the term were so at the time of their composition. Rather than assume that a document such as the Qur'an simply entered the world "from heaven" as a consensually normative work, a more basic question might be, how and by what processes did the Qur'an become normative and for whom? At what point did it become attached to the persona of Muhammad, who is rarely mentioned within it? And how does the Qur'an fit with other documents that would eventually also become normative (e.g., the hadiths or sayings/deeds of Muhammad)?

Most self-respecting Islamicists acknowledge that all the information we have about the first two centuries of Islam—this includes the Qur'an—comes from compilations and writings whose present recensions date from little earlier than the third Islamic century (i.e., 800 CE). Despite this acknowledgement, many attempt to circumvent it by placing their faith in the truth claims of the later sources to preserve earlier ones in a reasonably reliable manner. This, however, is extremely problematic because (1) many of these early sources are treated as if they formed a composite and accurate whole; and (2) this basic "methodology" turns out to be no methodology at all. Instead it is tantamount to a parroting of what later Muslims themselves believe. It fundamentally ignores a major question between fact and fiction. In the words of Koren and Nevo, it refuses to articulate what the later Muslim community "*thought* had happened or *wanted to believe* had happened or *wanted others to believe* had happened" (Koren and Nevo 1991: 89).

But this, nevertheless, creates real and perhaps intractable problems. It is at this point that again Neusner's name ought to be invoked. According to Wansbrough, if "what we know of the seventh-century Hijaz [the area of Mecca, Medina and environs] is the product of intense literary activity, then that record has got to be interpreted in accordance with what we know of literary criticism" (Wansbrough 1987: 14–15). These sources, in other words, are not history, but salvation history, a subgenre of literature, and the most appropriate way to analyze them are by means of form criticism, redaction criticism, and literary criticism—in much the same manner that they have been used in the study of early Christianity and Judaism. Wansbrough is, rightly in my opinion, opposed "to that school of sanguine historiography in which the pursuit of reconstruction is seldom if ever deflected by the doubts and scruples thrown up in recent (and not so recent) years by practitioners of form-criticism, structuralism and the like" (Wansbrough 1980: 361).

It is also important not to go to later interpretations of, for example, the Qur'an to try and shed light on it. At the same time, however, we must realize and acknowledge that all we have of the earliest Islamic period are later interpretations. The problem has been to assume that they simply offer eyewitness accounts of what "really happened" without employing any sort of theoretical or methodological criteria by which to adjudicate their veracity or lack thereof. Once again, the work of Neusner proves helpful in this context. Rather than proceed with the assumption that these texts represent a normative Islam at this early stage, we ought instead to understand them as single works that constitute different, even competing, versions of what its framers thought Islam should be. If we do not do this, we risk confusing distinct systems. This means that, say, the Qur'an represents *a* type of Islam in the eighth century CE (not the seventh, as is usually assumed), and that we ought to be aware that other types of Islams—other types of religious and/or philosophical systems—existed concurrently with it (Neusner 1988a: 3). Each one of these *Islams* thought itself to be and described itself as the authentic veritable Islam.

Neusner Beyond Rabbinics

It is important to be clear that I am not simply invoking Neusner and his methods because I think that scholarship on Islam ought to be only textual and only premodern. Neusner, as mentioned, wrote on all aspects of Judaism—ancient, medieval, and modern. He was, for example, extremely critical of American Jews (and their leaders), and American Jewish education that stressed the creation of an American identity based on the twin pillars of the Holocaust and Zionism (e.g., Neusner 1985, 1997). "Why American Jews," he writes, "sustain the contradictory position of deeming the State of Israel to be critical to their own existence as a distinctive, self-sustaining group in American society, and also insisting that they and their future find permanent place within American society, has to be worked out" (Neusner 1997: 3). These are issues, as should be immediately evident to those not in Jewish studies, that are extremely relevant and hard-hitting. In all of his writings Neusner's comments are informed by the larger discourses associated with the academic study of religion. Yet, not once did Neusner apologize for Judaism. He did not try to create a new Judaism, one that was in alignment with his own political or ideological views; nor did he try to pass off unsupportable musing as the stuff of history. It is for these reasons—in addition to the painstaking work he did to bring Jewish texts and interpretations to light for scholars of religion regardless of their data set—that Neusner is relevant to the academic study of Islam

Conclusions

I have engaged in this analysis to try and make the academic study of Islam more, not less familiar, to those working in the academic study of religion. In so doing, I have tried to redirect what seems to me an ominous turn in the academic study of Islam, especially as carried out in departments of religious studies, that seeks to put protective walls around its object of study. This confusion of scholarship with theology and of ends with means will, I submit, end badly for the academic study of Islam. Rather than engage in such an irenic and largely feel-good approach to the textual sources of Islam, it is necessary to begin the process of systematic description, analysis, and interpretation. Juxtaposed against the tendency to take these texts at face value, as accurate accounts of what they purport to describe, we need to subject these sources to the types of analysis encouraged by form and source criticism. These types of analysis are neither foreign to the study of the New Testament and, since the pioneering work of Jacob Neusner, to rabbinic texts. Why, then, should they be so foreign to the study of early Islam? And why must they be written off as a form of "Orientalist" hegemony? Such questions, I submit, have the potential to shed tremendous light on Islamic constructions both in the past and in the present. Like many of the formative texts from other religious traditions, the texts of Islam are also the product of attempts to organize and understand various social worlds. The question that Neusner and his students asked of rabbinic material must be asked of Islamic material. If they are not, the result is simply a failure of nerve.

Notes

1. Though this can be questioned by some, most notably Sherman A. Jackson in the previous chapter. His less liberal version of Islam (and presumably of gender and sexuality), however, comes with its own set of problems. It is, though, equally theological in intent.
2. As with the academic study of Islam, I again confine my analysis of Judaism to what goes on within departments of religious studies. The study of Judaism, in both Europe in the nineteenth and America in the twentieth century, is an extremely convoluted phenomenon. I have tried to get at some of the historical and theoretical issues behind

these formations in Hughes (2013b). On some of the problems in Jewish studies today, see Hughes (2014a).
3. Although it is important to point out that Neusner never had his own congregation. He once told me that this was because he did not have the "temperament" for it. He became a rabbi because at the time (the 1950s) that was pretty much the only option for someone who wanted to engage in higher learning in Jewish studies in America. I am currently writing an intellectual biography of Neusner (Hughes 2016) and the present chapter is an attempt to connect an individual who thought a lot about disciplinarity to a field that thinks very little about it.
4. For autobiographical comments from Neusner on how he found the study of Judaism when he entered the Jewish Theological Seminary in 1954, see Neusner and Neusner (1995: 70–75).
5. Although Neusner spends considerable time in many of his works dealing with these issues, this formulation comes from Neusner (1999: 24).
6. Born in West Hartford, Neusner writes with obvious irony that "West Hartford for young Jews could have presented a malign face, had we looked at how things really were. I grew up before and during World War II, when America, inhospitable to many minorities and utterly indifferent to the presence of blacks, chose the Jews for special abuse: we had all the money, we were not bleeding in the war, and we had caused it all" (Neusner and Neusner 1995: 60).
7. The staggering results of this may be found, for example, in Neusner (1974–77, 1977–80, 1979a, 1979b, 1982–93, 1984–95, 1985, 1986a, 1986b, 1987a, 1987b, 1988b, 1988c, 1989a, 1989b, 1989c, 1990).
8. Neusner had already worked out the details earlier in an article (Neusner 1979b) published in the University of Chicago's *History of Religions*. It provides a convenient expression of what he would do for much of the next decade.
9. See, for example, the collection of essays in Kramer (1999), in addition to Hughes (2006: 9–32).
10. In a leading introductory textbook to Islam, which I mentioned earlier in the context of Chapter 1, we read that "It is painful for Muslims to witness certain types of historico-critical, philological, and otherwise 'Orientalist' scholarly treatment of their sacred book." See Denny (1994:148). This is not to conflate an introductory textbook with a specialized study, but it does call attention to a particular posture in Islamic religious studies, a posture that I have been highly critical of in this study.
11. This is often referred to as the "authenticity debate." At least three different camps have stakes in this debate. The first contends that even though the earliest sources of Islam may come from a later period, they nonetheless represent reasonably reliable accounts concerning the matters on which they comment or describe. For example, the biography (*sira*) of Muhammad, which dates at the very earliest to a couple of generations after his death, is held up as a reliable account of Muhammad's life and times. Another camp contends that the Muslim historical record of the first two centuries is problematic. The social and political upheavals associated with the rapid spread of Islam fatally compromise the earliest sources. These sources, according to this position, are written so much after the fact and with distinct ideological or political agendas that they provide us with very little that is reliable with which to re-create the period they purport to describe. The third camp acknowledges the problems involved with the early sources but tries to solve them using form and source criticism, both of which seek to determine the original form and historical context of a particular text.

12. One recent example of this that has had tremendous results, albeit largely and unsurprisingly ignored by the status quo, is Shoemaker (2012).
13. The problem here, however, is that given the current political moment, many non-academics critical of Islam use such ideas to try and undermine the tradition. They will pick up, for example, on the notion that we cannot verify Muhammad's identity or existence as proof that Islam was "made up." Needless to say, this is both ridiculous and decidedly non-scholarly. Islam is neither more nor less "made up" than any other religious tradition.
14. E.g, Wansbrough (1977), Crone and Cook (1977), and, more recently, Nevo and Koren (2003), Powers (2009), and Shoemaker (2012).
15. See, for example, Robinson (2005: 100–104).
16. Such a dismissive posture of this approach is itself based on dishonesty. See Hughes (2012c: 10–33). On more serious—though, I think, equally misguided—criticisms of this type of approach see, for example, those discussed in Berg (1997).
17. Recent years have seen some interest in these questions, much of which was inspired by Crone and Cook's *Hagarism* (1977). See, for example, Hoyland (1997) and Conrad (1992). Though it is worth pointing out that none of this takes place within the discipline of religious studies, a discipline that, as we have seen, tends to be very critical of such investigations. Moreover, much of it is carried out by scholars with training in History, Near Eastern, Late Antique and/or Medieval Studies, and not Islamic religious studies per se.
18. Here I follow the comments in Shoemaker (2012: 3).

—6—

Turf Wars

This final chapter is an attempt to deal with many of the aforementioned issues, albeit from the perspective of greater theoretic distance. For ultimately many of the problems that I have broached and discussed in the previous pages are but a set of examples, derived from my own chosen field, that are representative of what I consider to be some of the larger issues endemic to the academic study of religion. Since this latter field lacks a consensual theoretical framework, it is not surprisingly wracked by a set of academic "turf wars" over how to negotiate data that is constructed, in one way or another, as religious. These turf wars say less about what we study than what we purport to study, and they reveal less about the world around us than they do about ourselves. The questions we ask of the observable world ultimately determine how we see it and how it reveals itself to us. It should, thus, come as little surprise that we are ultimately the creators of our own meaning. This is perhaps another way of saying that we, as scholars of religion, do not find religion "out there"; on the contrary, we conjure it into existence by the theoretical choices, methodological moves, and rhetorical flourishes we chose.

How we derive this meaning, whether as scholars of religion or as scholars of the humanities more generally, is contingent upon the theoretical and methodological grids that we employ.[1] However, these grids are not value neutral and, because they are often employed to examine that which we value or hold dear, they are necessarily connected with a host of desires, longings, and other baggage. Because of this neither theory nor method are immune from the political or the ideological. This is why it is necessary, as I have remarked at several junctures during this study, to be upfront about the principles and assumptions that guide our analyses. If we want to engage in an internal Islamic reformation, let's be upfront about it. If we think that converting to Islam allows us to overcome the racial or sexual prejudices of America or anywhere else for that matter, again this is something that a reader has every right to know. Our scholarly positionings have real intellectual consequences and shape, both consciously and unconsciously, how we approach data. Unless we engage in intellectual honesty, the larger scholarly community of which we are presumably all a part of has no means at its disposal to adjudicate or evaluate the work produced by others.

© Equinox Publishing Ltd. 2015

This does not mean that theory is a relativistic activity in which anything goes. It is not equivalent to opinion; one cannot just say, "I have my theory about Islam, and you have yours." Scholarship is an endeavor in which one must show one's work and be able to demonstrate to others how one got from there to here. But if the study of Islam is caught up in the reformation of Islam or if one's personal politics trump any attempt for objectivity, theoretical debates become little more than a form of existential warfare. It is at this point, moreover, that one can invoke the specter of "Orientalism" or what many consider to be its new iteration, "Islamophobia." Charges such as these silence critique, thereby turning critics into personal enemies. There are ways of talking about religions, changing the focus slightly, that are more empirical than others. If a theory is predicated on inner experience or based on one's experience as a Muslim or convert to Islam, then it is not open to everyone. How can one adjudicate an experience? Who gets to say what is a valid or invalid experience?[2] Any theorizing based on amorphous criteria that not everyone can partake of is, I submit, bad theorizing. Some sort of vague or personal experience cannot be the only authentic descriptor for understanding religion, at least in the secular context of the contemporary university. Critical scholarship, in other words, cannot be based on a vast array of feelings, moods, perceptions, dispositions, and states of consciousness that can be neither empirically nor scientifically verified.

We must not lose sight of the fact that theory and method are what permit us to conjure data into existence, to frame what we think of as significant (or not), and, of course, to discredit those with whom we disagree. At a time when the academic study of Islam—indeed, like the humanities more generally—is at a critical crossroads, this chapter seeks to present some of the stakes of what we do. When the theological agenda presented in the previous chapters represents the current status quo, it is important that a set of discourses be articulated to offer an alternative. Numerous private conversation and email correspondences have let me know that many are not happy with the status quo in Islamic religious studies, and that many are searching for new scholarly paradigms.

Rather than assume that theory and method are objective points of reference, despite claims to the contrary, it is perhaps more appropriate that we look into how they operate discursively in the field. It is one thing, after all, to say that one's colleague has mistranslated a gerund as a present participle, but quite another thing to claim that he or she is a crypto-theologian or a crypto-phenomenologist. It is within this context that the present chapter seeks to investigate the amphibolous nature of the term "theory." Frequently, for example, we hear at least internally within the subfield of Islamic religious studies the urgent call for more methodological and theoretical sophistication on the part of scholars of Islam, especially on the part of "insiders." However, it soon becomes quite clear that by "theory" such individuals mean little more than the theological construction of good religion and, if we are lucky, how we ought to move beyond a Sunni-centric position that marginalizes minority positions. But, again, all of these calls are internal to the subfield. They are theological and largely out of sync with the larger academic study of religion. To return to the previous chapter, it is similar to what Neusner first encountered when he began his pioneering study of Judaism, namely, the study of Jewish texts using internal criteria that consisted of traditional dialectic and commentary.

There are very few calls in Islamic religious studies that posit leaving behind existing criteria to study Islam so as to begin the process of asking different sets of questions, questions that are derived from external hermeneutical grids. Instead what passes for "theory" in Islamic religious studies' circles is little more than thought experiments with a veneer of light postcolonialism and a hint of 1970s-style religious feminism. The former refuses to ask hard questions and the latter presupposes that religion was originally egalitarian before being corrupted by misogynist male elites.[3] All of this is put in the service of a constructive theology that knows its conclusions (Islam = peace and love) beforehand.

For those involved in the critical study of religion, however, this approach is neither good enough nor sophisticated enough. The critical study of religion is not interested in reifying religion or Islam, but in querying the various discourses that bring such phenomena into existence in the first place. Islamic religious studies, to the contrary, is only interested in criticism when it is creating an Orientalist straw man; however, it never wants to turn the genealogical spotlight on itself. What are the implications, for example, of how we divide up and arrange our contingent social worlds? If we reduce theory in the academic study of religion to the invocation of Talal Asad or, on occasion, Jonathan Z. Smith, we are not doing theory. Instead we engage in a form of fetishization, one where "in" scholars are mentioned with the aim of gaining some sort of intellectual legitimacy. However, such theorists, whom so many in Islamic religious studies are keen to mention up front, seem to have absolutely no subsequent influence on their work. If they did, the contours of their work would be rather different than they currently are. One cannot use Asad or J. Z. Smith as theorists if one's aim is to create an egalitarian and pluralistic Islam.

If honesty and self-reflexivity form the hallmark of scholarship, I would like to see more of it among scholars of Islamic religious studies. A constructive theology of Muslim women ought not to masquerade as a critical and historical study of, say, sexual ethics in Islam. A plea for gender justice or the inclusion of gays, lesbians, and transgendered Muslims ought not to pretend to be a historical study of Islam at the time of Muhammad. Framed as theological studies, these may indeed be perfectly respectable works (I would then defer to the field of theology to judge their claims); framed as academic investigations, they are not. It is also problematic when many of these works are published as academic studies (and by academic presses) in American universities and colleges that, at least in theory, have laws governing the separation of Church and State. Much of the work I have examined in this study is crypto-theological at best, and nakedly theological at worst. While these approaches might well be fine for religiously affiliated schools, they are decidedly not for public universities or for academic centers.

The Politics of Theory and Method

The debates over the proper way to study, frame, and generally represent Islam, I want to suggest, swirl around theory and method whether we acknowledge it (as I have tried to here) or not (as the majority of those in Islamic religious studies do). It is unfortunate that many within Islamic religious studies frequently portray these debates using the language of hostility to "their" religion. While these debates should be intellectual, involving as they do the act of scholarly representation, they often have the potential to be much more than this because in critiquing Islamic religious studies, one is also perceived to be critiquing the Islam that it seeks to manufacture. This latter aspect has real and practical repercussions when it comes, for example, to what topics one can or cannot write on for a dissertation, on applying to and interviewing for jobs as an early career scholar, on publication through peer review, and ultimately assessment when it comes to tenure and promotion. This is why academic disciplines are so conservative. There are real consequences if one opposes or tries to undermine the theoretical position of the status quo. At the bottom of all this is not simply theory and method, but *whose* theory and *whose* method. Since everyone claims to be doing theory and method (even philological work is both theoretical and methodological), these debates get to the heart of generational divides, training divides (i.e., where one did one's graduate training and with whom), gender divides, political divides, and so on.

Since theory and method are the two tools by which we extract data, at stake is our orientation to that data or whether it should even be regarded as data in the first place. If we are historically minded, for example, we ought to be acutely aware that the words, terms and categories that we use to classify the world are of our making and do not necessarily exist naturally "out there." The very term "religion," for example, is a Western concept that has been forced on other cultures so that they may understand themselves in light of our terms of reference. If cultures did not have an autochthonous term for religion prior to contact with the modern West, however, they could not possess "religion." If we are less historical minded, and perhaps more interested in phenomenological comparisons, there is a tendency to regard deep-seated connections between phenomena in different cultures that point to some ahistorical and transcendent connection. Using the previous example, some will try to argue that cultures can have the concept of religion *before* the introduction of the term.[4] This is necessarily an intractable debate. History versus phenomenology. However, it is a debate that I believe needs to be occasioned within Islamic religious studies, and it is a debate that needs to be addressed on the level of theory.

Much of the previous chapters has critiqued the dearth of historical specificity in Islamic religious studies. Rather than see social actors trying to make sense of the world through inherited narratives, I instead argued that there is a tendency in Islamic religious studies (as there is in religious studies more generally) to talk about amorphous and metaphysical notions that exist outside of the domain of history. These include vague concepts such as the sacred, the spiritual, the mystical, the transcendent, and the like. How can such concepts, many of which are predicated on experiential or emotive states, be concretized, quantified, and studied? Rather than examine the assumption of maintaining that certain human beliefs, actions, behaviors, and institutions ought to be distinct from others, many are content to think that they really do occupy a different realm. Indeed, as the previous chapters have tried to show, many scholars are in fact quite happy to contribute to this type of mythmaking. In the case of Islam, this means that there exists somewhere a pristine Islam—unsullied by history, culture, misogyny, homophobia—and that certain people (Muslims, converts, and their non-Muslim cheerleaders) have special access to it.

The practical and conceptual consequences of this is the refusal on the part of many scholars dealing with the study of Islam within the academic study of religion to take seriously their own historical situatedness. They can point to historical actors who got it wrong on account of their misogyny or homophobia, but then these contemporary scholars refuse to situate themselves and their own historical creations. They are content, for example, to create an Islam that has absolutely no existence in the historical record and attempt to hold it up as the true Islam. Despite claims to the contrary, I have never seen a shred of proof that "Islam" at the time of Muhammad was egalitarian or gay-friendly.[5] These noble lies, as I have called them in this study, then do real intellectual heavy lifting in the present. They show, for example, genuine Islamophobes that Islam is not a hostile or violent religion (though I doubt that many of these Islamophobes will actually be convinced); they are used to help students, colleagues, the media—basically anyone who will listen—realize that Islam, on a fundamental level, is not antagonistic to the West and its values; and, perhaps just as importantly, it allows these scholars a certain amount of capital since they now position themselves as the de facto interpreters or reformers of their tradition.

Yet, when presumably secular scholars of a religious tradition become responsible for articulating what gets to count, and not count, as Islam, it is extremely problematic. Rather than critique the very term "religion" as part of a/the legacy of Orientalism, scholars of Islamic religious studies are surprisingly content to assume that there is such a concept of religion and that it somehow exists independently of the modern (again Western) nation state.[6] This means that their critique of Orientalism, as I have argued throughout this study, is less a real or valid critique than it is an attempt to carve out the intellectual and sociological space for what it is they presume they are doing. If their vaguely constructed Orientalism was engaged in textual or philological study, they are not; if Orientalism was interested in Islamic origins, they are not; if Orientalism was not interested in matters of gender or sexuality, they are; and so on.

As a result, many of these scholars problematically have to imagine Islam as a religion that existed prior to the invention of the category "religion" by European intellectuals in the seventeenth century.[7] As Brent Nongbri cogently puts it, "If a concept is defined as 'beyond language,' it is, then, by definition not something that can be discussed" (Nongbri 2013: 23). Yet, rather than regard "religion" as a Western category of hegemony (among other things), many in Islamic religious studies are content to use it presumably because it offers them a convenient narrative into which equally problematic constructs (e.g., egalitarianism, pluralism, justice) can be neatly inserted. Religion, or at least "good" religion, is something real and is supposed to be based on equality, justice, pluralism, and so on. In holding this position, however, scholars of Islamic religious studies inadvertently maintain a host of Christian assumptions that reflect the all too Christian heritage of the term "religion."

Religion is not a universal term, it is—as scholars such as Dubuisson and Arnal and McCutcheon, among others, have shown us—a Western folk taxon that, for some reason, has been elevated to the level of universal category. Rather than remove it from our acts of redescription, we valorize it, thereby further reifying it. Although many in Islamic religious studies claim to be critical of Western categories, they are more than willing to use such categories when it comes to imagining, for example, Muhammad's Islam to somehow be religion before the existence of religion. This necessarily involves the use of a set of Western-derived terms—"culture," "religion," "belief," "experience"—to make sense of what they think religion would have looked like in sixth-century Arabia.[8] The paradox, of course, is that they use these categories and simultaneously insist that critical or non-Muslim scholars engage in acts of misrepresentation. Needless to say, they engage in the exact same activity.[9] According to Arnal and McCutcheon,

> What must not go unnoticed in all of this is that, despite what some liberal-minded observers might read as a laudable, critical subaltern attitude toward Western imperialism, such critics are surprisingly conservative in their responses, for they seem to have little choice but to play by an alien, imported set of rules—rules that presume this thing that some of us happen to call religion to be a universal possession of all humankind. (Arnal and McCutcheon 2013: 9)

In a subfield that is, as we have seen, wracked by debates concerning the appropriate political representation of Islam, theory and method return us, not surprisingly, to the muck and mire of charges revolving around apologetics and Orientalism. Orientalism, thus, becomes a rhetorically useful stratagem to carve out space for what is considered to be the "proper" way to study and represent Islam. "Whatever we may be doing," so the claim goes, "it is not Orientalism." Moreover, scholars of Islamic religious studies, in invoking all of the traditional Western (even Orientalist) language encountered in the previous paragraph, paradoxically position themselves not only as the proper interpreters of Islam, but also as the proper way to be a Muslim.

Theory and Method: A Primer

Since so much of Islamic religious studies is relatively theory-lite when compared to the critical approaches taken by some in the academic study of religion, my goal in this section is to provide some of the larger context necessary for, hopefully, raising a set of questions that I trust is relevant for the academic study of Islam. My intended audience here is young scholars interested in Islam and who are looking for a brief introduction to the field of theorizing about "religion," as a way to show them some of the larger themes, issues, and players. Again, my point is not that all is good in the academic study of religion, and that the study of Islam simply needs to absorb better its discourses and/or first principles. There are, as I have duly noted, many categorical and taxonomic problems associated with the academic study of religion, and my own thinking about the field comes down firmly on the side of those *critical* theorists that follow in the wake of J. Z. Smith's pioneering *Map Is Not Territory* (Smith 1978) and *Imagining Religion* (Smith 1982). Smith is unwilling to assume an essence to religion that manifests itself in different cultural settings. For him, the study of religion is not about finding and interpreting a set of eternal meanings or symbols, but about constant reflection on choice and selection, including the various motivations and implications that attend to such choice and selection.

The discipline of religious studies, perhaps like every discipline, is caught in a complex web of contested entanglements. How best to analyze our objects of study? For some, perhaps the majority of the field, the goal is to appreciate the religious lives and worlds that people in different areas/traditions have made for themselves and, perhaps but not necessarily, to compare these to those lives and worlds that are more familiar to students in the North American classroom.[10] Such an approach frequently involves talk of the "sacred" or other such perceived universal characteristics that all of the religions of the globe, in one way or another, are again perceived to share. For others, myself included, talk of concepts such as the "sacred" or the "divine" are problematic in the extreme—as indeed is the very term "religion," which is often regarded as little more than a Western frame of reference and of little heuristic value.[11] Still others are interested in a model that stresses the origins of religion and how to provide a purely "scientific" model for its study.[12]

It is important to remember, however, that these three models are not untouched by one another; rather, they tend to overlap and, not infrequently, in rather problematic ways. So, for example, someone committed to the first model might have no qualms invoking some of the theorists associated with the second or even third models if they think it can help them prove a point. Perhaps the most obvious case of this conflation is what I like to call the trope of "Jonathan Z. Smith" that is invoked frequently at will and for all kinds of purposes in the academic study of religion, many of them in ways that are contradictory or counter-intuitive.

The point I wish to make here is that all who engage in these three models or approaches think they are doing something to which we might provide with the amorphous label "theory and method." Moreover, all believe that they are engaging with or using "theory and method" correctly and those in the other two approaches are not. At stake in the, for lack of a better term, "theory and method wars" is who we, as scholars of religion, are and what it is we do. How, in other words, is religion to be studied? Who has the authority to study it? And what are the ends of its study?

Why do we engage in theory and method? One reason we do so, I would like to suggest, is to draw boundaries between what is inside and outside. Like any other technique of "othering," these discourses permit us to define our discipline and ultimately ourselves and our place therein. We are not philosophers or sociologists, we might say, but scholars of religion, whatever that might mean. Within this context, theory and method—howsoever they are defined—have largely provided us with the means to patrol our borders, thereby permitting us—whoever we are—to say who is allowed to contribute and who is not, thereby excluding those with whom—for various disciplinary or political reasons—we do not agree. Yet, rather than assume that a boundary is a natural object as opposed to, say, a line on a map that is of our own creation, we need to reflect upon its instability, showing how rather than be fixed, its main function is to help form and maintain identity—be it national, religious, ethnic, or—in our case—disciplinary. Because these borders and identities are ultimately fictive, they must be protected, made to appear stable, and ultimately mythologized.

Of course, such boundary marking and othering does not just occur at the disciplinary level. It also occurs at the subdisciplinary level. This means that within religious studies, in specific traditions such as Buddhism, Islam, and so on, there exist distinct theoretical and methodological concerns that define who is part of the conversation and who is not. The same could, perhaps, be said for theory and method itself. Do the discourses associated with theory and method function as a subdiscipline, as some want them to? Or are they something that all in the field partake of regardless of area of expertise, as others do? If the latter, all in the field have a say; if the former then we have sentinels on the boundary who define the terms of membership and who punish transgression.

Up until fairly recently, religious studies has always had a fairly stable set of theorists that form the core of any department's annual undergraduate or graduate seminar devoted to the generic topic of some variation on the theme of "theory or method," or alternatively "theories and methods." This usually involves the trademark journey from Rudolph Otto's numinous creaturely feeling and *mysterium tremendum* ([1917]1969), through to Durkheim's primitive classification and collective effervescence ([1912]1995), Freud's patricide and totemism ([1930]1961), Frazer's search for the illusive and ever-expanding Golden Bough ([1890]1933), and Weber's ideal types and breakthroughs ([1922]1964). And it usually ends with Eliade's kratophanies, hierophanies, and irreducibility of the sacred ([1957]1987) or, if students are lucky, the work of J. Z. Smith mentioned earlier.[13]

These are the theorists that pretty much everyone in the academic study of religion has cut their teeth on. Obviously what they go on to do with them is their own business. Yet, if one works on theory today, it is still incumbent upon one to struggle with them, argue with them, and, if necessary, reject them (in addition, of course, to more recent thinkers such as Asad, Bourdieu, Lincoln, Masuzawa, and McCutcheon). They cannot simply be ignored or written off as irrelevant *if* one is engaging in theory as it takes place within the context of religious studies. These theorists form the bedrock of what we do and, in an ideal world, enable us to talk to one another. If the study of Islam wants to be better integrated into the academic study of religion, it needs to wrestle with these theorists and show how they are relevant (or even irrelevant) to Islamic data. My concern is that too many in Islamic religious studies simply ignore them as irrelevant. There are, as I shall argue shortly, real costs in doing this.

Although many in the field would agree on the Otto to Eliade chapter of the field, things take a turn—perhaps we might call it a postmodern turn—after we pass J. Z. Smith. While many cite him, it is not at all clear why they do. Often, as Arnal and McCutcheon argue, this is to speak of religions as opposed to religion or Buddhisms instead of Buddhism (i.e., using the plural as opposed the singular form of these nouns). But, as they write, "the erstwhile singular family identity in each case is just deferred to the level of genus; identity of some sort remains intact, unspoken, and thus untheorized" (Arnal and McCutcheon 2013: 11-12). While Neusner certainly began this discussion, as the work of Arnal and McCutcheon shows we can now take his initial observations much farther. Yet, once we move beyond Smith, the canon begins to break down and we get into a situation in which the majority of people working in theory and method are not so much trying to construct theories or methods, but to dismantle those of an earlier generation that continue to be used or recycled in one way or another. I think of individuals like Russell McCutcheon, Daniel Dubuisson, Donald Lopez, Tim Fitzgerald, and Tomoko Masuzawa. Because of the deconstructive nature of some of this work and the fact that it is often uncomfortably pointed at colleagues in the field, it is deemed problematic. It is often politically charged and it seeks to undermine the status quo and the regnant discourses the status quo produces. Because it is contemporary and because it seeks to undermine the category "religion" and all that travels in its wake, it is often deemed "angry."

It is this last category that most interests me and, indeed, I think I would try to situate myself in it if my colleagues therein will permit me entrance. What is the alternative to this theorization? One alternative, as the above study has shown, is to ignore it altogether and engage in a largely theological or quasi-theological agenda that is interested in theoretical models that downplay the historical and the critical. Another option, something we also see a lot in religious studies, is to revert to an area studies model where one engages in textual work within one's subfield and in such a way that it does not entertain larger disciplinary questions. One can, for example, produce critical editions of texts or translations—many of which are much needed and will be invaluable to others in the field—but with little interest in other issues, which may be perceived as an irritant.

We cannot, in short, simply invoke the names of theorists, we must actively engage their work. This does not necessarily mean that their concerns will necessarily always be our concerns. Even though much theory and method in religious studies is inattentive to women, to gender, to race, to discrimination, and to anti-Semitism, this need not mean that we must. That theory and method has perhaps not traditionally theorized these categories certainly does not mean that we should not in the future. The future of theory, framed somewhat differently, is not a closed book. Scholars of Islam must begin to enter these conversations.

Islamic Religious Studies

Now the question arises, what is the relevance of this discussion for the academic study of Islam as it has come to be understood with departments of religious studies? I have recounted what I have in this chapter to show how the generic term "theory and method" operates discursively in the field. In Islamic religious studies the term is deployed when it is required to defend the status quo, but little more. If and when the walls of the status quo are under threat or breached, the term quickly becomes pejorative and can be lumped into the pit of other terms that threaten, such as "critical," "insensitive," "reductive," "disinterested," and "political." But all of these terms I would argue are the hallmarks of sober scholarship. In this case, criticism of "theory and method" becomes paradoxically a way of avoiding criticisms, of securing regnant discourses, and of engaging in scholarship in the usual way.

Islamic religious studies is largely uninterested in the types of theoretical questions that are creating such a commotion in the academic study of religion. These questions have forced some, certainly not all, to rethink the very nature of traditional concepts, such as "religion," "faith," "experience," "identity," and "authenticity." Instead of querying such terms, many in Islamic religious studies are content to deploy them as if they existed naturally in the world as opposed to being of our own construction. Many, for example, are willing to point out the extra-intellectual aspects of nineteenth century Orientalism, but they are completely unwilling to turn the hermeneutical mirror on themselves. Presumably this can be done because it was perceived that *"the* Orientalists" were hostile to Islam,[14] whereas these contemporary scholars are in the habit of constructing good Islam. Their moves that privilege and deny, however, are phenomenologically identical to those whom they criticize.

Theory and method both require systematic and sustained analysis that is not afraid to ask hard questions of data and in ways that are uninhibited to ask why this datum in particular and why not, say, another one. Theory, in other words, should not enable us to arrive at the same spot from which we depart. It does not permit us with faddish theorists to justify or legitimate a set of conclusions we have arrived at before even beginning our analysis. Once we begin to theorize, the world that we have constructed in our image should be a different world. There cannot be some necessary and universal thing that transcends our contingent terminology and petty methodological disputes.

One cannot pretend, in other words, that neither theory nor method exists. In fact, as I have argued through this chapter, they are all that exist because they are the only tools at our disposal that permit us mediated access to the world we seek to describe and that we subsequently try to bring into existence for our own scholarly projects. And this is why they are so important. There cannot be experiences or inner feelings that drive disciplines or fields because this means that only some people can have access to them—in the case of Islamic religious studies, Muslims and, presumably, converts to Islam—whereas others cannot.

What happens when we permit certain people to be the de facto interpreters of tangible human actions, behaviors, and situations?

What we *all* possess is language, systems of signifiers, and semantic structures that are of our own making and that have distinct genealogies to them. Without understanding this, all we have is unverifiable claims. Certainly the humanities may lack the rigor of the sciences or even social sciences, but this does not mean that we can make things up. The "noble lies" that scholars of Islamic religious studies tell themselves, I have suggested, are precisely that: manufactured claims that are untestable, unverifiable, and have absolutely no existence in the historical record. They are the products of their own imaginations that they deploy with the intention of correcting gross misrepresentations in the media and other places.

The problem, though, is that these are no longer just for popular consumption, but apparently for scholarly consumption as well. These undertheorized representations are presented as authentic not just to the media, but now to the scholarly world as well. These noble lies then risk metastasizing into untruths to justify and legitimate a group of scholars that style themselves to be Muslim reformers. Because of this need to reform the tradition from within, as it were, these scholars engage in all of the rhetoric that is traditionally ascribed to theologians. Authenticity is posited instead of queried; rather than talk about operational acts of identification, they instead talk about identity; and truth claims are thought to be real as opposed to constructed.

I would not have as hard a time with this if the scholars engaged in constructive Muslim theology would admit that that is what they are doing. Instead, they use the rhetoric of religious studies, coupled with a disdain for traditional historical and text-critical scholarship that they write off, to pretend to be engaging in scholarly activity. They are not, and this is why they largely talk to one another as opposed to entering larger disciplinary conversations either in religious studies or the humanities more generally.

Scholars of Islamic religious studies are incapable at the current moment in engaging in these type of critical endeavors because they are so caught up in imagining "good" Islam and then adjudicating it in a variety of synchronic and diachronic texts. Attention has not yet turned to more critical questions because such questions are either judged to be "Western" or irrelevant. Yet, claims such as these to the contrary, the very language and categories used to cobble this good Islam together are, I have tried to suggest, decidedly Western and, as others have suggested, the product of the modern (= Western) political state (e.g., Žižek 1994: 14–17).

The loser in all of this, it seems to me, is the *academic* study of Islam or Islamic studies (as opposed to Islamic religious studies).[15] The study of Islam ought to be more in tune or in sync with thinking about other religions. For example, the regnant discourse in Judaism is not about ascertaining an egalitarian or pristine Judaism that provides the seeds for modern Judaism. Although this was certainly done in the nineteenth century, these conversations took place in seminaries as opposed to universities. The same could be said about pretty much every other religion studied within the context of religious studies. This is why, as I tried to argue in the previous chapter, the work of Jacob Neusner was so important. He did more than anyone to integrate Judaism into the types of questions that religious studies was asking at the time. Even those who disagreed with him had to provide the reasons for their disagreement. Islamic religious studies needs someone like Neusner—someone who cannot be neatly written off as an "Orientalist" because of his own insider credentials—to begin the process of asking new questions of old data.

We return again to the issue of relevance. What are the consequences—intellectually, institutionally, socially, even religiously—of not theorizing data in ways that are of relevance to other scholars in religious studies or even the humanities more generally? If we simply manufacture stories that equate an originary and pristine Islam with notions of democracy, liberalism, gender justice and equality for all regardless of sexual preference, we are not engaging in scholarship, but mythopoesis. Scholars of Islamic religious studies will slowly find themselves marginalized within the academic study of religion and, I would go so far as to say, within the larger field of Islamic studies as carried out in the contexts of Near East Studies departments or in Europe.

The study of Islam as it is currently undertaken in departments of religious studies is at a critical crossroads. Either it can carry on in the path of liberal Muslim theologizing or it can begin the process of engaging the types of theorists, and the questions that they ask, that I have presented in this chapter. This will not only open the field up to those interested in theoretical concerns in the academic study of religion and who are not interested in manufacturing good Islam, it will also have the effect of encouraging scholars of Islam to have larger disciplinary conversations.

The scope and nature of these conversations, I submit, will determine the future of the study of Islam as carried out in departments of religious studies. The present (and I trust provocative) study has been an attempt to begin this larger and necessary conversation.

Notes

1. According to my understanding, the term "method" and, by extension, "methodology" refers to the scholarly practices that have made and continue to make the academic study of religion possible. Sociology is a method, discourse analysis is a method, deconstruction is a method. "Theory," on the other hand, refers to the varied causal and naturalistic accounts used to account for the origins and transmission of what is commonly referred to as "religion." Totemism is a theory, animism is a theory, cognitive science is a theory. On this reading, theory is not the same thing as method and vice versa. One can, ostensibly, do theory without method and vice versa.
2. See the excellent essay by Sharf (1998). In this regard, see also the more philosophical analysis found in Proudfoot (1985).
3. In another study (Hughes 2012c) I distinguish "light" postcolonialism from postcolonialism. Whereas the latter is interested in investigating, often severely, the very notion of identity, the former upholds it.

4. See the critique of this concept of "religion before religion" in Nongbri (2013: 25-45).
5. I have "Islam" in quotation marks because Islam only became codified as a "religion"—legally, religiously, theologically—in the centuries after Muhammad's death.
6. See, for example, Asad (1993: 39), Dubuisson (2003: 9-16), Fitzgerald (2007a: 71-82), and more recently Arnal and McCutcheon (2013: 1-16) and Nongbri (2013: 97-105).
7. On the invention of the term religion, see Masuzawa (1993: 37-45), Stroumsa (2010: 24-38), and Nongbri (2013: 35-45).
8. This, for me, is the problem with Donner (2010). He reifies terms such as "belief" and "experience" in ways that seem anachronistic, although, to be clear, I do not define Donner, who works in a department of Near Eastern studies, as a scholar of Islamic religious studies. This is not simply because he works in Near Eastern studies, but because his interests are outside of the narrow confines of Islamic religious studies.
9. Here I am influenced by Arnal and McCutcheon (2013: 9-11).
10. One of the more recent and perhaps most articulate pleas for this kind of approach was made in Orsi (2005).
11. See, for example, McCutcheon (1997), Lincoln (1999), and Arnal and McCutcheon (2013).
12. Here I think of Boyer (2001) and, most recently, of L. Martin and Wiebe (2012).
13. We see all these figures on clear display in *Eight Theories of Religion* by Daniel Pals (2008).
14. This, of course, is patently false as I argued in Chapter 2 above. Names of "Orientalists" with sensitivity to Islam include Geiger, Goldziher, Horovitz, to name only a few.
15. Note that I have consciously removed "religious" from this phrase as a way to signal that hopefully the future will be Islamic studies as opposed to Islamic religious studies.

References

Abd-Allah, Umar F. 2006. *A Muslim in Victorian America: The Life of Alexander Russell Webb.* New York: Oxford University Press. http://dx.doi.org/10.1093/0195187288.001.0001.
Abou El Fadl, Khaled. 2005. *The Great Theft: Wrestling Islam from the Extremists.* San Francisco, CA: Harper.
Adams, Charles J. 1967. "The History of Religions and the Study of Islam." In Joseph M. Kitagawa, Mircea Eliade, and Charles H. Long (eds.), *The History of Religions: Essays on the Problem of Understanding*, 177–93. Chicago, IL: University of Chicago Press.
Afsaruddin, Asma. 2008. *The First Muslims: History and Memory.* Oxford: Oneworld.
Ahmad, Aijaz. 1992. "*Orientalism* and After: Ambivalence and Metropolitan Location in the Work of Edward Said." In idem, *In Theory: Classes, Nations, Literatures*, 159–219. New York: Verso.
Ahmed, Leila. 1993. *Women and Gender in Islam: Historical Roots of a Modern Debate.* New Haven, CT: Yale University Press.
Ahmed, Leila. 2011. *A Quiet Revolution: The Veil's Resurgence, from the Middle East to America.* New Haven, CT: Yale University Press.
Alfarabi, Abu Nasr. 1963. "The Enumeration of the Religious Sciences." In Ralph Lerner and Muhsin Mahdi (eds.), *Medieval Political Philosophy*, 24–30. Ithaca, NY: Cornell University Press.
Ali, Kecia A. 2006. *Sexual Ethics and Islam: Feminist Reflections on Qur'an, Hadith, and Jurisprudence.* Oxford: Oneworld.
Appiah, Kwame Anthony. 2006. *Cosmopolitanism: Ethics in a World of Strangers.* New York: Norton.
Armstrong, Karen E. 2000. *Islam: A Short History.* New York: The Modern Library.
Arnal, William E., and Russell T. McCutcheon. 2013. *The Sacred is the Profane: The Political Nature of "Religion."* New York: Oxford University Press.
Asad, Talal (ed.). 1973. *Anthropology and the Cultural Encounter.* Amherst, NY: Humanity Books.
Asad, Talal. 1993. *Genealogies of Religion: Discipline and Reasons of Power in Christianity and Islam.* Baltimore, MD: Johns Hopkins University Press.
Asad, Talal. 2003. *Formations of the Secular: Christianity, Islam, Modernity.* Stanford, CA: Stanford University Press.
Aslan, Ednan, Marica Hermansen, and Elif Medeni. 2013. *Muslima Theology: Voices of Women Theologians.* New York: Peter Lang.
Baudrillard, Jean. [1981] 1994. *Simulacra and Simulation.* Reprint. Ann Arbor, MI: University of Michigan Press.
Bayart, Jean-François. 2005. *The Illusion of Cultural Identity.* Trans. Steven Rendall, Janet Roitman, Cynthia Schoch, and Jonathan Derrick. Chicago, IL: University of Chicago Press.
Bayly, C.A. 2000. *Empire and Information: Intelligence Gathering and Social Communication in India, 1780–1970.* Cambridge: Cambridge University Press.
Bennington, Geoffrey, and Jacques Derrida. 1993. *Jacques Derrida.* Trans. Geoffrey Bennington. Chicago: University of Chicago Press.

Berg, Herbert. 1997. "The Implications of, and Opposition to, the Methods and Theories of John Wansbrough." *Method & Theory in the Study of Religion* 9 (1): 3–22. http://dx.doi.org/10.1163/157006897X00025.

Berg, Herbert. 2000. *The Development of Exegesis in Early Islam: The Authenticity of Muslim Literature from the Formative Period*. Richmond: Curzon.

Berman, Nina. 2004. "Thoughts on Zionism in the Context of German Middle East Relations." *Comparative Studies of South Asia, Africa and the Middle East* 24 (2): 133–44. http://dx.doi.org/10.1215/1089201X-24-2-133.

Berman, Nina. 2013. *German Literature on the Middle East: Discourses and Practices, 1000-1989*. Ann Arbor, MI: University of Michigan Press.

Berman, Russell. 1998. *Enlightenment or Empire: Colonial Discourse in German Culture*. Lincoln, NE: University of Nebraska Press.

Bérubé, Michael, and Cary Nelson (eds.). 1995. *Higher Education Under Fire: Politics, Economics, and the Crisis of the Humanities*. London: Routledge.

Bloch, Maurice. 2005. *Essays on Cultural Transmission*. Oxford: Berg.

Bloch, Maurice. 2008. "Why Religion Is Nothing Special but Is Central." *Philosophical Transactions of the Royal Society of London. Series B, Biological Sciences* 363 (1499): 2055–61. http://dx.doi.org/10.1098/rstb.2008.0007.

Bloch, Maurice. 2013. *In and Out of Each Other's Bodies: Theory of Mind, Evolution, Truth, and the Nature of the Social*. Boulder, CO: Paradigm.

Bourdieu, Pierre. 1984. *Distinction: A Social Critique of the Judgment of Taste*. Trans. Richard Nice. Cambridge, MA: Harvard University Press.

Bourdieu, Pierre. 1993. *The Field of Cultural Production*. Edited and introduced by Randal Johnson. New York: Columbia University Press.

Boyer, Pascal. 1994. *The Naturalness of Religious Ideas: A Cognitive Theory of Religion*. Berkeley, CA: University of California Press.

Boyer, Pascal. 2001. *Religion Explained: The Evolutionary Origins of Religious Thought*. New York: Basic Books.

Brenner, Michael. 2010. *Prophets of the Past: Interpreters of Jewish History*. Trans. Steven Rendall. Princeton, NJ: Princeton University Press. http://dx.doi.org/10.1515/9781400836611.

Brown, Jonathan A. C. 2009. *Hadith: Muhammad's Legacy in the Medieval and Modern World*. Oxford: Oneworld. http://dx.doi.org/10.1093/OBO_dataset_home.

Brubaker, Rogers, and Frederick Cooper. 2000. "Beyond 'Identity'." *Theory and Society* 29 (1): 1–47. http://dx.doi.org/10.1023/A:1007068714468.

Bulliet, Richard W. 1979. *Conversion to Islam in the Medieval Period: An Essay in Quantitative History*. Cambridge, MA: Harvard University Press. http://dx.doi.org/10.4159/harvard.9780674732810.

Butler, Judith. [1990] 1999. *Gender Trouble: Feminism and the Subversion of Identity*. New York: Routledge.

Chatterjee, Partha. 1993. *The Nation and Its Fragments*. Princeton, NJ: Princeton University Press.

Chaudhry, Ayesha S. 2014. *Domestic Violence and the Islamic Tradition*. New York: Oxford University Press.

Chidester, David. 1996. *Savage Systems: Colonialism and Comparative Religion in Southern Africa*. Charlottesville, VA: University of Virginia Press.

Chidester, David. 2014. *Empire and Religion: Imperialism and Comparative Religion*. Chicago, IL: University of Chicago Press.

Connolly, William. 2002. *Identity/Difference: Democratic Negotiations of Political Paradox*. Minneapolis, MN: University of Minnesota Press.

Conrad, Lawrence I. 1992. "The Conquest of Arwad: A Source-Critical Study in the Historiography of the Early Medieval Near East." In Averil Cameron and Lawrence I. Conrad (eds.), *The Byzantine and Early Islamic Near East: Papers of the First Workshop on Late Antiquity and Early Islam*, 317–401. Princeton, NJ: Darwin Press.

Conrad, Lawrence I. 1999. "Ignaz Goldziher on Ernest Renan: From Orientalist Philology to the Study of Islam." In Martin Kramer (ed.), *The Jewish Discovery of Islam: Studies in Honor of Bernard Lewis*, 137-80. Tel Aviv: Tel Aviv University Press.
Cook, David. 2005. *Understanding Jihad*. Berkeley, CA: University of California Press.
Cornell, Vincent J. 2004. "Practical Sufism: An Akbarian Foundation for a Liberal Theology of Difference." *Journal of the Muhyiddin Ibn 'Arabi Society* 36. Online at: http://www.ibnarabisociety.org/articles/cornellpracticalsufism.html
Cornell, Vincent J. 2010. "Reasons Public and Divine: Liberal Democracy, Shari`a Fundamentalism, and the Epistemological Crisis of Islam." In Carl W. Ernst and Richard C. Martin (eds.), *Rethinking Islamic Studies: From Orientalism to Cosmopolitanism*, 23-51. Chapel Hill, NC: University of North Carolina Press.
Crone, Patricia, and Michael Cook. 1977. *Hagarism: The Making of the Islamic World*. Cambridge: Cambridge University Press.
Day, Matthew. 2007. "Let's Be Realistic: Evolutionary Complexity, Epistemic Probabilism and the Cognitive Science of Religion." *Harvard Theological Review* 100 (1): 47-64. http://dx.doi.org/10.1017/S0017816007001423.
Day, Matthew. 2010. "The Sacred Contagion: John Trenchard, Natural History and the Effluvial Politics of Religion." *History of Religions* 50 (2): 144-61. http://dx.doi.org/10.1086/654907.
Denny, Frederick M. 1994. *An Introduction to Islam*. 2nd ed. New York: Macmillan.
Donner, Fred M. 2010. *Muhammad and the Believers: At the Origins of Islam*. Cambridge, MA: Harvard University Press.
Dubuisson, Daniel. 2003. *The Western Construction of Religion: Myths, Knowledge, and Ideology*. Trans. William Sayers. Baltimore, MD: Johns Hopkins University Press.
Dubuisson, Daniel. [1993] 2006. *Twentieth Century Mythologies*. 2nd ed. Trans. Martha Cunningham. London: Equinox.
Durkheim, Émile. [1912] 1995. *The Elementary Forms of Religious Life*. Trans. Karen E. Fields. New York: The Free Press.
Eliade, Mircea. [1957] 1987. *The Sacred and the Profane: The Nature of Religion*. Trans. Willard R. Trask. New York: Harcourt Brace Jovanovich.
Emerson, Steven. 2002. *American Jihad: The Terrorists Living Among Us*. New York: The Free Press.
Ericson, David F. 2011. *The Politics of Inclusion and Exclusion: Identity Politics in Twenty-First Century America*. New York: Routledge.
Ernst, Carl. 2003. *Following Muhammad: Rethinking Islam in the Contemporary World*. Chapel Hill, NC: University of North Carolina University Press.
Ernst, Carl, and Richard C. Martin (eds.). 2010. *Rethinking Islamic Studies: From Orientalism to Cosmopolitanism*. Chapel Hill, NC: University of North Carolina Press.
Esack, Farid. 2009. *On Being a Muslim: Finding a Religious Path in the World Today*. Oxford: Oneworld.
Fitzgerald, Timothy. 2000. *The Ideology of Religious Studies*. New York: Oxford University Press.
Fitzgerald, Timothy. 2007a. *Discourse on Civility and Barbarity: A Critical History of Religion and Related Categories*. New York: Oxford University Press.
Fitzgerald, Timothy, ed. 2007b. *Religion and the Secular: Historical and Colonial Formations*. London: Equinox.
Foster, Hal. 2012. "Post-Critical." *October* 139: 3-8. http://dx.doi.org/10.1162/OCTO_a_00076.
Frazer, James George. [1890] 1933. *The Golden Bough: A Study in Magic and Religion*. Abridged edition. London: Macmillan and Co.
Freud, Sigmund. [1930] 1961. *Civilization and Its Discontents*. Ed. and trans. James Strachey. New York: Norton.
Fück, Johann. 1955. *Die Arabischen Studien in Europa bis in den Anfang des 20 Jahrhunderts*. Leipzig: O. Harassowitz.
Geiger, Abraham. [1835] 1970. *Judaism and Islam*. Trans. F.M. Young. New York: Ktav.

Gill, Sam D. 1987. *Mother Earth*. Chicago, IL: University of Chicago Press.
Goitein, Shlomo Dov. [1955] 1974. *Jews and Arabs: Their Contacts Through the Ages*. 3rd ed. New York: Schocken.
Grewal, Zareena. 2014. *Islam Is a Foreign Country: American Muslims and the Global Crisis of Authority*. New York: New York University Press.
Haj, Samira. 2008. *Reconfiguring Islamic Tradition: Reform, Rationality, and Modernity*. Stanford, CA: Stanford University Press.
Hammer, Juliane. 2012. *American Muslim Women, Religious Authority, and Activism: More Than a Prayer*. Austin, TX: University of Texas Press.
Harvey, David. 1990. *The Condition of Postmodernity: An Enquiry into the Origins of Cultural Change*. Cambridge, MA: Blackwell.
Heyes, Cressida J. 2007. *Self-Transformations: Foucault, Ethics, and Normalized Bodies*. New York: Oxford University Press. http://dx.doi.org/10.1093/acprof:oso/9780195310535.001.0001.
Hidayatullah, Aysha A. 2014. *Feminist Edges of the Qur'an*. New York: Oxford University Press. http://dx.doi.org/10.1093/acprof:oso/9780199359561.001.0001.
Hoyland, Robert. 1997. *Seeing Islam as Others Saw It: A Survey and Evaluation of Christian, Jewish, and Zoroastrian Writings on Islam*. Princeton, NJ: Darwin Press.
Hughes, Aaron W. 2006. *Situating Islam: The Past and Future of an Academic Discipline*. London: Equinox.
Hughes, Aaron W. 2010. *The Invention of Jewish Identity: Bible, Philosophy, and the Art of Translation*. Bloomington, IN: Indiana University Press.
Hughes, Aaron W. 2012a. *Abrahamic Religions: On the Uses and Abuses of History*. New York: Oxford University Press. http://dx.doi.org/10.1093/acprof:oso/9780199934645.001.0001.
Hughes, Aaron W. 2012b. "The Failure of Islamic Studies Post 9/11: A Contextualization and Analysis." In William Arnal, Willi Bruan, and Russell T. McCutcheon (eds.), *The Failure of Nerve in the Academic Study of Religion: Essay in Honor of Donald Wiebe*, 129–46. Sheffield: Equinox.
Hughes, Aaron W. 2012c. "The Study of Islam Before and After September 11: A Provocation." *Method & Theory in the Study of Religion* 24 (4–5): 314–36. http://dx.doi.org/10.1163/15700682-12341234.
Hughes, Aaron W. 2012d. *Theorizing Islam: Disciplinary Deconstruction and Reconstruction*. Sheffield: Equinox.
Hughes, Aaron W. 2013a. *Muslim Identities: An Introduction to Islam*. New York: Columbia University Press.
Hughes, Aaron W. 2013b. *The Study of Judaism: Authenticity, Identity, Scholarship*. Albany, NY: State University of New York Press.
Hughes, Aaron W. 2013c. "Theory and Method in the Study of Religion: Twenty-Five Years On." In Aaron W. Hughes (ed.), *Theory and Method in the Study of Religion: Twenty Five Years On*, 1–17. Leiden: Brill. http://dx.doi.org/10.1163/9789004257573_002.
Hughes, Aaron W. 2014a. "Jewish Studies Is Too Jewish." *Chronicle of Higher Education*. March 24. Online at http://chronicle.com/article/Jewish-Studies-Is-Too-Jewish/145395/
Hughes, Aaron W. 2014b. "Sometimes Bad Scholarship Is Just Bad Scholarship: A Reply to Omid Safi." *Bulletin for the Study of Religion*. Posted on February 3, 2014. Online at http://www.equinoxpub.com/blog/2014/02/when-bad-scholarship-is-just-bad-scholarship-a-response-to-omid-safi/.
Hughes, Aaron W. 2016. *Jacob Neusner: An American Jewish Iconoclast*. New York: New York University Press.
Hughes Seager, Richard. 1995. *The World's Parliament of Religion: The East/West Encounter*. Bloomington, IN: Indiana University Press.
Hussain, Amir. 2006. *Oil and Water: Two Faiths, One God*. Kelowna: Copper House.
Jackson, Sherman A. 2005. *Islam and the Blackamerican: Looking Towards the Third Resurrection*. New York: Oxford University Press. http://dx.doi.org/10.1093/acprof:oso/9780195180817.001.0001.

Jackson, Sherman A. 2009. *Islam and the Problem of Black Suffering*. New York: Oxford University Press. http://dx.doi.org/10.1093/acprof:oso/9780195382068.001.0001.
Jameson, Frederic. 1991. *Postmodernism: Or, The Cultural Logic of Late Capitalism*. Durham, NC: Duke University Press.
Joy, Morny. 2001. "Postcolonial Reflections: Challenges for Religious Studies." *Method & Theory in the Study of Religion* 13 (1): 177–95. http://dx.doi.org/10.1163/157006801X00183.
Karim, Jamillah. 2008. *American Muslim Women: Negotiating Race, Class, and Gender with the Ummah*. New York: New York University Press.
Karim, Jamillah. 2010. "Can We Define 'True' Islam?: African American Muslim Women Respond to Transnational Muslim Identities." In Carl W. Ernst and Richard C. Martin (eds.), *Rethinking Islamic Studies: From Orientalism to Cosmopolitanism*, 114–30. Chapel Hill, NC: University of North Carolina Press.
Kassam, Zayn R. 2010. "Introduction." In Zayn R. Kassam (ed.), *Women and Islam*, xi–xxxvi. Santa Barbara, CA: Praeger.
King, Richard. 1999. *Orientalism and Religion: Post-Colonial Theory, India, and the Mystic East*. New York: Routledge.
Koren, Judith, and and Yehuda D. Nevo. 1991. "Methodological Approaches to Islamic Studies." *Der Islam* 68: 87–107.
Kramer, Martin (ed.). 1999. *The Jewish Discovery of Islam: Studies in Honor of Bernard Lewis*. Tel Aviv: Moshe Dayan Center.
Kruks, Sonia. 2001. *Retrieving Experience: Subjectivity and Recognition in Feminist Politics*. Ithaca, NY: Cornell University Press.
Kugle, Scott Siraj al-Haqq. 2010. *Homosexuality in Islam: Critical Reflections on Gay, Lesbian, and Transgender Muslims*. Oxford: Oneworld.
Kugle, Scott Siraj al-Haqq. 2014. *Living Out Islam: Voices of Gay, Lesbian, and Transgender Muslims*. New York: New York University Press.
Laden, Anthony. 2001. *Reasonably Radical: Deliberative Liberalism and the Politics of Identity*. Ithaca, NY: Cornell University Press.
Laroui, Abdallah. 1976. *The Crisis of the Arab Intellectual: Traditionalism and Historicism*. Trans. Diarmid Cammell. Berkeley, CA: University of California Press.
Lewis, Bernard. 2003. *What Went Wrong? The Clash Between Islam and Modernity in the Middle East*. New York: Perennial.
Lieberman, Saul. 1984. "A Tragedy or a Comedy." *Journal of the American Oriental Society* 104 (2): 315–19. http://dx.doi.org/10.2307/602175.
Lincoln, Bruce. 1994. *Authority: Construction and Corrosion*. Chicago, IL: University of Chicago Press.
Lincoln, Bruce. 1996. "Theses on Method." *Method & Theory in the Study of Religion* 8 (3): 225–7. http://dx.doi.org/10.1163/157006896X00323.
Lincoln, Bruce. 1999. *Theorizing Myth: Narrative, Ideology, and Scholarship*. Chicago, IL: University of Chicago Press.
Lincoln, Bruce. 2003. *Holy Terrors: Thinking About Religion After September 11*. Chicago, IL: University of Chicago Press.
Lopez, Jr. Donald S. 1998. *Prisoners of Shangri-La: Tibetan Buddhism and the West*. Chicago, IL: University of Chicago Press.
Lopez, Donald S., Jr. 2001. "Jailbreak: Author's Response." *Journal of the American Academy of Religion* 69 (1): 203–14. http://dx.doi.org/10.1093/jaarel/69.1.203.
Manji, Irshad. 2003. *The Trouble With Islam: A Muslim's Call for Reform in Her Faith*. New York: Saint Martin's Press.
Marchand, Suzanne L. 2009. *German Orientalism in the Age of Empire: Religion, Race, and Scholarship*. Cambridge: Cambridge University Press.
Martin, Craig. 2010. *Masking Hegemony: A Genealogy of Liberalism, Religion, and the Private Sphere*. London: Equinox Publishing.
Martin, Craig. 2012. *A Critical Introduction to the Study of Religion*. London: Equinox Publishing.

Martin, Craig. 2014. "Genealogies of Religion, Twenty Years On: An Interview with Talal Asad." *Bulletin for the Study of Religion* 43 (1): 12. http://dx.doi.org/10.1558/bsor.v43i1.12.
Martin, Luther H. 1987. *Hellenistic Religions: An Introduction*. New York: Oxford University Press.
Martin, Luther H., and Donald Wiebe. 2012. "Religious Studies as a Scientific Discipline: The Persistence of a Delusion." *Journal of the American Academy of Religion* 80 (3): 587–97. http://dx.doi.org/10.1093/jaarel/lfs030.
Martin, Richard C. (ed.). 1985. *Approaches to Islam in Religious Studies*. Tucson, AZ: University of Arizona Press.
Martin, Richard C. 2010. "Islamic Studies in the American Academy: Personal Reflections." *Journal of the American Academy of Religion* 78 (4): 896–920. http://dx.doi.org/10.1093/jaarel/lfq089.
Martin, Richard C., Mark R. Woodward, and Dwi S. Atmaja. 1997. *Defenders of Reason in Islam: Mu'tazilism and Rational Theology from Medieval School to Modern Symbol*. Oxford: Oneworld.
Mas, Ruth. 2012. "Why Critique?" *Method & Theory in the Study of Religion* 24 (4–5): 389–407. http://dx.doi.org/10.1163/15700682-12341246.
Masuzawa, Tomoko. 1993. *In Search of Dreamtime: The Quest for the Origin of Religion*. Chicago, IL: University of Chicago Press.
Masuzawa, Tomoko. 2005. *The Invention of World Religions: Or, How European Universalism Was Preserved in the Language of Pluralism*. Chicago, IL: University of Chicago Press. http://dx.doi.org/10.7208/chicago/9780226922621.001.0001.
Mattson, Ingrid. 2013. *The Story of the Qur'an: Its History and Place in Muslim Life*. 2nd ed. Oxford: Wiley-Blackwell.
McCauley, Robert N., and E. Thomas Lawson. 2002. *Bringing Ritual to Mind: Psychological Foundations of Cultural Forms*. Cambridge: Cambridge University Press. http://dx.doi.org/10.1017/CBO9780511606410.
McCloud, Amina Beverly. 2000. "The Scholar and the *Fatwa*: Legal Issues Facing African American and Immigrant Muslim Communities in the United States." In Gisela Webb (ed.), *Windows of Faith: Muslim Women Scholar-Activists in North America*, 136–44. Syracuse, NY: Syracuse University Press.
McCloud, Amina Beverly. 2006. *Transnational Muslims in American Society*. Gainesville, FL: University Press of Florida.
McCutcheon, Russell T. 1997. *Manufacturing Religion: The Discourse on Sui Generis Religion and the Politics of Nostalgia*. New York: Oxford University Press.
McCutcheon, Russell T. (ed.). 1999. *The Insider/Outsider Problem in the Study of Religion: A Reader*. London: Continuum.
McCutcheon, Russell T. 2003. *The Discipline of Religion: Structure, Meaning, Rhetoric*. New York: Routledge. http://dx.doi.org/10.4324/9780203451793.
McCutcheon, Russell T. 2007. *Studying Religion: An Introduction*. London: Equinox.
Moore, George Foot. [1927] 1954. *Judaism in the First Centuries of the Christian Era: The Age of the Tannaim*. 3 vols. Cambridge, MA: Harvard University Press.
Moosa, Ebrahim. 2003. "The Debts and Burdens of Critical Islam." In Omid Safi (ed.), *Progressive Muslims: On Justice, Gender and Pluralism*, 111–27. Oxford: Oneworld.
Moosa, Ebrahim. 2005. *Ghazali and the Poetics of Imagination*. Chapel Hill, NC: University of North Carolina Press.
Neusner, Jacob. 1962. *A Life of Rabban Yohanan Ben Zakkai, Ca. 1–80 CE*. Leiden: Brill.
Neusner, Jacob. 1970. *Development of a Legend: Studies on the Traditions Concerning Yohanan Ben Zakkai*. Leiden: Brill.
Neusner, Jacob. 1974–77. *A History of the Mishnaic Law of Purities*. 22 vols. Leiden: Brill.
Neusner, Jacob. 1977–80. *The Tosefta*. 6 vols. NY: Ktav.
Neusner, Jacob. 1979a. *A History of the Mishnaic Law of Holy Things*. 6 vols. Leiden: Brill.

Neusner, Jacob. 1979b. "Map Without Territory: Mishnah's System of Sacrifice and Sanctuary." *History of Religions* 19 (2): 103–27. http://dx.doi.org/10.1086/462839.
Neusner, Jacob. 1982-93. *The Talmud of the Land of Israel: A Preliminary Translation and Explanation*. 25 vols. Chicago, IL: University of Chicago Press.
Neusner, Jacob. 1984–95. *The Talmud of Babylonia: An American Translation*. 36 vols. Chico, CA: Scholars Press for Brown Judaic Studies.
Neusner, Jacob. 1985. *Israel in America: A Too-Comfortable Exile?* Boston, MA: Beacon Press.
Neusner, Jacob. 1986a. *Sifré to Numbers: An American Translation*. 2 vols. Atlanta, GA: Scholars Press for Brown Judaic Studies.
Neusner, Jacob. 1986b. *The Fathers According to Rabbi Nathan: An Analytical Translation and Explanation*. Atlanta, GA: Scholars Press for Brown Judaic Studies.
Neusner, Jacob. 1986c. "The Mishnah: Methods of Interpretation." *Midstream* 1986 (October): 38–42.
Neusner, Jacob. 1987a. *The Mishnah: A New Translation*. New Haven, CT: Yale University Press.
Neusner, Jacob. 1987b. *Pesiqta de Rab Kahana: An Analytical Translation and Explanation*. 2 vols. Atlanta, GA: Scholars Press for Brown Judaic Studies.
Neusner, Jacob. 1988a. *Judaism: The Evidence of the Mishnah*, 2nd edition. Atlanta, GA: Scholars Press for Brown Judaic Studies.
Neusner, Jacob. 1988b. *Mekhilta Attributed to R. Ishmael: An Analytical Translation*. 3 vols. Atlanta: Scholars Press for Brown Judaic Studies.
Neusner, Jacob. 1988c. *Sifra: An Analytical Translation*. 3 vols. Atlanta, GA: Scholars Press for Brown Judaic Studies.
Neusner, Jacob. 1989a. *Esther Rabbah: An Analytical Translation*. Atlanta, GA: Scholars Press for Brown Judaic Studies.
Neusner, Jacob. 1989b. *Lamentations Rabbah: An Analytical Translation*. Atlanta, GA: Scholars Press for Brown Judaic Studies.
Neusner, Jacob. 1989c. *Ruth Rabbah: An Analytical Translation*. Atlanta, GA: Scholars Press for Brown Judaic Studies.
Neusner, Jacob. 1990. *Song of Songs Rabbah: An Analytical Translation*. 2 vols. Atlanta, GA: Scholars Press for Brown Judaic Studies.
Neusner, Jacob. 1995. *The Documentary Foundation of Rabbinic Culture: Mopping Up After Debates with Gerald L. Bruns, S. J. D. Cohen, Arnold Maria Goldberg, Susan Handelman, Christine Hayes, James Kugel, Peter Schaefer, Eliezer Segal, E. P. Sanders, and Lawrence H. Schiffman*. Atlanta, GA: Scholars Press for Brown Judaic Studies.
Neusner, Jacob. 1997. *Stranger at Home: "The Holocaust," Zionism, and American Judaism*. Atlanta, GA: Scholars Press for Brown Judaic Studies.
Neusner, Jacob. 1999. *Rabbinic Judaism: Structure and System*. Atlanta, GA: Scholars Press for Brown Judaic Studies.
Neusner, Jacob, and Noam M. M. Neusner. 1995. *The Price of Excellence: Universities in Conflict During the Cold War Era*. New York: Continuum.
Nevo, Yehuda D., and Judith Koren. 2003. *Crossroads to Islam: The Origins of the Arab Religion and the Arab State*. Amherst, NY: Prometheus Books.
Nongbri, Brent. 2013. *Before Religion: The History of a Modern Concept*. New Haven, CT: Yale University Press. http://dx.doi.org/10.12987/yale/9780300154160.001.0001.
Orsi, Robert A. 2005. *Between Heaven and Earth: The Religious Worlds People Make and the Scholars Who Study Them*. Princeton, NJ: Princeton University Press.
Orsi, Robert A. 2011. "The Problem of the Holy." In Robert A. Orsi (ed.), *The Cambridge Companion to Religious Studies*, 84–106. Cambridge: Cambridge University Press. http://dx.doi.org/10.1017/CCOL9780521883917.006.
Otto, Rudolph. [1917] 1969. *The Idea of the Holy: An Inquiry into the Non-Rational Factor in the Idea of the Divine and Its Relation to the Rational*. Trans. John W. Harvey. London: Oxford University Press.
Owen, Roger. 1973. "Studying Islamic History." *Journal of Interdisciplinary History* 4 (2): 287–98. http://dx.doi.org/10.2307/202268.

Pals, Daniel L. 2008. *Eight Theories of Religion.* 2nd. ed. New York: Oxford University Press.
Pipes, Daniel. 2002. *Militant Islam Reaches America.* New York: Norton.
Plato. 1993. *The Republic.* Trans. Robin Waterfield. Oxford: Oxford University Press.
Powers, David S. 2009. *Muhammad Is Not the Father of Any of Your Men: The Making of the Last Prophet.* Philadelphia, PA: University of Pennsylvania Press. http://dx.doi.org/10.9783/9780812205572.
Prakash, Gyan. 1999. *Another Reason: Science and the Imagination of Modern India.* Princeton, NJ: Princeton University Press.
Preus, J. Samuel. 1987. *Explaining Religion: Criticism and Theory from Bodin to Freud.* New Haven, CT: Yale University Press.
Proudfoot, Wayne. 1985. *Religious Experience.* Berkeley, CA: University of California Press.
Ramadan, Tariq. 2007. *In the Footsteps of the Prophet: Lessons from the Life of Muhammad.* New York: Oxford University Press.
Ramadan, Tariq. 2010. *What I Believe.* New York: Oxford University Press.
Rippin, Andrew. 2012. "Provocation and Its Responses." *Method & Theory in the Study of Religion* 24 (4–5): 408–17. http://dx.doi.org/10.1163/15700682-12341247.
Robinson, Chase. 2005. *'Abd al-Malik.* Oxford: Oneworld.
Rodinson, Maxime. 1987. *Europe and the Mystique of Islam.* Trans. Roger Venius. Seattle, WA: University of Washington Press.
Ruml, Mark. 2006. "Respectful Methodology: Methodological and Ethical Issues in the Study of Aboriginal Religious Traditions." *Oral History FORUM d'histoire orale* 26: 64–80.
Safi, Omid (ed.). 2003. *Progressive Muslims: On Justice, Gender, and Pluralism.* Oxford: Oneworld.
Safi, Omid. 2009. *Memories of Muhammad: Why the Prophet Matters.* New York: HarperOne.
Safi, Omid. 2014. "Reflections on the State of Islamic Studies." *Jadaliyya.* Posted on January 31, 2014. Online at http://www.jadaliyya.com/pages/index/16269/reflections-on-the-state-of-islamic-studies#.Uuvw6CkjVY4.
Said, Edward W. 1978. *Orientalism.* New York: Vintage.
Said, Edward W. 1993. *Culture and Imperialism.* New York: Alfred A. Knopf.
Sanders, E.P. 1990. *Jewish Law from Jesus to the Mishnah.* Philadelphia, PA: Trinity.
Schatzki, Theodore R. 2008. *Social Practices: A Wittgensteinian Approach to Human Practices.* Cambridge: Cambridge University Press.
Schilbrack, Kevin. 2014. *Philosophy of Religion: A Manifesto.* Oxford: Wiley-Blackwell.
Schorsch, Ismar. 1994. *From Text to Context: The Turn to History in Modern Judaism.* Hanover, NH: University Press of New England.
Shaikh, Sa'diyya. 2012. *Sufi Narratives of Intimacy: Ibn 'Arabi, Gender, and Sexuality.* Chapel Hill, NC: University of North Carolina University Press. http://dx.doi.org/10.5149/9780807869864_shaikh.
Sharf, Robert. 1998. "Experience." In Mark C. Taylor (ed.), *Critical Terms for Religious Studies,* 94–116. Chicago, IL: University of Chicago Press, 1998.
Shoemaker, Stephen J. 2012. *The Death of a Prophet: The End of Muhammad's Life and the Beginnings of Islam.* Philadelphia, PA: University of Pennsylvania Press. http://dx.doi.org/10.9783/9780812205138.
Simmons, Gwendolyn Zoharah. 2000. "Striving for Muslim Women's Human Rights—Before and After Beijing: An African American Perspective." In Gisela Webb (ed.), *Windows of Faith: Muslim Women Scholar-Activists in North America,* 197–225. Syracuse, NY: Syracuse University Press.
Simmons, Gwendolyn Zoharah. 2003. "Are We up to the Challenge?: The Need for a Radical Re-Ordering of the Islamic Discourse on Women." In Omid Safi (ed.), *Progressive Muslims: On Justice, Gender, and Pluralism,* 235–48. Oxford: Oneworld.
Singleton, Brent D. 2007. "Brothers at Odds: Rival Islamic Movements in Late Nineteenth Century New York City." *Journal of Muslim Minority Affairs* 27 (3): 473–86. http://dx.doi.org/10.1080/13602000701737293.

Smith, Jonathan Z. 1978. *Map Is Not Territory: Studies in the History of Religions*. Chicago, IL: University of Chicago Press.
Smith, Jonathan Z. 1982. *Imagining Religion: From Babylon to Jonestown*. Chicago, IL: University of Chicago Press.
Smith, Jonathan Z. 1990. *Drudgery Divine: On the Comparison of Early Christianities and the Religions of Late Antiquity*. Chicago, IL: University of Chicago Press.
Smith, Jonathan Z. 2003. *Relating Religion: Essays in the Study of Religion*. Chicago, IL: University of Chicago Press.
Smith, Jonathan Z. 2007. "The Necessary Lie: Duplicity in the Disciplines." In Russell T. McCutcheon (ed.), *Studying Religion: An Introduction*, 74–80. London: Equinox. The essay is also available online at http://teaching.uchicago.edu/?/ctl-archive/course-design-tutorials/assessing-and-improving/smith.
Soroush, Abdolkarim. 2002. *Reason, Freedom, and Democracy in Islam: Essential Writings of Abdolkarim Soroush*. Trans. Mahmoud Sadri and Ahmad Sadri. New York: Oxford University Press.
Spencer, Robert. 2007. *The Truth About Muhammad: Founder of the World's Most Intolerant Religion*. Washington, DC: Regnary Publishing.
Steinmetz, George. 2007. *The Devil's Handwriting: Precoloniality and the German Colonial State in Qingdao, Samoa and Southwest Africa*. Chicago, IL: University of Chicago Press. http://dx.doi.org/10.7208/chicago/9780226772448.001.0001.
Strenski, Ivan. 1987. *Four Theories of Myth in Twentieth Century History: Cassirer, Eliade, Lévi-Strauss, and Malinowski*. Iowa City, IA: University of Iowa Press.
Stroumsa, Guy G. 2010. *A New Science: The Discovery of Religion in the Age of Reason*. Cambridge, MA: Harvard University Press.
Styers, Randall. 2004. *Making Magic: Religion, Magic, and Science in the Modern World*. New York: Oxford University Press. http://dx.doi.org/10.1093/0195151070.001.0001.
Sullivan, Winnifred Fallers. 2005. *The Impossibility of Religious Freedom*. Princeton, NJ: Princeton University Press.
Thurman, Robert A. F. 2001. "Critical Reflections on Donald S. Lopez Jr.'s *Prisoners of Shangri-La: Tibetan Buddhism and the West*." *Journal of the American Academy of Religion* 69 (1): 191–202. http://dx.doi.org/10.1093/jaarel/69.1.191.
Tolan, John. 2002. *Saracens: Islam in the Medieval European Imagination*. New York: Columbia University Press.
Tourage, Mahdi. 2013. "Performing Belief and Reviving Islam: Prominent (White Male) Converts in Muslim Revival Conventions." *Performing Islam* 2 (1): 207–26.
Turner, Bryan S. 1994. *Orientalism, Postmodernism, and Globalization*. New York: Routledge. http://dx.doi.org/10.4324/9780203427255.
Urbach, Ephraim. 1975. *The Sages: Their Concepts and Beliefs*. Trans. Israel Abrahams. Jerusalem: Magnes Press.
Wadud, Amina. 1998. *Quran and Women: Rereading the Sacred Text from a Woman's Perspective*. New York: Oxford University Press.
Wadud, Amina. 2006. *Inside the Gender Jihad: Women's Reform in Islam*. Oxford: Oneworld.
Wansbrough, John. 1977. *Quranic Studies: Sources and Methods of Scriptural Interpretation*. Oxford: Oxford University Press.
Wansbrough, John. 1980. "Review of Josef van Ess, *Anfänge muslimischer Theologie: Zwei antiqadaritische Traktate aus dem ersten Jahrhundert der Higra*." *Bulletin of the School of Oriental and African Studies. University of London. School of Oriental and African Studies* 43: 361–3. http://dx.doi.org/10.1017/S0041977X00115733.
Wansbrough, John. 1987. *Wansbrough, Res Ipsa Loquitur: History and Mimesis*. Jerusalem: The Israel Academy of Sciences and Humanities.
Webb, Gisela (ed.). 2000. *Windows of Faith: Muslim Women Scholar-Activists in North America*. Syracuse, NY: Syracuse University Press.
Webb, Mohammad Alexander Russell. 1892. *The Three Lectures*. Madras, India.

Webb, Mohammad Alexander Russell. 1893. *Islam in America*. New York: Oriental Publishing Co.
Weber, Max. [1922] 1964. *The Sociology of Religion*. Trans. Ephraim Fischoff. Boston, MA: Beacon Press.
Wiebe, Donald. 1984. "The Failure of Nerve in the Academic Study of Religion." *Studies in Religion/Sciences religieuses* 13: 401–22.
Wiebe, Donald. 1999. *The Politics of Religious Studies*. New York: Palgrave.
Wiebe, Donald. 2006. "An Eternal Return All Over Again: The Religious Conversation Endures – A Critical Assessment of Recent Presidential Addresses to the AAR." *Journal of the American Academy of Religion* 74 (3): 674–96. http://dx.doi.org/10.1093/jaarel/lfj091.
Wiese, Christian. 2005. *Challenging Colonial Discourse: Jewish Studies and Protestant Theology in Wilhelmine Germany*. Leiden: Brill.
Yelle, Robert. 2013a. *The Language of Disenchantment: Protestant Literalism and Colonial Discourse in British India*. New York: Oxford University Press.
Yelle, Robert. 2013b. *Semiotics of Religion: Signs of the Sacred in History*. London: Bloomsbury.
Žižek, Slavoj (ed.). 1994. *Mapping Ideology*. London: Verso.

Author Index

Adams, Charles, 17, 49
Ali, Kecia, xvii, 18, 61, 87–90
Arnal, William E., and Russell
 T. McCutcheon, 51, 120, 123
Asad, Talal, xvi, 4, 19, 51–53, 78, 117, 122

Bayart, Jean-François, 5
Berman, Nina, 44
Bloch, Maurice, 5
Bourdieu, Pierre, 5, 122
Brown, Jonathan A. C., xvii, 61, 90–92
Bulliet, Richard, 62
Butler, Judith, 4, 5, 19, 22, 33, 78

Chatterjee, Partha, 47
Chaudhry, Ayesha, 26–28, 31
Clark, Justice Tom, 7–8, 34n3
Cornell, Vincent, 61, 70–72

Derrida, Jacques, 8, 9
Dubuisson, Daniel, 5, 12n3, 19, 53, 120, 123
Durkheim, Émile, 122

Eliade, Mircea, 122, 123
Ernst, Carl, and Richard C. Martin, xvi, 6, 30, 48–49, 50–51, 109

Fitzgerald, Timothy, 19, 53, 123
Foster, Hal, 49
Foucault, Michel, 42
Frazer, James George, 122
Freud, Sigmund, 122

Gill, Sam, 48
Grewal, Zareena, 18–19

Hammer, Juliane, 61, 69
Hidayatullah, Aysha, 28–29, 31
Hoyland, Robert, 110

Jackson, Sherman, xvii, 79–82

Karim, Jamillah, 29–31
Koren, Judith, and Yehuda Nevo, 110–111
Kruks, Sonia, 22
Kugle, Scott, 6, 18, 40, 61, 63–67, 68, 81

Lewis, Bernard, 45
Lincoln, Bruce, 4, 7, 19, 24, 53, 61, 63, 122
Lopez, Donald S., xvi, 10, 37–40, 43, 48, 95, 123

Marchand, Suzanne, 44, 47
Mas, Ruth, 54
Masuzawa, Tomoko, 5, 122, 123
Mattson, Ingrid, xvii, 61, 84–87
McCloud, Beverly Aminah, 40, 61, 67–68
McCutcheon, Russell T., 5, 9, 19, 53, 59–60, 63, 122, 123
Moore, George Foot, 103–104

Neusner, Jacob, xvii, 10, 95–114, 117, 123, 126
Nongbri, Brent, 119

Orsi, Robert A., 16
Otto, Rudolph, 122, 123

Plaskow, Judith, 83
Plato, xi, xiii–xiv

Radford Ruether, Rosemary, 83
Ramadan, Tariq, 20
Renan, Ernst, 44
Rippin, Andrew, 8

Safi, Omid, xvii, 31–32, 76–77, 78, 79, 80, 82, 90, 92
Said, Edward, xiii, xvi, 2, 4, 6, 16, 32, 37–56, 77, 91, 92

© Equinox Publishing Ltd. 2015

Schatzki, Theodore R., 5
Shoemaker, Stephen, 107, 114n12, 114n18
Simmons, Gwendolyn Zoharah, 18, 62, 70
Smith, Jonathan Z., xiv, 5, 19, 32, 53, 63, 75, 117, 121, 122, 123
Sullivan, Winnifred, 5

Thurman, Robert, xvi, 10, 37–40, 43, 48, 95

Urbach, Ephraim, 103

Wadud, Amina, xvii, 61, 62, 63, 82–84, 87
Wansbrough, John, 111
Webb, Gisela, 67, 70
Webb, Mohammad Alexander Russell, 57–59
Weber, Max, 122

Subject Index

American Academy of Religion (AAR), 10, 47, 49, 76, 77, 79
apologetics, xvi, 1, 16, 18, 26, 32, 41, 61, 78, 95, 110, 120
   see also Islamic religious studies
Arab-Jew, 8
authenticity, xv, xii, 3, 8, 9, 10, 22, 23, 26, 37, 40, 59, 90, 91, 99, 109, 124, 125
   and rhetoric of, xvi, 3, 26, 61, 64, 71, 80, 100
   see also Islamic religious studies, normativity
authority, xiii, 5, 6, 26, 27, 39, 43, 51, 59, 60, 64, 67, 69, 104, 107, 108, 121,

blogosphere, 23–24
Boko Haram, xi–xii, xv

Canada, 9
colonialism, 23, 32, 45, 50, 54, 68
   see also postcolonialism
converts, xiii, xvi–xvii, 4, 10, 11, 45, 46, 50, 57–74, 78, 79, 82, 84, 119, 124
   as scholars, 62–63, 67, 95
   see also insiders and outsiders
conversion, xvi, 4, 11, 18, 45, 57–74, 92
   and advocacy for new religion, 61, 78
   and authority, 59, 63
   and Islamic religious studies, 61, 63
   movement from outsider to insider, 59, 62–63, 78
   as social act, 59, 62–63
   theorizing, xvii, 4
crisis in the humanities, 7–8

disciplinary lying, xiv
discourse analysis, 7
documentary hypothesis, 97–102

East Asian religions, 59

fiqh (jurisprudence), 28, 31, 89
First Nation studies, 59
footnotes, 23–25

gender jihad, 23, 82
gender justice, xiii, 23, 25, 26–31, 40, 82–84, 87, 117

Hamas, xii, 84
hijab, 2, 31, 50
history, xii, xvi, 7, 15, 22, 24, 33, 37m 47, 48, 53, 54, 82, 86, 100, 102, 103, 112, 118, 119
   versus salvation history, 107, 111
humanities, xiii, xvi, 2, 7, 17, 19, 21, 33, 40, 48, 49, 59, 95, 96, 106, 109, 115, 116, 125, 126

identity, 4, 5, 8, 9, 11, 16, 17, 21, 22, 23, 25, 30, 31, 32, 47, 50–51, 52, 62, 63, 65, 66, 69, 109, 111, 122, 123, 124, 125
identity politics, xv, xviii, 3, 4, 6, 10, 15–36, 41, 59, 72, 75, 95
ideology, 2, 6, 8, 24, 46, 67, 84, 107, 115, 116
insiders and outsiders, xvi–xvii, 5–7, 8–11, 45, 59, 75–94, 96
   defined, 59–60
   porous nature of, 78–79
   see also converts, conversion, Islamic religious studies, religious studies
insider/outsider debate, 59–62
   and Islamic religious studies, 60
ISIS, xi–xii, xv
Islam, xi, xiii, xvii, 1, 3, 5, 7, 11, 17, 18,, 23, 26, 29, 31, 39, 47, 51, 57, 58, 59, 65, 66, 69–70, 72, 77, 78, 79, 82, 84, 87, 97, 107, 117, 119, 125
   "authentic" version of, xii, xv, xvi, xviii, 1, 3, 20, 25, 26, 29, 30, 40, 41, 44, 47, 52, 60, 63–64, 67, 75, 90, 92, 125

© Equinox Publishing Ltd. 2015

and bastardization of, xii, 2, 17
beyond intellectual justification, xiii, 21, 29
as exemplum in the study of religion, xvii, 11, 39,
hijacking of, xv, 17, 20
and pluralism, 1, 9, 25, 76
polyvalent nature of, xiv, 6, 25, 40, 107
see also authenticity, converts, conversion, Islamic religious studies
Islamic religious studies, xiii, xv–xvi, 1–2, 5, 6, 7, 15–36, 40, 45–46, 48–50, 52, 59, 60, 62, 63, 65, 70, 72, 75–76, 77, 78, 86, 88, 92, 96, 97, 108–109, 112, 116, 117, 118, 119, 120, 124–126
compared to Jewish studies, 96–97, 105–106
and converts to Islam, xiii, 57–74, 95, 119
and constructive theology, xviii, 18–19, 20, 64, 71, 82–84, 85, 88, 106–108, 125
and the creation of a progressive Islam, xiii, 3, 4, 5, 7, 9–11, 20, 25, 40, 52, 63–64, 70–71, 83, 88, 108, 120
and crisis in the humanities, 7–8
at crossroads, 95
definition of, 17–21
and Edward Said, 37–56
and a gay-friendly Islam, 63–67, 81
and the humanities, 2, 7, 18, 21, 33, 40, 48, 78, 95, 116
and misunderstanding of Talal Asad, 51–53
and non-Muslims in, 2–3, 72, 78, 119
and political correctness, 65, 107, 108
presentism of, 21, 108–109
and problems of disciplinarity, 47–48, 85–86, 119
and "reformation", 1–2, 5, 18, 20, 27, 65, 69, 71, 82, 84, 95, 115, 116, 119, 125
regnant discourses within, xvi, 4, 20, 40, 78, 108
and the reification of identity, 25–27, 52
and rhetoric of authenticity, xiii, xvi, 52, 108
and role models in, xvii, 72, 78, 90, 95
and the secular university, xiii, xv, 85–86
and September 11, 2001, 10–11, 17–18, 20, 76, 108

theory in, 4, 6, 15, 19, 20, 40, 47–53, 59, 106–107, 116, 119, 120, 124–126
see also apologetics, converts, conversion, humanities, identity politics, Islam, normativity, religious studies
Islamic Studies, xii, 95, 108, 126
see also Islamic religious studies
Islamophobia, xiii, xvi, 11, 23, 39, 91, 116,
charges of, xvi

Jamaat-e-Islami, xii
Jewish studies, xvii, 12n1, 59, 95–114
and apologetics, 95–96
before and after Neusner, 96
compared with Islamic religious studies, 95–97, 105–106
and the humanities, 96, 97
see also Neusner, Jacob
Journal of the American Academy of Religion (JAAR), 37–38

Middle Eastern Studies Association (MESA), 77
Mishnah, 96, 97, 100, 101, 102–105
Muhammad, xiii, 16, 20–21, 33, 66, 75, 80, 81, 86, 107, 110, 117, 120

Near Eastern Studies, 15, 50, 126
New Testament, 100
noble lies, xiii–xiv, xv, 3, 39, 76, 119, 125
normativity, xii, xvi, 1, 3, 9, 10, 22, 31, 76, 84, 88, 90, 103, 108, 110, 111
see also authenticity

Orientalism, xiii, xv, xvi, 4, 6, 16, 19, 21, 37–56, 61, 67, 92, 96, 108, 112, 116, 119, 120, 124
Osama bin Laden, xv

politics of representation, 41–42
postcolonialism, 48–49, 54, 117
see also colonialism
post-criticism, 49, 50

al-Qaeda, xii
Qur'an, xvi, 9, 16, 17, 18, 26–28, 31, 33, 40, 44, 46, 54, 64, 67, 82–83, 84–87, 107–108, 109, 111
and early Islam, 17

and later misogynist interpreters, 18, 28, 27, 33, 54, 64, 68
locus of "good" Islam, 39, 40, 54, 72, 83, 84

rabbinic Judaism, 96–97, 98, 99, 101, 102, 103
religious studies, xii, xiii, xvii, 3, 5, 15, 19, 25, 39, 48–49, 53, 58, 59, 61, 62, 72–73, 76, 79, 88, 97, 99, 104, 106, 109, 112, 115, 118, 121, 122, 123, 125, 126
   and area studies, 99, 104
   and creation of "good" religion, 4, 19, 120
   critical wing of, 19, 88
   and humanities, 115–116
   and Islam, xiii, 5, 40, 53
   and redescription, xiii
   and theology, 15, 97, 106–108
   theory and method in, xviii, 98
   see also insiders and outsiders, theory and method
romanticization, xvi

the "sacred", 15–16, 61, 77, 118, 121
Salafism, 18, 20, 71, 87
School District of Abington Township, Pennsylvania v. Schempp, 7–8, 34n3
secularism, 51–52
September 11, 2001, xv, 2–3, 6, 9, 17, 20, 32, 76, 108, 109

al-Shabaab, xii
sharia, xi, 80
   and U.S. Constitution, 80–81
South Asian religions, 59
Sufism (= "good" Islam), xvi, 18, 23, 33, 66, 71, 79

Taliban, xii, 1
Talmud, 96, 100, 101, 103
theory and method, 28, 76–77, 98, 101, 115–128,
   and academic "turf wars", 115–116, 121
   amphibolous nature of, 116, 121
   contested nature of, 115, 121
   and the creation of "religion", 115, 118
   debates within, 118–120
   defined, 126n1
   and ideology, 115, 116
   and importance of self-reflexivity, 115, 117
   politics of, 118–120
   relativism of, 77, 116
   as sub-discipline, 122
   see also Islamic religious studies, religious studies
Tibetan Buddhism, xvi, 37–39

University of Calgary, 9–11
   and anti-Semitism, 11, 12n13

"the West", 45, 68, 91, 125

www.ingramcontent.com/pod-product-compliance
Lightning Source LLC
Chambersburg PA
CBHW071848230426
43671CB00012B/2113